Qualitative Content Analysis in Practice

Qualitative Content Analysis in Practice

 Margrit Schreier

Los Angeles | London | New Delhi
Singapore | Washington DC

First published 2012

Apart from any fair dealing for the purposes of research or private study, or criticism or review, as permitted under the Copyright, Designs and Patents Act, 1988, this publication may be reproduced, stored or transmitted in any form, or by any means, only with the prior permission in writing of the publishers, or in the case of reprographic reproduction, in accordance with the terms of licences issued by the Copyright Licensing Agency. Enquiries concerning reproduction outside those terms should be sent to the publishers.

SAGE Publications Ltd
1 Oliver's Yard
55 City Road
London EC1Y 1SP

SAGE Publications Inc.
2455 Teller Road
Thousand Oaks, California 91320

SAGE Publications India Pvt Ltd
B 1/I 1 Mohan Cooperative Industrial Area
Mathura Road
New Delhi 110 044

SAGE Publications Asia-Pacific Pte Ltd
3 Church Street
#10-04 Samsung Hub
Singapore 049483

Library of Congress Control Number: 2011920596

British Library Cataloguing in Publication data

A catalogue record for this book is available from the British Library

ISBN 978-1-84920-592-4
ISBN 978-1-84920-593-1

Typeset by C&M Digitals (P) Ltd, Chennai, India
Printed and bound by CPI Group (UK) Ltd, Croydon, CR0 4YY
Printed on paper from sustainable resources

CONTENTS

ABOUT THE AUTHOR

Margrit Schreier is Professor of Empirical Methods at Jacobs University Bremen. She started out with a BA in English Language and Literature (at New College, Oxford), before she went on to study Psychology at Heidelberg University (Dipl. Psych., Dr.) where she first became interested in qualitative research methods. She was also co-director of the Methods Center of the Bremen International Graduate School of Social Sciences (BIGSSS) and Editor-in-Chief of the *Journal of Media Psychology*. She has taught research methods courses for 15 years, including qualitative methods, experimental design, and mixed methods, to students from a variety of social science disciplines, and has given workshops on qualitative content analysis and other methods topics at GESIS, the Leibniz Institute for the Social Sciences, for more than five years. Her other research interests include the didactics of teaching qualitative research methods, media reception, the empirical study of literature, and health-related research. She has been a principal investigator in several DFG-funded research projects on these topics, and she has authored and co-authored an introductory methods textbook and more than 90 book chapters and articles. When she is not working, she enjoys cooking and photography. She is also a classical homeopath and has been surprised to find that homeopathy allows her to apply many of her methods skills – including qualitative content analysis!

PREFACE

It has been a long time since my first encounter with qualitative content analysis (QCA) in the early 1990s as a student at Heidelberg University. Little did I anticipate at the time that I would one day teach the method, even less that I would write a textbook on the topic... Back then I was simply intrigued by what the method had to offer: a very systematic way of making sense of the large amount of material that would invariably emerge in the process of doing qualitative research.

As I began to teach qualitative research methods, including QCA, it quickly became clear that there was a need for a textbook on the topic. When I was talking to my German students, they obviously didn't know about the rich history of the method. When I was talking to my international students, chances were that they had never even heard of it. When I mentioned it to my students from the humanities, they would take it to mean a rich description of a work of art. When I mentioned it to my students from communication studies, they would say: Qualitative content analysis? But content analysis is a quantitative method, right?

At this point, I might simply have let things rest. Why try to convince students of the merits of a method they were barely familiar with? But alongside these confused looks, mostly from undergraduate students, I was increasingly approached by graduate students who wanted to use QCA in their work – but didn't know how exactly to go about it. I began to teach university courses and workshops on QCA on a regular basis, and it is above all from the studies and questions of the participants in these classes that this book has grown. There exist quite a few textbooks on quantitative content analysis, down to the details of how to actually go about it – but these focus on the quantitative version of the method. There also exist textbooks on QCA, but they tend to focus on the different traditions and concepts in QCA and less on the research process (and, sadly, one major exception was quickly sold out and never saw a second edition). In each class, students were asking me similar 'how to' questions. At first, I kept on thinking: If there only was a textbook I could use! And gradually this turned into: I must get down to it and write that textbook!

So this is what this book is meant to be: a hands-on textbook, guiding students and other researchers through the process of conducting their own

QCA. It contains only a little about the history and the methodological background of the method because a lot has already been written about this. Instead, I focus on describing how QCA fits into the broader landscape of qualitative research, and I then move on to what makes up the major part of the book: a detailed description of the steps involved in QCA, illustrated by examples that are taken from published papers by other authors as well as from my own work and the work of several students. Many of these examples are originally in German; all translations from German into English are my own. An additional chapter containing more detailed descriptions of these examples can be accessed on the Sage website: www.sagepub.co.uk/schreier

I would like to thank Norbert Groeben who first introduced me to QCA; Ruth Rustemeyer whose book on QCA has inspired me over the years; Guenter Mey and Sascha Schroeder who have kept on asking me when I will finally get down to it and write my own; Özen Odağ for her steady reassurance over the years of working together that this book is worthwhile; Jürgen Hoffmeyer-Zlotnik and Patricia Lueder from GESIS as well as Guenter Mey (again) and Katja Mruck from qualitative-research.net for inviting me to teach QCA; Claudia Gronewold, Simone Heil, Marie-Luise Herrmann, Özen Odağ (again), Marina Otten, and Katrin Viertel for letting me draw upon and quote extensively from their research; Adele Diederich and Jeannette Winkelhage for letting me draw on our joint research and working papers on prioritising in medicine; Immacolata Amodeo and Petra Lietz for their moral support; Patrick Brindle from Sage for his enthusiasm in getting the book project off the ground; Katie Metzler from Sage for her editorial suggestions, which have transformed a rather stuffy academic text into what is now hopefully a readable textbook; Irina Chiaburu for her tireless help with databases, files, and photocopying; Meropi Tzanetakis and several anonymous reviewers for their feedback on the manuscript in various draft stages; Jacobs University Bremen for granting me a sabbatical to write the book; and finally and above all, the many students and workshop participants whose questions over the years have inspired this book. I hope you will find it useful!

Margrit Schreier
Bremen
June 2011

1
INTRODUCTION: WHAT IS QUALITATIVE CONTENT ANALYSIS?

Chapter guide

You are a qualitative researcher, and probably you have already collected part of your data. Now you want to know: What does it all mean? There are many qualitative methods out there for analysing your data and interpreting its meaning, and qualitative content analysis (QCA) is one of them. This first chapter will give you a basic idea of the method and what it involves, before going into more detail in the following chapters. More specifically, we will look at:

- some basic features of QCA;
- the origin of quantitative content analysis in the social sciences;
- how QCA emerged from quantitative content analysis.

The chapter will conclude with an overview of the book.

Some basic features of QCA

QCA is a method for describing the meaning of qualitative material in a systematic way. You do this by assigning successive parts of your material to the categories of your coding frame. This frame is at the heart of QCA, and it covers all those meanings that feature in the description and interpretation of your material.

KEY POINT

QCA is a method for systematically describing the meaning of qualitative material. It is done by classifying material as instances of the categories of a coding frame.

In the following, we will look in more detail at:

- the kind of material to which you can apply QCA;
- the goals of QCA;
- how QCA is done.

What material is suitable for QCA?

In most general terms, QCA will be an option if you have to engage in some degree of interpretation to arrive at the meaning of your data. In a way, this is almost a tautology. Data never 'speaks for itself', it does not 'have' a specific meaning. Meaning is something that we, the recipients, attribute to the words that we hear or read, to the images that we see. This is a complex process in which we bring together our perception of the material with our own individual background: what we know about a topic, the situation in which we encounter it, how we feel at the time, and much more. Meaning is not a given, but we *construct* meaning. The assumption that meaning is not something that is inherent in a text, that the recipients take an active part in constructing meaning, was first put forward by Fredric Bartlett, a psychologist, as early as 1932. Ever since, it has become a staple of theory and research on reading and text comprehension (see Goldman, Graesser & van den Broek, 1999, on reading, processing and understanding different kinds of texts).

But meanings can be more or less standardised. Highly standardised meanings are also meanings by convention, and they also require some degree of interpretation. But because the meaning is such a standard one, the process of meaning construction no longer requires any effort; it has become automatic, and pretty much everyone with the same cultural background will agree that this is what the material means. When you are dealing with highly standardised meanings, there is really no need to apply a method like QCA (or any other qualitative method for data analysis). This would be the case, for instance, if you were interested in finding out about the number of men and women shown in magazine advertisements: little interpretation is needed to decide whether the persons in the picture are male or female. With such material, quantitative content analysis would be a good method to use (see Chapter 2 for the difference between qualitative and quantitative content analysis).

QCA comes into its own when you are dealing with meaning that is less obvious. If you were interested in finding out whether women in magazine advertisements are more often placed in trivial contexts than men, for instance, you would be dealing with a much less standardised meaning. What exactly is a trivial context? Not everyone would agree on this, and often you will only be able to tell whether a context is trivial or not by examining the image in some detail. It is in this sense that QCA is a suitable method for describing material that requires some degree of interpretation. When you are engaged in qualitative research, your data will usually be of the type that requires some interpretation.

As long as your material is of this kind, QCA will be an option. It does not matter, for instance, how you came by your data: whether you generated it in the process of doing your research (by doing interviews, or creating observation protocols) or whether you sampled material from other sources (such as newspapers or documentary archives). QCA can be applied to a wide range of materials: interview transcripts, transcripts of focus groups, textbooks, company brochures, contracts, diaries, websites, entries on social network sites, television programs, newspaper articles, magazine advertisements, and many more (for an overview of qualitative methods for data collection see Marshall & Rossman, 2006, Chapter 4; on the interview in particular see Wengraf, 2001; Witzel & Reiter, in press).

It also does not matter whether your material is verbal or visual. When QCA was first developed, it was used for analysing and interpreting texts, such as newspaper articles (see below). Today, too, QCA is most often applied to verbal data, such as interview transcripts, emails, archival material, and the like. This is why the data for QCA is often referred to as 'text'. But this is merely a matter of convenience and of habit, and many authors have stressed that content analysis can just as well be used for analysing visual material (for example, Krippendorff, 2004; Shapiro & Markoff, 1997). It is helpful to keep this in mind when reading about the 'text' or the 'textual material' to which QCA is applied: 'Text' is used as a generic term here, covering all kinds of qualitative material, visual as well as verbal.

Checklist: When to use QCA

- When you are dealing with rich data that requires interpretation
- On verbal data
- On visual data
- On data that you have sampled from other sources (documents, internet, etc.)
- On data that you have collected yourself (interviews, focus groups, etc.)

The goals of QCA

In most general terms, the aim of QCA is to systematically describe the meaning of your material. The systematic nature of content analysis, including QCA, is a point on which pretty much all authors who have written about the method over the years agree (to name only a few: Früh, 2007; Groeben & Rustemeyer, 1994; Holsti, 1969; Krippendorff, 2004; Mayring, 2000; 2010; Shapiro & Markoff, 1997). But this very broad goal needs to be qualified in two respects.

In the first place, QCA will help you describe your material only in certain respects which you have to specify. QCA does not allow you to describe the full meaning of your material in each and every respect. This characteristic points to an important difference between QCA and other qualitative methods for data analysis, especially methods that are rooted in a hermeneutic tradition. These methods take you along a spiral path, taking more aspects into account and arriving at a yet more comprehensive sense of your material at every step. QCA is not like this. With QCA, your research question specifies the angle from which you examine your data. If other important aspects strike you during the analysis, you can change your coding frame and include these as well. But these will again be specific, selected aspects. QCA does not give you a holistic overview of your material. Früh (2007) and Groeben (1987) write about this in more detail.

Focusing on selected aspects of your material is what distinguishes QCA from many other qualitative methods for data analysis. On the one hand, selected aspects are less compared to the full, comprehensive meaning of a text. On the other hand, qualitative data are very rich anyway – so rich that it is impossible for all practical purposes to really capture their full meaning. Also, qualitative research tends to produce a *lot* of data. And it is easy to get lost in what can be hundreds of pages of interview transcripts. When you are dealing with a lot of very rich material, it can actually be very useful to focus on selected aspects only, and QCA helps you do so.

There is a second sense in which the very general goal of describing the meaning of your material needs some qualification. This concerns the question of what your description is for: does it stand on its own, or do you use your description as a basis for conclusions about an external social reality? Do you, for instance, simply want to describe advertisements depicting men and women and the contexts in which they are shown? Or do you want to use the information that women are (or are not) shown in trivialising contexts more often than men to infer something about the values held by the culture and society in which these magazines are published?

This has been a highly controversial topic, with authors such as Groeben and Rustemeyer (1994), Lisch and Kriz (1978) and Rössler (2005) arguing that QCA can never do more than describe the material to which it is applied, and others such as Früh (2007), Krippendorff (2004) and Merten (1995) claiming that QCA proper invariably involves conclusions that go beyond the material under study. This controversy has its roots in the different disciplinary origins of the authors, and we will return to it in the context of validity issues (see Chapter 9). For the time being you should simply be aware that your answer will probably depend on your material. If you have generated your material in the research process, a simple description will often be enough. If you have conducted interviews, for example, you will probably use QCA to describe what your participants have said. But if you have sampled your material from other sources, chances are that you will want to go beyond description. If you are analysing company brochures, for example, you will usually want to say something about the company, not just about the brochures. Likewise, if you are analysing gender depiction in magazine advertisements, you will be interested in gender stereotypes and gender roles in that society, not just in describing the advertisements. In this case, QCA may not be enough to substantiate your conclusions. You may need additional evidence to show that the brochures do indeed provide valid information about the company, and that magazine advertisements adequately reflect upon the gender roles and stereotypes that are prevalent in society (they may well lag behind actual developments!).

What QCA involves

In our everyday interactions with others, we are constantly engaged in deciphering meaning and in interpreting communication. But what we do on an everyday basis is largely intuitive: we do not always listen carefully, we may jump to conclusions, and sometimes we hear what we want to hear, and not what the other person is actually saying. Qualitative data analysis is like everyday understanding in its concern with meaning. But at the same time it goes beyond our everyday activities. Each method of qualitative data analysis specifies a distinctive way – a *method* – of overcoming the shortcomings of our everyday understanding. The way in which QCA does this is as follows: first, it requires you to 'translate' all those meanings in your material that are of interest to you into the categories of a coding frame; second, it has you classify successive parts of your material according to these categories. The way in which this is done highlights three important characteristics of QCA: it is a systematic method, it is flexible, and it reduces data.

KEY POINT

QCA is systematic, flexible, and it reduces data.

QCA is systematic

The *systematic* nature of QCA is probably its most distinctive feature (see above). QCA is systematic in three important respects.

In QCA, you examine *all* your material and decide for each part where in the coding frame it fits (Rustemeyer, 1992; Shapiro & Markoff, 1997). This is very important and a point to which we will come back several times in the course of this book. Unless you examine each and every part of your material, chances are that you will overlook those parts that do not fit the concepts and ideas that you bring to your research. And you invariably have such notions, even if you do not have any hypotheses.

Regardless of your material and your research question, QCA always involves the *same sequence of steps* (for content analysis in general see Neuendorf, 2002; for QCA in particular see Rustemeyer, 1992): deciding on a research question; selecting your material; building a coding frame that will usually comprise several main categories, each with their own set of subcategories; dividing your material into units of coding; trying out your coding frame through double-coding, followed by a discussion of units that were coded differently; evaluating your coding frame in terms of the consistency of coding and in terms of validity and revising it accordingly; coding all your material, using the revised version of your coding frame, and transforming the information to the case level; interpreting and presenting your findings. Deciding on a research question, selecting your material, and interpreting and presenting your findings are an important part of all research, regardless of the method you are using. All other steps are specific to QCA.

Steps in QCA

1　Deciding on your research question
2　Selecting your material
3　Building a coding frame
4　Dividing your material into units of coding
5　Trying out your coding frame
6　Evaluating and modifying your coding frame
7　Main analysis
8　Interpreting and presenting your findings

When we engage in understanding and interpretation of meaning in every-day contexts, we bring to this process our individual personalities, needs and moods; and all of this takes place in a specific situation. You may flare up at a chance remark that would not bother the next person in the least; and perhaps you only flared up today because you had a big fight with your partner the day before. In QCA, you go beyond your individual understanding at the given moment by checking whether your understanding stands the test of *consistency*. This can be consistency with how another person understands the same passage; it can also be consistency with what you take the passage to mean at another time (see Chapter 9 in more detail on how to go about this).

Consistency in this sense refers to what has been called *reliability*. The origins of reliability are in quantitative research where the criterion is used to assess the quality of instruments (see, for instance, Bryman, 2008, pp. 149ff.; Cresswell, 2009, pp. 190ff.). In general terms, an instrument is considered to be reliable to the extent that it yields data that is free of error. Checking for consistency between coders or between different points in time is one way of assessing the reliability of your coding frame. Note that this is not to say that your own, individual understanding is not worthy of consideration! It definitely is, and this plays an important role as you build your coding frame (see Chapter 5). But when it comes to classifying your material according to this coding frame, the goal of QCA is to go beyond individual understanding and interpretation (on the role of consistency and reliability in QCA see Boyatzis, 1998; Mayring, 2010; Rustemeyer, 1992).

QCA is flexible

At the same time, QCA is also a highly *flexible* method – flexible in the sense that you will always have to tailor your coding frame to your material (Boyatzis, 1998; Rustemeyer, 1992). This is because you not only want your coding frame to be reliable – you also want it to be *valid*. In the methodological literature, an instrument is considered valid to the extent that it in fact captures what it sets out to capture (Krippendorff, 2004, Chapter 13; Neuendorf, 2002, Chapter 6; see Chapter 9 below for a more in-depth discussion of the role of validity in QCA). Your coding frame can be regarded as valid to the extent that your categories adequately represent the concepts in your research question, and to achieve this you have to adapt your frame so as to fit your material.

This is an important difference from quantitative content analysis. Here, concept-driven coding frames are sometimes used, and standardised coding frames have been developed, such as the coding frames by Gottschalk and Gleser (1967) for assessing the expression of emotions in textual material. Their assumption is that expressions of basic emotions and their indicators remain the same, regardless of the person expressing them and the context in which they are expressed. But in QCA, you are always to some extent concerned with describing the specifics of your material. And to do so, your coding frame has to match your material. Because of this, coding frames in QCA are always partly data-driven. You can make use of theory or of coding frames developed by other researchers, but you have to adapt these to the material that you are studying.

QCA reduces data

Finally, QCA *reduces* data – and in this respect it is different from other methods for qualitative data analysis (Früh, 1992; Groeben & Rustemeyer, 1994). Most methods for qualitative data analysis are concerned with opening up your data, discovering new things about it, bringing it together in novel ways. This usually involves producing even more data – data about your data, as it were (see Chapter 2). QCA is different. It focuses your analysis on selected aspects, and in this process it reduces your material in two ways:

- In the first place, you do not take into account all the information provided by a case (be it a document, an interview transcript, etc.). Instead, you limit your analysis to those aspects that are relevant with a view to your research question.
- Second, the categories of your coding frame will usually be at a higher level of abstraction than the more concrete information in your material. By classifying the specific, concrete information in your material according to your coding frame, you lose these specifics. This is the price you pay for being able to compare one specific piece of information to another (within the same case or as part of another case). In the process of coding, you classify all specific information as instances of higher-order categories. Building a coding frame in QCA is all about finding the right

balance here. You will make your categories sufficiently abstract to allow for comparison and sufficiently concrete so as to preserve as many specifics as possible (see Chapters 4 and 5).

But note that as you engage in reducing specifics through the process of classification, you are at the same time producing new information (Früh, 1992). This is information *across cases*, telling you how your cases compare to each other with respect to the categories in your coding frame. You may lose specific information on the individual level, but you gain information on the aggregate level!

───────── **Example of how you reduce your material using QCA** ─────────

McDonald, Wearing and Ponting (2009) wanted to find out which elements of wilderness settings contribute to what has been called a peak experience: a brief experience of happiness, fulfilment, and spiritual insight. They asked 39 persons who had visited a wilderness setting to describe in their own words the most wonderful experience they had had there. They then used QCA to analyse these descriptions in a data-driven way, resulting in what they call seven core themes, i.e. seven important aspects of peak experiences in wilderness settings. This analysis reduces the interview material by focusing only on characteristics of peak experiences. Other aspects of the participants' responses were not included in the analysis, such as how they came to choose this wilderness setting in particular, or potential negative effects of their experience, such as forgetting to make an important phone call. It also reduces the material by subsuming all the individual details of the participants' experiences under these seven core themes. Theme 2, for instance, refers to escape from the man-made world. Different aspects of the man-made world are summarised here: the presence of other people as such, the sheer number of other people in a large city, as well as man-made media. At the same time, creating this category also produces new information, namely information about what there is in the man-made world that people want to escape from: number of people, the omnipresence of the media, and an inability to focus on one's surroundings because of a constant input from the outside world. Creating the category relates these to each other.

SUMMARY

QCA is a method for systematically describing the meaning of qualitative material. This is done by classifying parts of your material as instances of the categories of a coding frame. The method is suitable for all material that requires some degree of interpretation. This can be verbal or visual, and it can be material that you generated for your research, or material that you sampled from other sources. QCA requires that you focus your analysis on selected aspects of your material, as indicated by your research question; in this respect it differs from other qualitative methods of data analysis. QCA is systematic, flexible, and it reduces data. The method is systematic in three ways: all relevant material is taken into account; a sequence of steps is followed during the analysis, regardless of your material; and you have to check your coding for consistency (reliability). It is flexible in that your coding frame must be adapted so as to fit your material, i.e. to be valid. And it reduces your material by limiting your analysis to relevant aspects of the material. Also, through classifying specific information as an instance of a category, you subsume the specific information under a more general concept. At the same time, categorising also produces new information about how your cases compare.

The origins of quantitative content analysis in the social sciences

We will now look at the history of quantitative content analysis, originating in communication studies. The history of the method can be divided into three broad phases: a first phase of early applications, lasting from approximately the eighteenth century until the early twentieth century; a second phase when quantitative content analysis came into its own as a research method, lasting until the late 1940s; and a third phase of interdisciplinary and methodological elaboration that is continuing until the present day. Developments during these phases actually overlap to some extent. This is why only approximate beginnings and ends of phases are given.

First phase: Early applications

People were interested in the systematic analysis of text a long time before 'content analysis' was formally developed as a method in the social sciences (for more detail see Krippendorff, 2004; Merten, 1995).

In the late seventeenth and eighteenth century, Church potentates were worried that non-religious or unorthodox material might be distributed in the name of the Church. To prevent this, they commissioned analyses of religious texts. In eighteenth-century Sweden, for instance, a collection of hymns was analysed for the frequency of certain key words (such as *God, Kingdom of Heaven*) to determine whether these songs were in line with Church teachings (it was concluded that they were; see Dovring, 1954).

---------- **Example of an early use of newspaper analysis** ----------

In 1893 Speed published an analysis of the themes covered by different New York newspapers, comparing the years 1881 and 1893. He concluded that over time the coverage of themes such as gossip and scandal had increased at the expense of religious and scientific content (Speed, 1893).

As the newspaper gained in popularity and turned into the first 'mass medium' in the second half of the nineteenth century, there was also an increasing interest in the content distributed by this medium. Journalism schools were founded, and founders and teachers wanted to instil in their students ethical standards of journalism and 'objective' reporting. Scientists also wanted to know whether newspaper content was in fact objective, ethical, and 'edifying'. In this context, quantitative descriptions and differentiations of newspaper content became the focus of early content analysis.

Often, this involved comparisons, both within one newspaper (by following its development over time) and by comparing different newspapers in terms of the themes that were covered. In determining the relative importance of the different themes, researchers did not rely on the number of articles alone. They also took into account number of words, percentage area of a page taken up by an article on a given topic, letter size of headlines, placement on the page, and the like (Merten, 1995, Chapter I.2 provides many detailed examples).

Second phase: Content analysis coming into its own

During the second phase, content analysis was developed into a research method in the empirical social sciences. Two developments contributed to this: the rise of the social sciences and an increasing interest in the effects of communication content in the media (Krippendorff, 2004; Lissmann, 2008; Merten, 1995).

In the 1930s and 1940s, other social science disciplines such as sociology and psychology were gaining in importance, and researchers from these disciplines introduced new concepts, such as social stereotypes or attitudes. These social science concepts affected the analysis of communication content in two ways. First, these concepts were theory-based, requiring far more sophistication of conceptualisation and measurement than had been customary in early quantitative newspaper analysis. Second, the concepts suggested new directions in the analysis of mass media content. The concept of stereotypes, for instance, created an interest in how certain key issues were represented in media products. Simpson (1936), for example, analysed representations of black Americans in the press, and Martin (1936) examined the representation of nationalism in children's books from different countries.

──────── **Example of the use of stereotypes in early content analysis** ────────

For her analysis of nationalism in children's books, Martin (1936) selected 24 popular children's books from 12 different countries in their English translation (among them *Pinocchio, Heidi, Jungle Book*). For her analysis, she identified symbols of nationalism which she then analysed in three respects: according to subject, whether the symbol referred to the country of origin or a different country, and whether the evaluation of that country was positive or negative. Altogether, she identified approximately 1,000 such symbols in each of the books! As it turned out, books from the different countries did not differ significantly in the amount and type of national symbolism used. But Martin did find more nationalist symbolism in children's books that were published after times of crisis (compared to books published before or during a national crisis).

The concept of attitude proved to be of special importance for the further development of content analysis. Whereas in the past, analysis of newspaper content had been limited to themes, Lasswell (1941) now examined how such themes were evaluated (see also the above example of Martin's analysis of children's books). For each theme, he also recorded the direction of the evaluation, differentiating between negative, neutral, and positive evaluations. This analysis of the evaluative dimension of representations in the media has become standard in quantitative content analysis in communication studies.

Whereas early analysis of newspaper content had been limited to the content itself, the 1930s brought an increasing interest in inferences from communication content to the recipients. This new interest was linked to the advent of the new media of radio and film. There was now increasing competition within the media landscape, raising the question of how to attract and hold the interest of the audience. More media also meant more advertising, and with more advertising there came a concern with designing maximally effective messages.

The increasing interest in the effects of media messages was also closely related to the Second World War. In 1939, the US Government made Harold Lasswell head of the department for the analysis of wartime communication. Lasswell had already begun to develop propaganda analysis in the 1920s (Lasswell, 1927). Under his directorship, ongoing content analysis of propaganda issued in Nazi Germany was carried out (e.g. Lasswell & Jones, 1939; see also the overview in Schramm, 1997). Unlike the previous quantitative analysis of newspaper content, propaganda analysis required that communication content be placed in the context of both its production and its reception.

With propaganda analysis, Lasswell not only opened up a new substantive area for the application of content analysis (the first among many). He also began to refine the method, adding considerations concerning sampling, the building of categories, and assessing agreement between coders as a quality measure. This marked the beginning of a period of methodological reflection on content analysis as a research method, starting in the year 1941.

KEY POINT

1941 was the 'birth year' of content analysis.

This was the year when content analysis really came into its own. A conference on mass communication was held in Chicago which was attended by all leading scholars in the field, and the focus of the conference was on content analysis (Waples, 1942). Soon afterwards, Berelson and Lazarsfeld (1948) published a first introduction to the method. Based on this book, Berelson (1952) published what was to become the first leading textbook on content analysis.

Third phase: Interdisciplinary and methodological elaboration

From the 1940s, content analysis began to attract attention as a research method outside communication studies. This trend continued during the subsequent years, and content analysis came to be used in many diverse disciplines such as political science, psychology, education, and literary studies (Krippendorff, 2004; Merten, 1995).

In political science, Lasswell's propaganda analysis had already paved the way for content analysis. The beginnings of the use of content analysis in psychology were marked by the work of Gordon Allport (1942; 1965). He used personal structure analysis (a variant of content analysis: Baldwin, 1942) to analyse 301 letters written by one woman ('Jenny'), identifying key themes and drawing conclusions from these themes on Jenny's attitudes and personality. Other landmark applications of content analysis in and to psychology include Bales's development of a multidimensional coding frame for analysing the verbal interactions between the members of small groups (interaction process analysis: Bales, 1950), and using the method for analysing free responses to the Thematic Apperception Test (Smith, 2008), a personality test for assessing the strength of people's motives (such as power, success, or affiliation).

In educational research, content analysis was, for instance, used to analyse texts in terms of their readability. Flesch (1948) developed a readability formula that was based on average sentence length, average word length, number of personal words, and number of personal sentences in a text. At the same time, this is an example of content analysis that does not in fact focus on textual content features, but on the formal characteristics of a text. Formal features were also the focus in applying content analysis to literary studies where it has, for example, been used to differentiate between potential authors of texts of unknown authorship. Yule (1944) used stylistic content analysis to establish that of two authors, Thomas à Kempis and Charlier de Gerson, the former was more likely to have written the text *De Imitatione Christi*.

This use of content analysis in different disciplines was accompanied by an increasing methodological differentiation. To adapt the method to the research questions that were asked in the different disciplines, ever new variants of content analysis were developed, such as contingency analysis (Osgood, 1959), value analysis (White, 1944), the semantic differential (Osgood, 1952), and others already mentioned above (readability analysis; personality structure analysis; analysis of motives, etc.). Overall, these developments were characterised by increasing attention to the context in which communication content is produced or received, and by changing the focus of the analysis from the frequency of selected textual characteristics to their interrelation. These elaborations of the method were discussed at a second landmark conference on content analysis which took place in 1955 (Pool, 1959). Later conferences in 1967 and 1974 increasingly focused on the use of computers in content analysis (Gerbner et al., 1969; Stone, 1975).

SUMMARY

The history of content analysis can be divided into three phases: early applications, content analysis coming into its own, and interdisciplinary and methodological elaborations. Early applications focused on the quantitative description and differentiation of newspaper content, often from a comparative perspective. The second phase was characterised by more sophisticated conceptualisation and measurement as well as an increasing interest in the effects of content on the recipients. During the third phase, content analysis came to be used in other social science disciplines. As the method was applied to novel kinds of research questions, ever more variants were developed. This was accompanied by increasing attention to the context of production and reception and to the interrelation of selected textual characteristics.

The emergence of qualitative content analysis

Critique of quantitative content analysis

In his textbook on content analysis, Berelson (1952, p. 18) defined the method as follows: 'Content analysis is a research technique for the objective, systematic, and quantitative description of the manifest content of communication.' But this definition, with its strong focus on content analysis as a quantitative method, was contested even in that same year by Kracauer (1952). Kracauer argued against a purely quantitative type of content analysis on three grounds:

- Meaning is often complex, holistic, and context-dependent.
- Meaning is not always manifest and clear at first sight. Sometimes it is necessary to read a text in more detail to determine what exactly it means.
- Some aspects of meaning may appear only once in a text. This does not necessarily imply that such aspects are less important than aspects that are mentioned more frequently.

Based on these considerations, Kracauer favoured a more qualitative type of content analysis that does not limit itself to manifest content and frequency counts. This suggestion was taken up by George (1959) who had been one of the researchers engaged in the analysis of wartime propaganda. The analysis of propaganda, George argued, requires an analysis of strategy, and strategy often manifests in what he called non-frequency indicators, namely the single occurrence of a certain phrase or word throughout a text. In fact he preferred the term 'non-frequency' to the term 'qualitative' in characterising the variant of content analysis that he was proposing: 'We employ the term "non-frequency" to describe the type of nonquantitative, nonstatistical content analysis which uses the presence or absence of a certain content characteristic or syndrome as a content indicator in an inferential hypothesis' (George, 1959, p. 8). In this way, George took up one of Kracauer's criticisms of quantitative content analysis, namely its focus on frequency counts (for a similar conceptualisation of qualitative content analysis see Holsti, 1969).

Development of QCA

On the one hand, these early criticisms of quantitative content analysis established a sharp dichotomy between a quantitative and a qualitative variant of the method, reflecting the division between adherents of the quantitative and the qualitative research paradigm. On the other hand, this sharp contrast becomes blurred on closer inspection. Berelson himself wrote that some research questions require a more qualitative approach, and George, by choosing the term 'nonfrequency analysis', attempted to evade the distinction altogether. As quantitative content analysis evolved and became more sophisticated, it was increasingly applied to less manifest content. In consequence, many proponents of quantitative content analysis argued that the distinction between a qualitative and a quantitative type of content analysis was artificial, that 'qualitative' and 'quantitative' was merely a matter of degree (cf. Früh, 2007; Holsti, 1969; Krippendorff, 2004; Lisch & Kriz, 1978; Merten, 1995; see also the overview in Groeben & Rustemeyer, 1994). In this way, especially in England and the US, quantitative content analysis opened up towards these first attempts at establishing a qualitative version of the method and ultimately came to embrace it.

Because of this development and the continuing dominance of quantitative content analysis, QCA has not been well known as a research method, especially in English-speaking countries, until recently. Many qualitative researchers do not mention QCA at all (cf. Gibbs, 2007; Mason, 2002; Miles & Huberman, 1994; Silverman, 2000) or present a very quantitative version of the method (compare the descriptions in Berger, 2000, or in Bernard & Ryan, 2010). Other authors equate QCA with the whole range of qualitative methods for data analysis, subsuming other methods such as discourse analysis, conversation analysis, or objective hermeneutics under QCA (Krippendorff, 2004; Lamnek, 2010). Yet other authors describe what is essentially QCA, but call it by a different name, such as 'thematic coding' (cf. Boyatzis, 1998; Saldana, 2009) or 'qualitative media analysis' (Altheide, 1996). It is only recently that QCA has been described as a distinct method in the Anglo-American literature (e.g. Elo & Kyngäs, 2008; Hsie & Shannon, 2005), although some authors (e.g. Klotz & Prakash, 2008) continue to use the term in the same way as did Kracauer (1952) or George (1959), i.e. to refer to an analysis of the presence versus absence of specified themes or features.

On the Continent, especially in Germany, the situation has been different, and there have been a number of conceptualisations of a genuinely qualitative QCA. These include Ritsert's (1972) concept of an anti-ideological variant of the method (see also Vorderer & Groeben, 1987), Rust's (1980) development of a 'strict and qualitative' type of QCA, and flexible QCA (Groeben & Rustemeyer, 1994; Hussy, Schreier & Echterhoff, 2009; Rustemeyer, 1992; other variants can be found in Bilandzic, Koschel & Scheufele, 2001; Gläser & Laudel, 2009; Kuckartz, 2009; Mathes, 1992). A major proponent of QCA in Germany has been Philipp Mayring (2010). He distinguishes between several distinct variants of the method, such as summative and structural QCA. We will look at these in more detail in the context of developing a coding frame in QCA (Chapters 5 and 6).

What is different about QCA?

Who is right? Those who argue that there is no need for QCA because quantitative content analysis can do it all? Or those who have elaborated QCA as a distinct research method? There is certainly no sharp line dividing quantitative content analysis and QCA. Nevertheless all versions of QCA share some characteristics which distinguish the method from quantitative content analysis (see Table 1.1).

KEY POINT

There is no sharp line dividing quantitative and qualitative content analysis. Nevertheless all versions of QCA share some characteristics which make it a method in its own right.

The most important difference was suggested by Kracauer in the early 1950s: the focus of QCA is on *latent* meaning, meaning that is not immediately obvious, whereas quantitative content analysis focuses on manifest, literal meaning (Berelson, 1952; Kracauer, 1952; see the discussion in Groeben & Rustemeyer, 1994; Lisch & Kriz, 1978).

Because manifest meaning is fairly obvious at first sight, you can usually identify it by looking at a small segment of material, such as a single sentence or paragraph. To detect latent meaning, on the other hand, you often have to take context into account. This can be the entire text from which a passage is taken – or even the publication venue or additional background information. If you come across a passage praising the foresight of George W. Bush in the Iraq war, for instance, and

Table 1.1 Differences between quantitative content analysis and QCA

Quantitative content analysis	QCA
Focus on manifest meaning	Focus on latent meaning
Little context needed	Much context needed
Strict handling of reliability	Variable handling of reliability
Reliability checks more important than validity checks	Validity checks just as important as reliability checks
At least partly concept-driven	At least partly data-driven
Fewer inferences to context, author, recipients	More inferences to context, author, recipients
Strict sequence of steps	More variability in carrying out the steps

you know that this comes from a news broadcast in 2008 on the Fox News channel (known for its Republican sympathies), you will take the passage literally. But if you know that it comes from an article published in *Mad* (a major US satirical magazine), you will take it to be ironic and mean the very opposite of what it says. QCA therefore requires you to take *context* into account.

In quantitative content analysis, reliability by double-coding is the most important quality criterion. This is closely related to the focus of quantitative content analysis on manifest meaning. If two persons independently code the same passage, they are more likely to code it the same way if the meaning of the passage is manifest. The more hidden the meaning is, the more context you need in order to infer it, and the more likely it is that two people will read it differently (Neuendorf, 2002). In quantitative content analysis, high reliability is fairly easy to achieve because of the focus on manifest meaning; in QCA, when looking at latent meaning, reliability is more difficult to achieve. Therefore it is only to be expected that reliability is handled differently in QCA (see Chapter 9 for details). In the first place, in QCA consistency scores between coders are acceptable. Second, agreement between coders is not necessarily quantified. Third, in QCA validity is considered to be just as essential as reliability.

This takes us to the next characteristic of QCA, namely the importance of *validity* as a quality criterion (Holsti, 1969; Lisch & Kriz, 1978; Rustemeyer, 1992). This importance is closely related to the role of theory and description in quantitative content analysis and QCA, respectively. In quantitative content analysis, coding frames will usually be partly concept-driven, and you may want to use the method for hypothesis testing. In QCA, on the other hand, your coding frame will usually be partly *data-driven*, and you may want to use the method primarily for describing your material. Overall, theory and prior research play a greater role in quantitative content analysis, and working in a data-driven way is more important in QCA. In quantitative content analysis, theory validates the concept-driven parts of your coding frame. But in QCA you have to make sure that the data-driven parts of your coding frame really capture what is there in your material. Because of this, a validity check is just as important in QCA as a reliability check.

Some authors have argued that QCA is also more likely to be used in making inferences about the context of production, the authors, or the effects on the recipients (Groeben & Rustemeyer, 1994). If you want to draw such inferences that go beyond your material, checking for the validity of your conclusions becomes even more important.

Finally, quantitative content analysis always follows a certain series of steps. So does QCA (although some versions do not: see Altheide, 1996; Lamnek, 2010), but there is more variety in QCA. If you are building a data-driven coding frame, for instance, you may do so based on 5% of your material, 20%, or even all of it. In checking for the reliability of your coding, you may quantify the consistency of the coding, or you may simply sit down with the other coders and explain why you coded a passage in a certain way. Overall, QCA is therefore more *flexible* than quantitative content analysis.

SUMMARY

Already in 1952, quantitative content analysis was criticised on three accounts: meaning is often complex, it may be latent, and it may appear only once in a text. Non-frequency analysis, an early version of QCA, was suggested as an alternative. As quantitative QCA became more sophisticated, proponents of quantitative content analysis came to consider the distinction between quantitative and qualitative content analysis as a matter of degree. Especially in the Anglo-American context, quantitative content analysis encompassed QCA. On the Continent, especially in Germany, QCA was developed as a method in its own right. Recently, it has also come to be recognised as a distinct method of qualitative data analysis in an Anglo-American context. There is no sharp line dividing quantitative content analysis and QCA. Nevertheless all versions of QCA share certain characteristics: focus on latent meaning; attention to context; variable handling of reliability; validity checks just as important as reliability checks; at least partly data-driven; more inferences to context, author, and recipients; more flexibility in going through the steps.

Outlook: What lies ahead

By now, you have gained a first impression of what QCA is all about and how it evolved. In the following chapters, we will look at QCA and the steps involved in carrying out a QCA in more detail.

Although QCA is a qualitative research method, it has its roots in both the qualitative and the quantitative research tradition. In Chapter 2 we will look at some important features of qualitative research and examine in what way QCA does (or does not) exemplify these features.

While QCA is a highly useful method for qualitative data analysis, especially when you are dealing with a large-scale study, there are some research objectives for which it is more suitable than others – and some for which it is not suitable at all. In Chapter 3 we will compare QCA to other methods for qualitative data analysis. On this basis, I will help you decide whether QCA would be a good method for you to use, considering your material and your research question.

The following chapters will then guide you in actually carrying out your own QCA. In Chapter 4, I will explain in more detail what a coding frame is and how to structure a frame. On this basis, we will then look at the steps involved in building a coding frame in general (Chapter 5) and strategies for generating data-driven categories in particular (Chapter 6). To apply a coding frame, you first have to divide your material into smaller parts; this so-called process of segmentation will be covered in Chapter 7. Once you have generated a first version of your coding frame and segmented your material, you are ready to try out your frame in a trial coding. The trial coding is at the core of the pilot phase which we will describe in Chapter 8. Based on your trial coding, the next step is to evaluate your coding frame and modify it accordingly (Chapter 9). Chances are that your frame is now suitable for starting on your main analysis, i.e. assigning all your material to the categories of your frame (Chapter 10). Once you have completed your QCA, you will want to present your findings; Chapter 11 provides you with an overview of strategies for doing so.

Nowadays, qualitative researchers are increasingly making use of software to support their analysis. In Chapter 12 we will take a look at the kinds of software packages that are available today and how they can support you during the different steps of carrying out a QCA.

To illustrate the process of QCA, many examples will be used throughout the book. Nevertheless, you may find yourself wanting to look at more sample studies. You will find an additional chapter describing examples of studies using QCA from a variety of different social science disciplines on the website accompanying this book.

Frequently asked questions

Is content analysis really a qualitative method?

You will probably find as many opinions about this as there are researchers using the method. Content analysis as used in communication studies is typically quantitative content analysis. As I explain earlier in this chapter, QCA developed out of quantitative content analysis. And while there is no sharp line dividing QCA from quantitative content analysis, the various versions of QCA share a number of features which distinguish the method from quantitative content analysis. Because these are features that QCA shares with other qualitative research methods, I would argue that QCA is indeed a qualitative method. In the next chapter, we will look in more detail at what QCA has in common with the qualitative research tradition and where it differs from this tradition and is closer to the quantitative framework.

Can I use QCA if I am working on my own?

Yes, you can. Having said that, it is better if you can find someone to help you. This is so for two reasons. In the first place, you cannot possibly see all the relevant meaning that may be hidden away in your material. This is why, in qualitative research in general, it is better to have several people take a look at the material. Because we do not find meaning, but construct meaning, we all construct it in different ways. It is important to be aware of these different ways in which your material can be read as you are building your coding frame, and someone else can help you with this. Second, consistency is an important criterion during the pilot and the main analysis phase. This can be consistency between different coders or consistency across different points in time (for one coder). In QCA, you want to determine what each part of your material means with respect to your research question. And as you draw your conclusions, you will typically assume that others who share the same socio-cultural background would agree with your interpretation of your material. You have a stronger case if you can show that others (another coder) have indeed read your material in the same way. This does not mean that a second coder has to read and classify all your material. If someone else can code a part of it, this is quite enough (see Chapters 8 and 10).

Is QCA suitable only for analysing content?

I take it that you are referring to the distinction between content and form. In this case, an analysis of content would be about what is being said, whereas an analysis of form would be about how something is being said. Although the name suggests that QCA is only suitable for looking at the 'what', this is actually not the case: you can just as well use QCA to look at how something is being said or expressed in your material. Remember that even quantitative newspaper analysis relied on indicators such as letterhead size and percentage of a page taken up by the coverage of a given theme, i.e. on formal criteria. QCA is suitable for looking at any formal features of your material that you may be interested in: type of argument used, literary genre, the angle from which a picture is taken, typographic features, and much more.

--- **End-of-chapter questions** ---

- What are the three most important characteristics of QCA as a method of data analysis?
- What are the three phases in the development of quantitative content analysis as a research method?
- What were Kracauer's main points of criticism of quantitative content analysis?
- Name four characteristics that distinguish QCA from quantitative content analysis.

2
WHAT IS QUALITATIVE ABOUT QUALITATIVE CONTENT ANALYSIS?

Chapter guide

In the first chapter you have seen how there is no clear line dividing quantitative content analysis and QCA, and how some authors even dispute that QCA is a method in its own right. In this chapter, we will look at what exactly is qualitative about QCA. In the process, we will:

- examine some basic features of qualitative research;
- identify the main qualitative features of QCA.

What is qualitative research?

You will find some key features of qualitative research listed in Table 2.1. In the following, we will look at each of these in turn (for a more in-depth discussion of qualitative research and its characteristics, see, for example, Flick, 2009; Quinn Patton, 2002; Stake, 2010).

Qualitative research is interpretive

Qualitative research is concerned with interpretation in a number of ways. In the first place, data in qualitative research is not standardised, but requires an active effort at interpretation on the researcher's side. Quantitative research deals with numerical data, and there is little room for interpretation as to what a '3' means, or a '100'. Qualitative research deals with symbolic material – verbal data, visual data, artefacts – which leaves much room for interpretation. Moreover, it is often not possible to exactly pin down the meaning of symbolic material, nor do qualitative researchers necessarily want to do so. Several interpretations of the same material can be equally valid, each emphasising a different facet of the meaning of that data. Once we accept that the process of understanding, of attributing meaning, is a constructive one, that we bring to this process our own individual background, and that this background can be different in different situations, the idea of 'the correct' meaning of any piece of data loses its appeal (see also Chapter 1). Qualitative researchers are comfortable with the idea that there can be multiple meanings, multiple interpretations,

Table 2.1 Key features of qualitative research

Interpretive
Naturalistic
Situational
Reflexive
Has emergent flexibility
Inductive
Case-oriented
Puts emphasis on validity

and that these can shift over time and across different people. By the way, this is not to say that all interpretations would be equally valid! Finally, qualitative research is also interpretive in terms of its research questions. If you do qualitative research, you will often be dealing with research questions where you explore the personal meaning of experiences or the social meaning of public persons, or norms, or events.

KEY POINT

Qualitative research is interpretive in three ways: It deals with symbolic material that requires interpretation; different interpretations of the same material can be valid; and it deals with research questions exploring personal or social meanings.

While qualitative researchers emphasise the interpretive nature of their work, this is not to say that quantitative research is not interpretive! Although quantitative researchers are sometimes not fully aware of this, interpretation is part of any research process, be it qualitative or quantitative. When filling in a quantitative survey, the participants have to interpret the questions and the response options (I get headaches about twice a week. Does this mean that I get headaches 'often' or just 'sometimes'? And do my migraines qualify as 'headaches'?). And when they have completed their data analysis, quantitative researchers have to interpret their findings. The difference between qualitative and quantitative research is that in qualitative research, interpretation is at the heart of the research process, whereas in quantitative research it tends to be peripheral, and quantitative researchers are typically less aware of the role it plays in their work.

Qualitative research is naturalistic

Quantitative research often requires the participants to come to the lab, to fill out a questionnaire or to participate in an experiment. This is because the logic of quantitative research requires that anything that might distort or confound the results be eliminated from the research setting. And this is done by bringing the participants into a context that is under the control of the researcher.

Qualitative researchers, on the other hand, are interested in all those messy features that make up real-life contexts. They assume that it is this very context that makes their data meaningful and rich in information. Because of this, qualitative researchers often try to capture as much of this context as possible, for instance by going out into the field and observing, or by asking their participants to tell them about their lives. The context of an event is part of that event. If you go to a party on board a ship, for example, this will be a very different party from the one you usually go to at your club; and the fact that it takes place on board a ship is part of what makes it what it is. Typically, qualitative researchers also do not interfere with the real-world settings that they study – although there are some exceptions to this, such as action research or the qualitative experiment.

But again we are not dealing with a difference in absolute terms here. Quantitative research does not necessarily interfere with the research context. And qualitative researchers sometimes also ask their participants to come to the lab. This can be important in an interview study, for example, where the researcher might prefer a lab setting where interruptions are less likely. But in qualitative research, the researcher would probably not insist on meeting in the lab if the participant preferred to have the interview at home.

Qualitative research is situational

The situational nature of qualitative research is closely related to the previous two characteristics. Qualitative researchers think of interpretation as a process of actively constructing meaning, and they assume that meaning will vary depending on the person who does the interpreting and the context in which meaning is produced. If meaning depends on context, context in fact becomes part of the data. This includes as full a context as possible: the situation in which an event took place or something was said, the history behind the data, and the role of the researcher in the research situation. To understand the life story of an interviewee, for example, it would be important to know whether the interview took place in the lab or in the home of the interviewee and what meanings these different contexts hold for the interviewee. If she is an untidy person, she may feel embarrassed about having the interview at home. It would also be important to know something about her family history. And it would make a difference whether the researcher was also female, of the same ethnicity and age group. In qualitative research, all these different aspects of the context are part of the data.

If context is part of the meaning, this also implies that meaning is context-specific. While quantitative researchers are interested in generalisations that hold across different contexts, qualitative researchers are interested in the very particulars that quantitative researchers leave out as irrelevant. Qualitative research is guided by the assumption that conclusions which apply regardless of context will often be so general as to tell us virtually nothing. The particulars may translate to a few contexts only, but they give us a vivid impression of a specific setting or a specific person.

Qualitative research is reflexive

In quantitative research, objectivity is an important concern. The idea behind objectivity is to obtain data and findings that are independent of the researcher. It should not make a difference, for instance, whether you or your friend measures the pulse in a participant's ear while she is looking at a series of stimuli on the computer screen. If there is a difference, this is either considered to be error (which should even out across the full range of stimuli) or a mistake – perhaps one of you is not yet familiar with the apparatus.

Qualitative research, on the other hand, starts out from the assumption that in the social and behavioural sciences we conduct research on other human beings, and that as human beings we share certain features with our participants. We all think about the things that happen to us in life, we try to make sense of them, and we react differently to different people. When we are participants in a research setting, we of course react differently to different researchers. Some people we like, others make us feel uncomfortable, and it is only natural that we will open up more to someone we like. If we take part in an interview study about the way in which we experience chronic illness, we will focus on different aspects of our experience, depending on whether we are talking to a physician or a fellow sufferer. And we may well come to realise something new about the way in which we experience and cope with chronic illness during the interview, because the questions make us think about our experience in a different way.

From this perspective, objectivity does not really make sense, and reflexivity becomes important instead. This refers both to the reflexivity of our participants and to reflecting upon our own role as researcher. If we take the reflexivity of our participants seriously, we will consider them the experts on our research question, and we will treat them as our partners during the research process. We will also treat them in an ethically responsible manner: We will not hide information from them, for example, or trick them into telling us more than they feel comfortable with. When it comes to our own role as researchers, we should be aware that we invariably co-produce our data (unless we select it from an already existing data pool). And in this case it is crucial that we take into account and acknowledge our own part both in data collection and data analysis.

KEY POINT

Qualitative research acknowledges both the reflexivity of our participants by considering them our partners in the research process and of ourselves by acknowledging the ways in which we co-produce our data and our findings.

But note that this take on objectivity does not imply that 'anything goes' in qualitative research! It is very important in both qualitative and quantitative research that your data is valid (for more detail see below). In an interview, for example, your interviewee should feel free to say what is really going through her mind, and it is your responsibility as a researcher to create an atmosphere where this is the case. Also, your interpretations must always be grounded in your data, and you have to convince your readers that yours really is a plausible way of interpreting your material.

Qualitative research has emergent flexibility

In quantitative research, the idea is that you come up with a hypothesis, a design, and the measures for your most important variables, and then stick with these during the research process, until your study has been completed. But in the process, you are making quite a few assumptions. And it often happens that, as you are conducting your research, you become aware that some of these assumptions are 'off', that another scale, for example, would have been a better way to measure what you are after.

Qualitative research is different, because it has 'emergent flexibility'. This is to say that you continue to adapt and change all aspects of your research as you are collecting and beginning to analyse your data. Your research question may change as you collect more data. You may want to select your cases based on the data you have been collecting, as is done in grounded theory methodology; or you may decide to include more cases than you had originally planned, or adapt your strategy for case selection. The same applies to your methods for data collection and analysis. If you are conducting interviews, for example, you will add more questions if a new aspect of the phenomenon under study has caught your attention, and you will continue to adapt your instrument for data analysis until it really fits your material.

This adaptability of the qualitative research process has an important implication. You can only continue to adapt the research process if you do not proceed in a linear fashion. In quantitative research, you complete one step (data collection), before you get started on the next (data analysis). In qualitative research, all steps of the research process tie into one another in a cyclic manner. You complete all steps for a few cases only; then you look back, adapt your procedure, and apply this to the next cases.

Qualitative research is inductive

Emergent flexibility is closely related to the inductive nature of qualitative research. In terms of data collection this means that you do not pre-structure or standardise your measures. This is in contrast to the deductive, structured nature of quantitative research. In quantitative research, you derive the questions or categories that you use for data collection from theory or prior research; and in this way you specify the aspects of the phenomenon on which you are collecting your data. You also typically provide your participants with a set of response options, standardising the way in which they can respond. In qualitative research, on the other hand, you typically start data collection with some very open, non-directional questions; in this way, you leave it up to your participants which aspects of the phenomenon they wish to focus on. Even as your questions may then become more specific, you do not provide any response options, and your participants can reply in any way they wish.

As a qualitative researcher, you also do your data analysis in an inductive, data-driven way. This is to say that you decide on your key codes and concepts as you go through your material. This has also been called 'letting your categories emerge from your data' and contrasts with a concept-driven procedure. In concept-driven research, you decide on key categories based on theory and on prior research, checking to what extent your material fits these ideas.

KEY POINT

Qualitative data collection is inductive in using open, non-directional measures. Qualitative data analysis is inductive by letting key categories and concepts emerge from the data.

Note that quantitative research can also be inductive, and qualitative studies can contain concept-driven elements – although it would be rare to find a qualitative study that is purely concept-driven.

Qualitative research is case-oriented

Quantitative research is mostly variable-oriented. This is to say, you single out certain characteristics on which you want to focus, such as voting behaviour, personality characteristics, grade point average, or anything else that is of interest to you. Every such characteristic is a variable which can take on a certain number of values. You then study all cases in your sample with respect to these variables, and these variables only. You are not concerned with the cases as such, but with their average value on selected variables, or with the relation between your variables. The advantage of a variable-oriented approach is that you can easily include many cases in your study, sometimes several hundred cases.

Qualitative research, on the other hand, is case-oriented. This means that you are concerned with your cases in their entirety. The case-oriented way of doing research is also a holistic way, where the total is more than the sum of its parts: the case is more than any number of variables taken together to describe a case. Let us suppose that you are doing a study on the experience of unemployment. In a qualitative study, you would explore what unemployment means to the participants in your study, how it makes them feel, what they have done to find another job, how it has affected their family life, their social life, and much more. You look at your phenomenon under study not in isolation, but in relation to many other aspects of your participants' lives. In this way, you study each case in depth. Because in-depth case-oriented research is very time-consuming, qualitative studies typically include only a few cases, sometimes as few as one case only (the single-case study). The main advantage of a case-oriented research strategy is the in-depth understanding that you gain of your cases.

Qualitative research emphasises validity

In quantitative research, objectivity, reliability, and validity are important quality criteria. Objectivity requires that your data, your findings, and your interpretations are the same, regardless of who does the research, and I have already pointed out that this criterion is not upheld in qualitative research: if you believe that meaning is always contextual and that you as the researcher are invariably part of this context and play a role in creating your data, then your data, findings, and interpretations will necessarily be different for every researcher.

The criterion of reliability requires that your data and your findings are free of error. At first sight, this is certainly a reasonable requirement, and qualitative researchers want to avoid error and mistakes as much as quantitative researchers do. But quantitative and qualitative researchers differ in what they regard as 'error' and in how they assess it. In quantitative research, consistency (between raters or between different items that are intended to measure the same construct) and stability (of measurements across time) are common ways of assessing reliability. In qualitative research, stability over time is not usually a feasible criterion, especially where data collection is concerned. Because of the more in-depth and often personal nature of qualitative research, it would not make much sense to repeat your data collection at a later point in time (to ask the same person the same interview questions, for example). Also, because context is so important in qualitative research, it would not even be possible to exactly repeat a data collection process. Because the context has changed, the situation is no longer the same, and different questions might be appropriate.

Most qualitative researchers would agree that assessing reliability through stability of repeated measurements is not a feasible way of dealing with this criterion during data collection in a qualitative research context. In all other respects, however, there is little agreement on reliability among qualitative researchers. Some reject the notion of reliability and error altogether (Smith, 1984). Others accept the quantitative concept of reliability and suggest assessing it as consistency between observers (Silverman, 2001). Yet others argue in favour of a different notion of reliability. They suggest that to make your research reliable, it is important that you proceed in a systematic way, that you make all steps in your research transparent to your readers, and that you show how exactly you arrive at your conclusions (Steinke, 2004).

KEY POINT

In qualitative research, the quantitative criterion of objectivity does not apply. Concerning reliability, the opinions of qualitative researchers differ: Some reject it altogether, some accept it for qualitative research, some suggest a modified concept of reliability for qualitative research.

The third important criterion for assessing the quality of your research is validity. In quantitative research, this applies to your instruments for data collection (and sometimes analysis). These are considered valid to the extent that you succeed in measuring what you set out to measure. In qualitative research, you would not speak of 'measuring' the phenomenon you are looking at. Nevertheless validity is of crucial importance, and you can already guess at this by looking at some of the other characteristics of qualitative research: It is naturalistic; this means that as a qualitative researcher you study your phenomenon in its natural setting. It is also data-driven; this means that you base your conclusions on a close reading of your material. All this points to the importance of really capturing your phenomenon, i.e. of conducting research that is valid.

Moreover, in qualitative research the term 'validity' is sometimes used in a much more comprehensive sense (e.g. Gibbs, 2007). Validity in this comprehensive sense refers to your entire study and the soundness of your findings and your conclusions. To make your conclusions sound and acceptable, your data must of course be valid in the more narrow sense. But in addition, you have to make sure that you have gone about your research in a systematic way, that you make your procedure and your reasoning transparent to your readers, that your design and your method are appropriate to your research question, that you have taken negative cases and alternative interpretations into account. Validity in this broader sense also includes other quality criteria such as reliability.

KEY POINT

Validity is a very important criterion for assessing the quality of qualitative research. It is used in two senses: in a narrow sense, referring to the extent to which your instruments help you capture what you set out to capture, and in a broader sense, referring to the overall quality of your study.

Some final considerations about qualitative and quantitative research

There are many different ways of setting up a study, and what is commonly called 'qualitative' and 'quantitative' research are really just the end points on a continuum. It is only rarely that you will come across research that combines all the above qualitative or all the quantitative features. More often any specific empirical study will be a mix, and there is no sharp line dividing qualitative and quantitative research.

SUMMARY

Qualitative research is:

- Interpretive. It deals with symbolic material that requires interpretation; different interpretations of the same material can be valid; and its focus is on research questions where personal or social meaning is explored.
- Naturalistic. It preserves real-life context and does not manipulate the research setting.
- Situational. Context is always taken into account; and the focus is on particulars.
- Reflexive. The reflexivity of our participants is acknowledged; and you take into account how, as researcher, you co-create your data.
- Characterised by emergent flexibility. You can adapt all aspects of the research process during the study.
- Inductive. You use open measures for data collection; and in data analysis you let key concepts emerge from the data.
- Case-oriented. You study your cases in their entirety and in-depth.
- Focused on validity. Validity refers to both the extent to which your instruments capture what you want to capture and the overall quality of your study.

QCA in the context of qualitative research

Now that we have looked at some key characteristics of qualitative research, we will turn back to QCA. In Chapter 1 we described QCA as a systematic and flexible method of qualitative data analysis which reduces and summarises your material. How does QCA fit with these characteristics of qualitative research?

When answering this question, it is important to keep in mind that QCA is a *method*, whereas some of the above characteristics are meant to apply to research designs. A research design is the way in which a study is laid out, the sequence of steps that you plan in order to answer your research question (Cresswell, 2007; Flick, 2009, Part 3). A method is one step in that sequence. This can be the step of data collection or else, as with QCA, the step of data analysis. Because of this, those characteristics of qualitative research that describe research designs will usually not be applicable to QCA, nor to any other qualitative research *method* (as opposed to research design).

QCA and interpretation

Qualitative research has been described as interpretive in three respects. First, it is interpretive because it is concerned with understanding symbolic material that is not standardised, that requires some degree of interpretation. This key feature is shared by QCA: Whereas quantitative content analysis is used for classifying material that is comparatively standardised, QCA is used when the meaning of your material is less obvious, when interpretation is needed. Remember that QCA helps you describe your material only in certain respects, and that the method will give you the best results if your focus is on describing your material (see Chapter 1). Other qualitative methods such as hermeneutic interpretation or discourse analysis will give you a fuller, more comprehensive interpretation or will let you look beyond your material to the author or the situation in which the material was produced. But this is only a matter of degree, a matter of where you go with your interpretation. The key feature of being concerned with interpreting symbolic material is shared by all qualitative methods for data analysis, including QCA.

Qualitative research is also interpretive in that it is often concerned with personal or social meaning. QCA is also typically applied to research dealing with such questions. Studies where QCA is applied to material from public sources (such as legal documents, advertisements, news reports on the Internet) are often about social meaning (see the examples in Chapter 1); research where QCA is applied to material that is produced by an individual (interviews, biographies, diary entries, and the like) is often about personal meaning.

—————— **Example of using QCA to study personal meaning** ——————

Odağ (2007) used QCA in a study where she compared the ways in which women and men experienced the reading of different types of narrative texts. Employing the reminding method for data collection (Larssen & Seilman, 1988), the readers were asked to mark the text whenever a thought, an emotion, or a memory occurred to them. When they had finished reading, they were requested to go back to these marks and to briefly describe in writing what had been going through their minds. Odağ then used QCA to analyse these reading protocols in terms of quality of the reading experience, reference points of the experience, emotions mentioned, and many other features. By looking at how each individual reader experienced one of the texts, Odağ was concerned with describing personal meaning.

Another way in which qualitative research is interpretive is in acknowledging that different interpretations of the same material can be equally valid. In this respect, QCA differs somewhat from other qualitative methods. You can use QCA to categorise and describe your material on any number of features, i.e. main categories. But for each feature, you have to decide on one meaning; you have to code one out of the various subcategories for a given main category, and subcategories are meant to be mutually exclusive (see Chapter 4). The main strength of QCA is that it helps you analyse and describe the most important characteristics of large amounts of qualitative data. It does so precisely because it reduces and summarises your material, and this comes at the 'cost' of losing the potential multiplicity of meanings of your material.

KEY POINT

QCA shares the interpretive orientation of qualitative research in that it is used on symbolic material requiring some degree of interpretation and in its concern with social or personal meaning. It differs from other qualitative research by requiring the researcher to decide on one out of a potential multiplicity of meanings.

QCA and the naturalistic approach

Qualitative research typically preserves real-life context (which is considered important) and does not manipulate the research setting. Strictly speaking, this feature applies only to qualitative research designs, not to individual research methods. Nevertheless, quantitative researchers have sometimes used this characteristic to describe content analysis as a 'non-reactive' or 'unobtrusive' method (Holsti, 1969; Krippendorff, 2004), i.e. as a method that does not change the data in any way (remember that content analysis is considered a method for data collection in quantitative research). This is especially apparent when you apply QCA to material that you have selected from already existing sources (such as newspapers, archives, the Internet). When you apply QCA, you do not change these materials in any way.

Also, QCA requires that you take all the context into account that you need to know about in order to understand what your material means. This is another way in which the method can be considered naturalistic.

QCA and the situation or context

Qualitative research has been described as context-specific in two ways: qualitative researchers assume that meaning is context-specific; and qualitative research is interested in the particulars, not in general conclusions across contexts.

QCA fully shares the first of these two features. If you use QCA, you take as much context into account as you need to understand the material you are looking at. This can be an earlier paragraph in a piece of text, it can be information about the relationships between people who are talking to each other, or it can be information about the culture in which your material was produced. In fact, in QCA you are even supposed to think about how much context you will have to consider before you get started on your analysis (see Chapter 7 on 'context units').

When it comes to the second way in which context is relevant in qualitative research, things are a little more complicated. QCA was described in Chapter 1 as a method that reduces and summarises your data: you focus your analysis on those parts of your material that are relevant to your research question, and you take the meaning of these parts to a higher level of abstraction. By coding parts of your material as instances of a category in your coding frame, you make these parts comparable to other parts, for instance to what other people are saying on the same topic. But at the same time you lose some of their specific, unique meaning. Doing a QCA is always about finding a balance between these two extremes: preserving the unique and allowing for a certain degree of comparison. In this way, QCA is not as much concerned with the particular and specific as other qualitative research methods are. At the same time, by aiming for a balance between the specific and the general, it is much more concerned with specifics than quantitative research methods are. Because of this, QCA shares features of both qualitative and quantitative research in this respect.

KEY POINT

QCA is context-specific in that you have to explicitly take context into account in arriving at your interpretations. At the same time the method shares features of both qualitative and quantitative research in striking a balance between the specific and the general.

QCA and reflexivity

Qualitative research takes into account the reflexivity of your participants in two ways: by considering them as partners in research and by acknowledging the extent to which you co-produce your own data. The first of these facets of reflexivity does not apply to QCA or to other qualitative methods of data analysis. You can acknowledge the reflexivity of your research participants only where you are engaged in data collection. But QCA, as a method for data analysis, only comes into play at a later stage of the research process.

The second aspect of reflexivity – the part you take in co-producing your data – however, plays an important role in QCA. In a way, one might even say that reflexivity in this sense is a rationale underlying the method: QCA is important because researchers inevitably bring their own background and their own assumptions to any act of understanding. In the process of doing QCA, this reflexivity is acknowledged in creating a coding frame. It is generally a good idea not to do this on your own, but let someone else take a look at your material (cf. Chapter 5). This helps you consider your data from different perspectives and overcome the limitations of your own specific background and assumptions.

When it comes to doing the coding, the goal of QCA is to arrive at a socially shared, consensual understanding of your material. This socially shared understanding should transcend your individual background and assumptions. This is similar to what you do when interpreting and writing up your findings based on other qualitative research methods. Here, too, you are concerned with making a case for your interpretations, making them plausible to others and taking potential rivalling interpretations into account. At the same time, the way you do this is distinctive in QCA. In the first place, you acknowledge your role in co-producing your data by making the grounds for your interpretation transparent so that it can be shared by others. You do this by defining the meanings of your material as the categories of a coding frame. Second, you actually check for the plausibility of your interpretations by assessing their consistency, ideally by comparing your interpretation with someone else's.

QCA and emergent flexibility

Qualitative research typically has emergent flexibility: the research process is cyclic, and you can continue to adapt all aspects of your study in the process.

QCA, like many other qualitative methods (such as coding), combines linear and cyclic elements. It is linear in that there is a clear sequence of steps to the method. At the same time it is cyclic to the extent that you will find yourself going through some stages of the process more than once. As you build your coding frame and generate data-driven categories, you will go through a cycle of including more data and revising your frame, followed by the inclusion of yet more data and another round of revision, and so on (see Chapters 5 and 6). Likewise, the trial coding and the main coding are subsequent cycles of the same activity, i.e. categorising your units of coding by assigning them to one of the categories in your coding frame (see Chapters 8 and 10). Depending on how well the frame fits your material and the degree of consistency in applying the frame, you may have to add yet more cycles of coding.

QCA and the inductive nature of qualitative research

Most qualitative research is inductive, i.e. lets key concepts and categories emerge from the data. QCA shares this feature to a considerable extent.

When you use QCA, you will create at least a part of your categories in a data-driven way (see Chapters 5 and 6). In fact, this is one of the most important strengths of QCA: the method allows you to describe and classify large amounts of qualitative data, such as interviews. At the same time, QCA is only rarely used in an exclusively data-driven way. Especially when you are analysing interviews, your interview guide will point you to concepts which will guide you when creating some of your categories.

— Example of combining concept- and data-driven categories in QCA —

In a study about prioritising and decision making in health care, we conducted semi-structured interviews with participants from six different stakeholder groups (healthy members of the general population, patients, physicians, members of the nursing profession, politicians, and representatives of public health insurance companies). The aim of the study was to describe a broad range of criteria underlying priority setting decisions in health care (Diederich & Schreier, 2009). Following the full transcription of all interviews, we used QCA to analyse our material. In a first step, we made use of our interview guide to create an initial set of concept-based main categories (Winkelhage et al., 2008a; 2008b). In a second step, subcategories and some further main categories were added in a data-driven procedure. Because we wanted to use the same set of categories in analysing the responses of all six stakeholder groups, we developed the coding frame by going through the responses of one stakeholder group after another, adding more data-driven categories whenever additional aspects were mentioned. The final coding frame across all stakeholder groups and all interview questions consisted of 89 main categories and 435 subcategories.

QCA and case orientation

In qualitative research, you will usually look at cases in their entirety and in depth. QCA also lets you describe your material in considerable depth (compare the extensive coding frame we used in our prioritising study). But despite this detailed description, QCA follows a variable-oriented rationale. Each main category in a coding frame is the equivalent of a variable, and the subcategories for each main category make up the values of this variable. In this way, QCA makes you split your cases into variables and look at them through the lens of these variables.

At the same time, in QCA you will use a comparatively large number of variables considering the number of cases – Heil (2010) uses 578. Because you will often use so many variables, you can to a certain extent overcome the limitations of the variable-oriented approach when you interpret your findings. Once you get to this stage, you can synthesise your findings across all variables on a case-by-case basis, creating in-depth profiles for each of your cases in turn (see Chapter 11).

QCA and validity

In evaluating the quality of qualitative research, validity is typically emphasised instead of objectivity and reliability. In this respect, QCA again combines elements from both the quantitative and qualitative research traditions.

In the first place, both objectivity and reliability play a larger role in QCA than they do in qualitative research in general (see also Chapter 9 on evaluating your coding frame). In QCA, a consistency check is built into the procedure: you either have part of your material coded by another person, or you recode part of the material yourself after approximately 10–14 days. There is a twofold rationale behind this double-coding. In the first place, the idea in QCA is to arrive at an interpretation of your material that would be shared by most people with a similar cultural background (see above). You do not claim that this is *the* meaning of your material in absolute terms, but you would certainly claim that this is not just your individual understanding. Having your material double-coded by another researcher helps you check for this. And inter-subjectivity is commonly considered to be an approximation of objectivity.

Second, double-coding helps you assess the quality of your coding frame. If your code definitions are clear and subcategories do not overlap, two rounds of independent coding should yield approximately the same results. It does not matter whether this involves you and another researcher coding or you coding at two different points in time. Where the results of the two rounds of coding differ systematically, you will have to go over your coding frame again and revise it. Where the results of the two rounds of coding coincide, you can consider your coding frame to be reliable.

I mentioned earlier that qualitative researchers differ in their views on the role of reliability in qualitative research: some reject it altogether, some apply the criterion to qualitative research as well (and checking your coding frame for errors through double-coding is just such an application), and others modify the idea of reliability. One such modification involves the requirement that qualitative researchers work in a systematic way and make it transparent to their readers how they arrive at their interpretations and conclusions. Reliability in this latter sense of the term is also important in QCA. Because QCA always requires you to follow the same sequence of steps, regardless of your research question and your material, it is a very systematic method; and by being very systematic, QCA is also reliable.

━━━━━━━━━━━━━━━━━━━━━━ KEY POINT ━━━━━━━━━━━━━━━━━━━━━━

In QCA, reliability is important in two respects. As coding consistency, it tells you something about the quality of your coding frame. As a systematic, transparent way of proceeding it requires you to always follow the same sequence of steps.

Reliability and even objectivity (though in a modified sense) are therefore important criteria in QCA – but this does not come at the expense of validity. Instead, validity is just as important as reliability/objectivity, and in the importance it places upon validity, QCA is close to the qualitative research tradition. This refers to validity in the narrow sense of the term, i.e. the requirement that your coding frame captures what you set out to capture. The importance of validity is one of the reasons why your coding frame in QCA will usually be part data-driven. Unless you at least adapt your categories to your data, chances are that your coding frame will not be sufficiently valid (see Chapter 9 for more detail). The importance of validity is also related to the controversy surrounding the kinds of inferences that you can draw based on a QCA of your material: if you want to say something about the author, the situation in which your material was created, or its effects on the recipients, you will usually need additional evidence of validity, over and above the general fit between your data and your coding frame (Früh, 2007; Groeben & Rustemeyer, 1994).

━━━━━━━━━━━━━━━━━━━━━━ SUMMARY ━━━━━━━━━━━━━━━━━━━━━━

Like other qualitative research, QCA is interpretive in that it is applied to symbolic material that requires interpretation and in focusing on personal or social meaning; it is naturalistic in not changing your data in any way; it requires you to take context into account in arriving at your interpretations; it acknowledges your reflexivity by taking others' perspectives into account when creating your coding frame and by making the grounds for your interpretations transparent; your categories will be at least in part data-driven, i.e. inductive; and validity is an important criterion in evaluating your coding frame.

In other respects, QCA shares and combines features of both qualitative and quantitative research: It takes into account a large number of features, yet forces you to decide on one meaning for each of these features; it aims for a balance between the general and the specific; it combines linear and cyclic elements; it is part data-driven and part concept-driven; it is variable-oriented, and at the same time allows for an in-depth description of cases by combining a large number of variables; and reliability and validity are of equal importance as evaluation criteria.

Frequently asked questions

QCA involves numbers – doesn't this make it a quantitative method?

It is not true that QCA always involves numbers. But you are right: numbers can and often do play a role in QCA, and they do so in two ways – when quantifying coding consistency, and when presenting your results in a frequency format.

In the first place, numbers enter the picture if you quantify coding consistency in your research, for instance by calculating a kappa coefficient or a percentage of agreement (see Chapter 9). Coding consistency is indeed an important part of QCA. But this does not mean that you invariably have to quantify coding consistency. Alternatively, you and the other coder can simply sit down together and discuss those segments of your material that you coded differently. And even if you do quantify coding consistency, this does not automatically make QCA a quantitative method. It is simply one more respect in which QCA combines features from both qualitative and quantitative research.

Another way in which numbers are often believed to play a role in QCA is when you present your results. Many researchers do this by providing their readers with the coding frequencies for all their categories. But to start with, QCA does not require you to present your results in any particular way. There are many ways of doing this (they will be described in Chapter 11), and providing coding frequencies is only one of them. Moreover, presenting your results is not a part of QCA – presenting your results is a step that follows QCA. And although the results of QCA lend themselves well to being presented in a frequency format, the results of other qualitative methods for data analysis can also be presented as frequencies.

Can I use QCA in a qualitative study with a cyclic design?

Because QCA combines linear and cyclic elements, it is easiest to use the method with designs that resemble QCA in this respect, such as the qualitative survey (Jansen, 2010). But you can also adapt the method to a cyclic design. This would mean that you keep on building and revising your coding frame as you include additional cases and collect more data. When you have completed your data collection, you do one last round of revising your coding frame and then apply it to all your material.

--------------------- **End-of-chapter questions** ---------------------

- Which characteristics does QCA share with other qualitative research methods?
- In what respects does QCA combine features of qualitative and quantitative research?

3

WILL QUALITATIVE CONTENT ANALYSIS WORK FOR ME? DECISION AIDS

Chapter guide

QCA is a powerful method, especially when it comes to summarising and describing key aspects of your material. But no method is 'good' or 'not so good' as such. How useful a method is always depends on your research question. This chapter will help you decide whether QCA would be a good method for you to use by comparing it to other methods for qualitative data analysis.

There are many such methods out there, and it is impossible to compare QCA to all of them. This chapter will focus on methods that both are prominent in qualitative data analysis and may in fact come to mind as alternatives to QCA. Two methods that might come to mind in this context are document analysis and thematic analysis. These are not included in this chapter because they in fact overlap with QCA to a considerable extent. Document analysis refers to the analysis of a particular type of material (Bowen, 2009; Rapley, 2007), and QCA is one of the methods that can be used here. Thematic analysis (as described by Boyatzis, 1998) in fact refers to a particular type of QCA, namely QCA that focuses on the themes mentioned in your material. Instead, we will look at:

- QCA compared to coding;
- QCA compared to discourse analysis;
- QCA compared to (social) semiotics.

QCA and coding

Coding: a brief overview

Coding is probably *the* most widely known and popular method of qualitative data analysis (Coffey & Atkinson, 1996; Dey, 1993; Gibbs, 2007; Miles & Huberman, 1994; for an overview of different types of coding see Saldana, 2009). At the same time, it is also highly elusive. Some authors write of coding in general terms. Gibbs (2007), for instance, describes coding as the activity of identifying what your data is about. Dey (1993), on the other hand, makes a distinction between labelling and coding your data. He emphasises that coding is always a conceptual process: by creating a code, you identify a part of your data as an instance of a given concept. To add to the confusion, coding can be used as a method in its own right (Coffey & Atkinson, 1996; Miles & Huberman, 1994). Alternatively, it can also, in a more specific sense, be part of the process of building a grounded theory (Strauss & Corbin, 1998).

To differentiate between these different ways of coding, a distinction made by Coffey and Atkinson (1996) is helpful. They distinguish between coding to reduce data and coding as a conceptual device. The reductive type of coding is really a type of indexing: you file away bits and pieces of data under labels or codes. In reductive coding, the focus is on grouping together data addressing the same theme, i.e. on creating links between different pieces of data. This type of coding is purely descriptive, and it essentially reduces large amounts of material to a few general terms. Although it is very simple (it may even strike you as simplistic), reductive coding can help you get a first impression of what 'is there' in your material. In this way, it can be a useful first step and can help you prepare for a more in-depth conceptual analysis.

KEY POINT

'Coding' can refer to a variety of different procedures. In general terms, reductive coding and coding as a conceptual device can be distinguished. Coding in qualitative research usually refers to coding as a conceptual device.

Example of using coding as indexing

In our study about prioritising and decision making in health care, we included vignettes in our interview guide, illustrating treatment options and common dilemmas in medical care, and participants were asked for their opinions and the underlying reasons. One such vignette was about the case of Terri Schiavo, a patient suffering from an eating disorder who had been in a vigil coma for 15 years when intravenous feeding was discontinued. The following passage is taken from the response of one of our participants to this vignette. As described in Chapter 2, in fact QCA was used for data analysis, not coding. The codes that are shown here and in the following example were generated for illustration purposes only.

Well – I don't know what to say, really. I don't approve of this, of turning off her life support. Because this way, she was destined to die. But if you have watched this happen for 15 years, and if there isn't really any– But on the other hand, there have always been miracles, and people have always come back from coma. But on the other hand, if I know that their brain doesn't function properly – what kind of life is that, when the person wakes up. Now that I think about it, I would say it was right that they turned off her life support and that they let her die a dignified death. Well, I don't know whether it was dignified, really... (participant 101)

If you used coding as indexing, you would code this entire passage as *Terri Schiavo*. In this way, you would distinguish it from other passages where other topics are addressed. Coding as indexing can help you find all those passages within one interview where the participant mentions the case of Terri Schiavo. When analysing all interviews, it can help you locate and compare the passages where different participants talk about the case.

Coding as a conceptual device, on the other hand, is described by Coffey and Atkinson (1996) as a device for questioning your data, for opening up new meanings. Coding in this sense is not purely descriptive, but it is a way of relating your data to concepts. By so doing, it helps you think about how one concept you identify may be related to other concepts, and whether you can find evidence of these in your data as well. Also, you will think about how the various concepts are related. In this way, conceptual coding involves creating links between data and concepts, between concepts, and between data. All of this will help you to look at your material from new and different angles and to discover new aspects and ways of questioning your material. This is very much an analytical process that goes beyond the descriptive level and helps you generate theory about your data.

─────────── **Example of using coding as a conceptual device** ───────────

Here you see the same passage concerning Terri Schiavo as above, this time with potentially useful conceptual codes written in the margin.

Well – I don't know what to say, really. I don't approve	disapproval/reasons
of this of turning off her life support. Because this way,	inevitability of death
she was destined to die. But if you have watched this	approval/reasons
happen for 15 years, and if there isn't really any – But on	duration of coma
the other hand, there have always been miracles, and	miracles
people have always come back from coma. But on the	deliberation
other hand, if I know that their brain doesn't function	'proper life'
properly – what kind of life is that, when the person wakes	prerequisites of 'proper life'
up. Now that I think about it, I would say it was right that	approval
they turned off her life support and that they let her die a	
dignified death. Well, I don't know whether it was dignified,	'dignified death'
really... (participant 101)	

These few conceptual codes 'open up' the passage in a number of different ways. On a first level, the participant deliberates about the case and in the process utters different opinions, before she finally reaches a conclusion. She also gives various reasons supporting her initial disapproval (such as the inevitability of Terri Schiavo's death) and her final approval (such as the duration of the coma). Underlying these reasons, a number of more or less implicit assumptions emerge. She mentions miracles. A miracle would be an unusual, highly unlikely course of events. Its implicit opposite would be the normal, expected course of events. This might be a new perspective from which to look at the material: what emerges as 'normal' and what emerges as 'extraordinary' in the context of medicine and medical treatment. Other underlying categories include 'life' and 'death'. The participant rejects the idea of living if one's brain is not fully functional. She therefore clearly has normative ideas of what a 'life' should be like that she considers worth living. Along the same lines, she speaks about a 'dignified death' which she regards as desirable. This raises the question of what constitutes a dignified death, who dies such a dignified death, and what makes this desirable. At the same time, the notion of an 'undignified death' would also be interesting to pursue in this interview as well as in other interviews.

When you read about coding in the context of qualitative data analysis, the author will usually have coding in this conceptual sense in mind. Often, conceptual coding is only the first step in a more comprehensive process of data analysis. Miles and Huberman (1994), for instance, see coding as the starting point in looking for patterns in your material. This potential of conceptual coding for generating theory is particularly apparent in grounded theory. Here, you consider your data the visible indicators of underlying, more general concepts. You discover, refine, and link these concepts in an iterative process that combines three steps: open, axial, and selective coding. In this process, initial open codes are successively condensed into categories and subcategories (Berg & Milmeister, 2008; Breuer, 2009; Strauss & Corbin, 1998).

Comparing coding and QCA

Coding and QCA are similar in many ways, even down to the terminology. In both coding and QCA, 'categories' play a role, and the process of data analysis is referred to as 'coding'. But these are only superficial, and they are less important than the conceptual similarities:

- *Abstraction.* In both coding and QCA, codes/categories are created. This involves some degree of abstraction from your material.
- *Creating new links between data.* In the process of carrying out coding and QCA, you classify parts of your data as instances of these more abstract categories. In this way, you create new links between the data which are coded under the same category.
- *Hierarchical coding frame.* In both coding and QCA, you will usually create a hierarchical coding frame containing both main categories and subcategories.
- *Code definitions.* In both coding and QCA, you want to identify a code/category by a short label. In addition, you define each of your codes/categories.

But in many other respects, the two methods are quite different (see the summary in Table 3.1):

Table 3.1 Differences between coding and QCA

Coding	QCA
Analytic: How do categories relate?	Descriptive: How do data relate?
Codes are mostly data-driven	Codes are part data-driven and part concept-driven
Iterative/cyclic procedure	Linear procedure with cyclic elements
Focus on trustworthiness and credibility	Focus on consistency
– creating and applying codes are one step	– creating and applying codes are different steps
– focus of code definitions is on the conceptual level	– focus of code definitions is on how to recognise instances of the concept in the data
– codes are not mutually exclusive	– subcategories for the same main category are mutually exclusive
– no segmentation necessary	– before coding, material must be divided into units of coding

- (Conceptual) coding is always an analytic process. Its aim is to generate theory, to 'open up' your data. The focus is at least as much on the structure and the interrelations between your categories as on the interrelations between your data and your categories. QCA, on the other hand, is more of a descriptive method. QCA is more about summarising what is there in the data, and less about looking at your data in new ways or creating theory. The focus of QCA is on how your data relate to each other and how your data and your categories relate to each other. The focus of coding, on the other hand, is on how your categories relate to each other.

- Coding is an inductive, iterative method. Typically, codes and categories are not concept-driven, but data-driven; they are derived from your material. To arrive at your final set of categories and codes, you will go through your material many times; and you will continue to revise your codes and your coding as new ways of looking at your material emerge. With QCA, you can create your coding frame in a data-driven way and you may repeatedly return to include more data and generate additional categories. But some of your categories may also be concept-driven, especially main categories. Overall, deductive, concept-driven categories are much more common in QCA than they are in coding. Also, in QCA you want to arrive at a final set of categories as early as possible in the research process. If this is at all feasible, you want to avoid going through your material several times (although you will do so if necessary). Ideally, you will be able to finalise your coding frame based on a part of your material only (see Chapter 5).

- Coding and QCA emphasise different quality criteria. In coding, the emphasis is on trustworthiness and credibility. Others should be able to follow your analysis and your conclusions, but they need not necessarily have arrived at the same conclusions independent of you. On the contrary: it may even add to the depth of your analysis if you take into account different views and look at your material from different angles. In QCA, consistency is an important quality criterion (see Chapters 2 and 9). This implies that you compare how two independent coders categorise your material or how you categorise your material at different points in time. This comparison has important implications for the research process, and these implications make for additional differences between QCA and coding:

o In coding, creating your codes and categories and coding your material are combined into a single step; they are done simultaneously. In QCA, creating a coding frame and applying the frame to your material constitute separate steps in the research process.

o In coding, when defining your codes and categories, the focus is more on the conceptual level and less on how to recognise instances of the concept in your data. In QCA, on the other hand, the focus of your definitions is on the interrelation between your data and your categories. You create definitions to help you recognise instances of your categories in the data and to assign segments of your data to the appropriate categories.

o In coding, codes and categories need not be exclusive, and you can assign several codes simultaneously to the same section of your material. In QCA, the subcategories within one main category mutually exclude each other. This is to say that you can assign a given section of your material to one subcategory only.

o In coding, there is no need to divide your material into units of coding. In QCA, this is an important step: you can only compare the categories selected by two independent coders or at two points in time, if they relate to the same segments.

When to use coding and when to use QCA

Whether to use coding or QCA depends on your research question and on your material.

If your research question is descriptive, QCA would be the better choice. You are dealing with a descriptive research question when you are asking questions such as the following:

• What is a certain group of persons saying about a given topic? For example: What are clients' expectations of couple therapy (Tambling & Johnson, 2010)? What are the unexpected benefits experienced by patients who received alternative treatment for their back pain (Hsu et al., 2010)?

• How is a certain issue represented in certain types of sources? For example: How is family life presented on German television (Viertel, 2010)? How are the motives of terrorists presented in newspapers (Maerten, 2008)?

Descriptive questions are often comparative in nature:

• What does one group of persons say about a given topic compared to another group? For example: What are the preferences of different stakeholder groups concerning medical care (Heil et al., 2010)? In what respects do men compared to women experience the reading of different kinds of narrative texts (Odağ, 2007)?

• How has the representation of a given issue changed over time or how does it differ between sources? For example: How do men and women interact in an online environment (Guiller & Durndell, 2007)? How is the Airbus crisis represented in German and French newspapers (Görnitz, 2007)?

If, on the other hand, you are interested in creating theory, in analysing the various manifestations of a phenomenon, coding would the better choice. For example: What does 'flow' mean when surfing the web, and when do web users experience flow (Pace, 2004)? How do parents and their children reposition themselves *vis-à-vis* each other as the parents grow older (Dieris, 2006)?

KEY POINT

QCA is a good method to use if your research question is descriptive. If your research question is focused on theory and analysis, coding is better. Coding is also better if your material is very varied and diverse.

Also, your material may be more suitable for one method or the other. Remember that QCA helps you reduce your material by summarising it in relevant respects (see Chapter 1). If your categories are data-driven, you usually create a new category only if you come across the same aspect at least twice in your material (see Chapter 6). If you compare different participants or different sources, there must be sufficient similarity between them to apply the same coding frame. In short, QCA will be an option only if there is something in your material that can be summarised in the way that is characteristic of QCA. If there is not, if your material contains many diverse aspects, coding would be a better choice; the method would allow you to analyse what concepts underlie these diverse aspects and how they hang together.

———— Example of deciding between coding and QCA ————

A PhD student working with me is interested in how women in Indonesia conceptualise health, illness and different kinds of medical treatment (traditional herbal medicine, Western medicine, etc.). There are different ways in which she could develop her research question and design her research. A first option would be to focus on describing women's thoughts about these topics through conducting semi-standardised interviews. With a descriptive research question and several interviews covering the same topics, QCA would be a good method for analysing this material. Another option would be to focus on one type of treatment, to explore how different stakeholders within the Indonesian health care system conceptualise this and to analyse the factors that relate to the use of this treatment. This would be an analytic type of research question, requiring that she draw upon and compare different types of sources. In this case, with an analytic research question and highly variable material, coding would be a good method for analysing the material. After giving these (and some additional) options a lot of thought, the student decided in favour of an analytic research question and of constructing a grounded theory on the topic, using conceptual coding for her data analysis.

Can coding and QCA be combined?

Although coding and QCA clearly have different foci, there are situations in which elements from the two methods can be combined:

- *Generating categories in QCA.* When you are creating data-driven categories, you can make use of coding to help you generate categories (see Chapter 6). This is so because especially open coding (the first step of coding in grounded theory) is largely descriptive, like QCA; you would add an analytic dimension to your codes only during the later steps of axial and selective coding. You can therefore make use of the descriptive aspects of open coding in generating categories for QCA.
- *Defining codes.* Conversely, you can also bring elements of QCA into coding. One way to do this is to use the more extensive definitions of categories in QCA to refine the codes that you generate during coding. In coding, code definitions are typically limited to a label and description that emphasises the analytic aspects of your codes. If this is appropriate in terms of your research question, you can extend these definitions by including indicators (i.e. descriptions of how to recognise instances of your code in the data), a positive example, and possibly decision rules (see Chapter 5).

SUMMARY

Different types of coding are discussed in the literature. In qualitative research, coding is typically a conceptual device that opens up data in new ways and helps to create theory. Coding and QCA are similar in several ways. Both involve some degree of abstraction from your material, and both involve assigning a category/code and a segment of data to each other. But in other respects, the methods are quite different. Coding involves an analytic and iterative procedure, codes are typically data-driven, and consistency is less of an issue. QCA is descriptive, linear more than iterative; categories can also be concept-driven, and consistency is an important quality criterion. Accordingly, QCA is the method of choice with descriptive research questions, whereas coding is better suited for analytic research questions. You can also combine elements of the two methods: you can use coding to help with creating data-driven categories in QCA, and elements of QCA to refine definitions in coding.

QCA and discourse analysis

Discourse analysis: A brief overview

Even more than the term 'coding', the term 'discourse analysis' refers to a whole set of methods (see the overview in Van Dijk 1997a; 1997b). As the name implies, all these methods provide tools for the analysis of discourse. But discourse, in this context, is a technical term. The kind of discourse that becomes the object of discourse analysis is not, for instance, the type of conversation you have with another student or with your superior at work – although this can also be part of a 'discourse'. Phillips and Hardy (2002, p. 3), in an introductory textbook on discourse analysis, have defined discourse as 'an interrelated set of texts, and the practices of their production, dissemination, and reception'.

This definition highlights an important assumption that underlies all discourse analysis: discourse analysis does not deal with texts in and of themselves, but its fundamental concern is with the ways in which language and social reality are interrelated – what Phillips and Hardy have called 'the practices of [the] production, dissemination, and reception' of texts. One of the most basic assumptions underlying discourse analysis is that language does not represent reality, but that it contributes to the *construction* of reality, and to the construction of social reality in particular.

KEY POINT

Discourse analysis rests on the assumption that language does not represent reality, but contributes to the construction of reality.

This assumption has far-reaching implications. If language plays a part in constructing reality, we cannot perceive reality outside language, we can perceive only what we talk about and in the terms in which we talk about it. Moreover, our being in the world is not limited to talking; we also act within and towards our reality. And what we perceive to be possible ways of acting towards a certain phenomenon will also be constrained by the way in which we speak about it.

Example of a study using discourse analysis

Herzog et al. (2008) use discourse analysis to analyse 22 interviews conducted with the inhabitants of Valencia in Spain about drug-related behaviour. They are able to show that the participants clearly distinguish between two types of drug users in the neighbourhood. The first group consists of native inhabitants who take heroin. They are represented as victims of social policies and drugs, in danger of contracting AIDS. They are considered addicts who are not responsible for their behaviour; they are to be pitied and taken care of. The second group consists of persons who drink alcohol, especially at weekends. These are represented as immigrants, foreign to the community, who constitute a threat to the social order. They are represented as having a choice whether to consume alcohol or not, and when threatening the social order, they need to be controlled by the police. The analysis clearly shows how different ways of representing the two user groups are closely related to diametrically opposite evaluations and very different courses of action.

On the one hand, this provides 'language' with a lot of power. And of course it is not 'language' that does anything, but those who use language, who engage in producing and in disseminating texts. Power therefore rests with those who are in a position to produce and to distribute texts which carry a certain authority in society. These texts and the ways in which they refer to each other and reinforce each other's 'message' constitute what has been called the 'dominant discourse' on a given topic. But at the same time, the basic assumption that language shapes reality also provides everyone with a certain degree of power: We all use language every day, and in so doing, we can either contribute to the dominant discourse, or we can try to create an alternative reality, contributing to subordinate counter-discourse – which may one day become a dominant discourse.

The goal of discourse analysis in all its forms is to analyse the ways in which language contributes to the construction of social reality. The various types of discourse analysis differ, however, in the extent to which they highlight the issue of power. In this respect, two broad traditions can be distinguished. The first of these is predominantly descriptive, and the methods within this tradition often have their origin in linguistics (such as social linguistic analysis; van Dijk, 1997a). They are concerned with describing the way text and talk are organised, the ways in which people pursue conversational goals, and what kinds of strategies they use.

KEY POINT

The goal of discourse analysis is to analyse the ways in which language contributes to the construction of social reality.

The second type of discourse analysis, in the tradition of Foucault, is critical and typically rooted in the social sciences (Fairclough, 2003; Potter & Wetherell, 1987; van Dijk, 1997b, 2008; Wodak & Meyer, 2009). Critical discourse analysis in its many different manifestations focuses on instances of dominant discourse (also called 'hegemonic discourse'). It may use the same tools as descriptive discourse analysis. But unlike descriptive analysis, it does not limit itself to the analysis of language, but also includes the relationship between language, the processes of producing, receiving, and disseminating language, and the larger context in which this takes place. Critical discourse analysis also examines (and often criticises) the values that are transported by the dominant discourse and the ways in which the discourse shapes our perception of a given phenomenon.

Discourse analysis of both traditions makes use of a large number of analytic strategies which have also been described as methods in their own right, such as metaphor analysis (Todd & Harrison, 2008), deconstruction (Czarniawska,

Table 3.2 Differences between discourse analysis and QCA

Discourse analysis	QCA
Based on constructivist assumptions	No assumptions about reality or implicit realist assumptions
Descriptive or critical	Typically descriptive
Focus on processes	Focus on states
Analysis of what is and what is not there in the material	Analysis of what is there in the material

2004), analysis of rhetoric (Swartz, 1997), of syntax (Chilton & Schäffner, 1997), of argument structure (van Eemeren, Grootendorst & Snoeck Henkemans, 2002), and many more (for an overview see van Dijk, 1997a; 1997b).

Comparing discourse analysis and QCA

On several accounts, discourse analysis and QCA are fundamentally different (see Table 3.2 for a summary).

In the first place, QCA, unlike discourse analysis, does not make any assumptions about the nature of language, social reality, and how the two are related; at least, it does not do so explicitly. Implicitly, going back to the roots of content analysis in communication studies, the use of QCA is often based on realist assumptions. Researchers who use QCA frequently assume that there is a reality 'out there' (such as certain attitudes and feelings held by the participants) and that this reality is represented in the material under analysis. But this need not be the case – ultimately, QCA does not take a stance in this respect. Discourse analysis, on the other hand, is typically based on the constructivist assumptions described in the previous section. If you use discourse analysis, you will do so under the assumption that language shapes social reality.

Discourse analysis can be either descriptive or critical. In the social sciences in particular, the critical tradition has been developed. QCA, on the other hand, is above all a descriptive method, and this is how it is typically used. If you use QCA to analyse what your interviewees are saying about your phenomenon of interest, you are simply describing what is in your material. But this is only the way in which QCA is *typically* used. Like other methods, QCA can be placed in the service of a more critical analysis (see below on combining the two methods).

With its constructivist assumptions, the focus of discourse analysis is on the way in which social reality is constructed by using language. If you use discourse analysis, you are interested in the process of reality construction. QCA, on the other hand, with its implicit realist assumptions, is concerned with describing what is there. QCA is more static in its outlook.

Because of its focus on process and on how a given discourse operates, researchers who employ discourse analysis have as much of an interest in ways in which language is *not* used as in how it is used. In their analysis of drug discourse, for instance, Herzog et al. (2008) note that in speaking about immigrants who get drunk at weekends, the interviewees do not refer to them as members of the in-group, do not regard them as victims, and do not look upon them with pity. When you use discourse analysis, you analyse both what is there and what is not there in your material. QCA, on the other hand, focuses on describing what is there in your material.

When to use discourse analysis and when to use QCA

These differences between the two methods already provide some clear indications for when to use discourse analysis and when to use QCA.

If your research question is a descriptive 'what' question (such as: What are the interviewees saying here? What does the representation of a certain phenomenon look like?), QCA would be a good method to use. But if you are interested less in what is said and more in how it is said, that is how a certain phenomenon is constructed in and through discourse, discourse analysis would be preferable. An example would be the analysis of hegemonic strategies by which terrorism is constructed as the 'other' in international discourse on terrorism (Herschinger, 2011). Discourse analysis would also be the method of choice if you are concerned with the interrelation of language and social reality and how the one influences the other, especially if you are also interested in issues of power and ideology (e.g. Wodak's analysis of official notifications about residence permits for aliens in Austria: Reisigl & Wodak, 2001, Chapter 5).

─── **Example of deciding between discourse analysis and QCA** ───

Following up on our study about prioritising in health care, an MA student working with us was interested in the topic of health care in oncology for her MA thesis. One way to elaborate on this topic would be to examine how patients construct their illness, their hospital stay, and the treatment they received or are receiving. This would be a question with a focus on process. To realise this kind of study, she might have conducted narrative interviews with patients about their experience and followed this up with a discourse analysis, examining the metaphors the patients use. A different research question relating to the same general topic would be to examine patients' opinions concerning the medical care they received: What do the patients think about their hospital stay? This would be a descriptive 'what' question. To answer it, she could conduct semi-standardised interviews with patients, covering both positive and negative aspects of their experience as well as ideas about how the system might be improved. In a next step, QCA would be a suitable method for analysing these interviews. In the end, she opted for the second research question involving semi-standardised interviews and QCA.

Can discourse analysis and QCA be combined?

Despite the different foci of discourse analysis and QCA, it is possible to combine the two methods. This is so because of the strong concern of discourse analysis with the relation between language and social reality, especially when it comes to issues of power and ideology and the analysis of realisations of inequality in and through language. From this perspective, critical discourse analysis is less a method, and more an attitude towards research and your research question. Phillips and Hardy (2002, p. 10) put it like this: 'What makes a research method discursive is not the method itself but the use of that method to carry out an interpretive analysis of some form of text with a view to providing an understanding of discourse and its role in constituting social reality.'. In this way, QCA and discourse analysis can be combined by putting the method of QCA into the service of the critical-interpretive attitude underlying discourse analysis.

KEY POINT

QCA and discourse analysis can be combined by putting QCA into the service of the critical-interpretive attitude underlying discourse analysis.

One way of realising such a combination of the two methods is to conduct a discourse analysis and use QCA as a method, either by itself or alongside other methods such as rhetorical or metaphor analysis. The focus here is on discourse analysis; QCA is used in a subordinate function.

--------- **Example of using QCA towards critical discourse analysis** ---------

In a study of letters to the editor published in newspapers from the UK, the US, and Australia during the year following the 9/11 terrorist attacks, Hogan (2006) adopts the principles informing critical discourse analysis. The concern of the study is with uncovering power relations and forms of political control through language. To this end, QCA is used alongside an analysis of the discursive strategies employed by the letter writers. Through data-driven QCA, the actions advocated in the letters as a response to the terrorist attacks are identified (pacifism, international involvement, military, etc.). These actions are in turn classified as more or less supportive of the state, and on this basis the letters are divided into two groups. In a next step, the main discursive strategies employed in the two types of letters are identified (such as use of distancing mechanisms, use of connotation-rich lexical items), described in detail, and illustrated.

Another way of combining the two methods is to conduct a critical QCA. There exists a small tradition of QCA of German origin that is explicitly aimed at uncovering ideology (Ritsert, 1972; Vorderer & Groeben, 1987). The focus here is on QCA; linguistic phenomena that are considered to be contributing to ideology or power inequalities are conceptualised as categories in QCA. To put it differently, in critical QCA, categories do not refer to textual content, but to the form, the way something is expressed.

Example of a critical QCA

Sommer and Vorderer (1987) developed a coding frame for assessing the degree of reification expressed in texts where the speaker is referring to a situation in which she might be held accountable for an action. The coding frame consists of six categories: meaningful absence; lack of specific denotations; depersonalising; statification; repressive-regressive forms of distancing; miscellaneous. To validate the coding frame, they analysed four texts: an interview with a US Air Force captain about his involvement in the Vietnam War; an excerpt from the diary of R. Hoess, commander of the Auschwitz concentration camp; statements made by a US soldier who had been in immediate contact with the victims of the My Lai massacre in Vietnam; and a statement made by Willy Brandt, then Chancellor of the Federal Republic of Germany (FRG), justifying his signing of the contract between the Soviet Union and the FRG in 1970. They expected that reification language would occur more frequently in the first two texts, and they were able to confirm this expectation.

SUMMARY

Discourse analysis is based on the assumption that language does not represent reality, but contributes to the construction of reality. The goal of discourse analysis is to analyse the ways in which language and language users do this. It is important to distinguish between descriptive and critical discourse analysis, with critical discourse analysis being concerned with dominant discourse and issues of power. The method differs from QCA in its assumptions about the relation between language and reality, its critical outlook, its concern with process, and taking into account what is left unsaid. Discourse analysis should be used if you are interested in how a phenomenon is expressed in discourse, in how language and social reality are related, or in ideology. Despite these differences, the two methods can be combined by putting QCA into the service of the critical outlook characteristic of discourse analysis.

QCA and semiotics

Semiotics: A brief overview

Semiotics is concerned with the analysis of signs and the ways in which we all generate cultural meaning through using signs. Semiotic analysis is done by looking at the relationships between signs. The foundations of semiotics were laid by Ferdinand de Saussure and Charles Peirce who each developed their own definition of what a sign is and what kinds of signs there are. The fundamental idea in semiotics that a sign consists of a signifier (such as the word 'tree') and a signified (such as the concept of a tree) goes back to Saussure (see Chandler, 2007; Eco, 1978).

In the broadest sense, a sign is anything that conveys meaning by standing for something else. The language we all use and that I use in writing at this very moment consists of signs. The words I use stand for concepts and meanings. Words in language may be the first examples of signs in culture that come to mind, but they are by no means the only ones. Traffic signs, for instance, are signs by definition. The musical score in a film acts as a sign: try to not watch, but listen to a thriller, and the music will alert you to crucial parts of the plot. When you leave the house today, you yourself will be a 'signpost'. If you live in a culture where you have a choice in these matters, the clothes, the glasses, the shoes you wear, the mobile phone you use all tell other people something about you. A key idea in semiotics is that signs do not have meaning in absolute terms, but acquire meaning by the ways in which they are related to other signs.

KEY POINT

Semiotics is about the analysis of signs. A sign is anything that meaningfully stands for something else. A sign acquires meaning by the way in which it is related to other signs.

Semiotics is therefore not restricted to language, but includes the analysis of all kinds of cultural signs. Also, something can act as a sign and convey meaning even if you do not intend it to. Your clothes, for instance, give out a message, whether they were meant to or not. They may even give out a very strong message precisely because you were in a hurry and just put on anything that you could lay your hands on. In fact, some people may want to give out the message that they do not care about appearances and spend a lot of time putting together an outfit that looks as though it was haphazardly thrown on in the morning without a second thought...

Semiotic analysis makes use of a number of concepts that function as tools. They help you analyse how cultural meaning is generated by using signs:

- *Denotation and connotation.* 'Denotation' refers to the literal, descriptive meaning of a sign, whereas 'connotation' refers to the figurative, culturally ascribed meaning of a sign. Typically, connotative meanings are not made explicit, but are merely suggested. You have to infer them.
- *Intertextuality.* 'Intertextuality' refers to the ways in which texts are related to each other and borrow from each other. In semiotic analysis, it is important to take this into account.
- *Syntagmatic analysis.* In syntagmatic analysis, texts are analysed in terms of sequence, i.e. how their different parts follow upon each other, and how meaning is generated from sequence.
- *Paradigmatic analysis.* In paradigmatic analysis, the focus is on hidden opposites. Advertisements, for instance, often show young people who are having fun – not young people who ponder important world issues, or older people who are having fun. Seriousness and old age function as hidden opposites here.

Example of a study using semiotics

Momany, Bardaneh, and Migdadi (2009) conducted a semiotic analysis of how gender metaphors which draw upon women's bodies and experiences are used in Middle Eastern politics. Their focus was on analysing the connotations these metaphors would have for an Arab readership. They distinguish between what they call dysphemistic and euphemistic metaphors. Dysphemistic metaphors are used to present the protagonists and their politics in a negative light. Dysphemistic metaphors that draw upon the feminine typically have connotations of weakness, for instance by referring to prominent politicians as *chickens* or other small animals. Euphemistic metaphors, on the other hand, are used to portray politicians and their actions in a positive light. An example would be the reference to violence in terms of birth and midwifery, evoking images of happiness, peacefulness and relief at the event of childbirth.

Traditionally, the focus of semiotics is on the analysis of the sign itself. A more recent development is social semiotics (Kress & van Leeuwen, 1996; van Leeuwen, 2005). Here the focus shifts to the process and the means of generating meaning in social context. The metaphor analysis carried out by Momany et al. is actually an example of social semiotics because the focus of the analysis is on constructing meaning *vis-à-vis* a specific cultural audience.

Comparing semiotics and QCA

The two key terms in semiotics, denotation and connotation, make for a good starting point in comparing the two methods.

Where denotation is concerned, the two methods are quite similar in terms of their goals. Both semiotics and QCA can be used to describe (cultural) meaning. But they use somewhat different means to get there: in a semiotic analysis,

Table 3.3 Differences between semiotics and QCA

Semiotics	QCA
In-depth description of meaning	Description of meaning in selected respects
Analysis of individual specifics of each instance	Comparative analysis
Different researchers may differ in their interpretation – criterion of plausibility	Different researchers should agree on their interpretation – criterion of consistency
Analysis of what is and what is not there in the material	Analysis of what is there in the material
Analysis of multiple meanings from one perspective	Analysis of one meaning only from one perspective

you provide a detailed description of denotative meaning, whereas with QCA you highlight selected aspects of meaning. Also, in a semiotic analysis you would typically create an in-depth description of a few selected signs, whereas you can apply QCA to a larger amount of material, not going into depth to the same extent. Finally, semiotic analysis proceeds differently: you do not create a coding frame where you define relevant aspects of meaning.

The differences between the two methods become more pronounced when it comes to analysing connotative meaning (see Table 3.3 for a summary). QCA is a comparative method that helps you reduce your data. Semiotic analysis, on the other hand, by going into depth, expands upon the connotative meaning of each individual sign or message. Momany et al. (2009), for instance, look at how gendered metaphors are used to present Middle Eastern politics in a positive or a negative light. In this respect, the metaphors are examined from a similar angle. Yet each metaphor is analysed individually in terms of what its exact connotations are and what is suggested about the politics that are described in these terms.

Social semiotics in particular always looks at language in use. Whereas denotative meanings may be similar even for different kinds of audiences, this is not the case for connotative meanings. In fact you would even expect connotative meanings to differ between audiences, and different audience groups may interpret the same sign (in denotative terms) quite differently. A prominent case in point is the controversy surrounding the Danish Mohammed cartoons. These were perceived as highly offensive by some members of a Muslim audience, but not so by a Danish (potentially Christian) audience. Because of this focus on meaning in context, intersubjective agreement between independent researchers is not a relevant criterion in semiotics. Instead, it is important that you make it transparent how and why you arrive at your interpretation.

In semiotics, it is assumed that a sign derives its meaning from its position compared to other signs. Therefore, in semiotic analysis you explore the relations between one sign and other signs, assembling a holistic picture of a sign's meaning. In paradigmatic analysis in particular, this involves looking at the relations to other signs which have remained hidden and implicit. By taking into account the relationship between one sign and other signs, you can use semiotics to analyse the multiplicity of meanings that may be inherent in any one sign. In doing QCA, on the other hand, you focus on those images that you are analysing. You can use other sources as your context to some extent, and you can analyse implicit meaning. But you cannot take intertextuality into account in QCA to the same extent that you can in semiotics. Also, QCA focuses on what is there in your material; you cannot use it to analyse what is left unsaid (as with discourse analysis; see above). Finally, QCA is not suitable for analysing multiple meanings (Früh, 1992; Rustemeyer, 1992). Of course you can use QCA to analyse your material from different perspectives, generating several main categories. But because the subcategories in each of these main categories are meant to exclude each other, you cannot assign more than one meaning to your material under this one perspective.

When to use semiotics and when to use QCA

Again, the differences between the two methods help you decide when to use semiotics and when to use QCA:

- If you want to analyse meaning and the generation of connotative meaning in detail, semiotics would be the method to use. If, on the other hand, you want to analyse meaning only in certain respects, QCA would be your method of choice.
- The focus of semiotics is on the meaning of signs in cultural context. In principle, you can carry out a semiotic analysis on any kind of material, because any message is of course generated within some cultural context. But the meaning of signs in a cultural context is especially salient in products or messages that are intended for a wider audience, such as television series, newspaper articles, or advertisements. Semiotics is better suited for analysing this kind of material than, for instance, interviews.
- The focus of semiotics is on analysing various connotative meanings that are simultaneously conveyed. Some material is highly suitable for this kind of analysis, whereas other material is not at all suitable. This is related to the conventions that govern the production and reception of different kinds of texts and media products (Groeben & Schreier, 1992). Instructions on how to use a DVD player, for instance, are expected to have only one meaning. Poetry, on the other hand, is expected to convey different meanings simultaneously. If you are interested in analysing how different meanings are generated and transported simultaneously, you should use semiotics.

—— **Example of differentially using content analysis and semiotics** ——

In her PhD thesis, Özcan (2009) analysed the way in which women and men were visually represented in secular and Islamic Turkish newspapers. In the first part of her analysis, she focused on manifest, descriptive features of their representation. Here she looked at whether women and men were usually shown on their own, in single-gender or in mixed-gender groups, whether the women were shown wearing a headscarf, and the like. For this part of her analysis, Özcan used a quantitative type of content analysis, counting the number of men and women shown, the different kinds of headscarves, and other denotative features of the images. In a subsequent analysis, Özcan selected approximately 100 images for an in-depth analysis of gendered visual stereotyping. Here she used a combination of social semiotics and iconology, a method that was developed especially for the analysis of visuals (Panofsky, 1955/1983). Through her in-depth analysis she was able to demonstrate, for instance, that women wearing a headscarf are frequently shown in both Islamic and secular newspapers, but in different contexts and with different meanings. In Islamic newspapers, the religious meaning of the headscarf is usually dominant, whereas secular newspapers are more likely to show the headscarf as a symbol of Muslims in Europe.

Can semiotics and QCA be combined?

Semiotics and QCA share the goal of describing denotative, literal meaning, and this shared goal points towards a first way of combining the two methods. In fact, the above study by Özcan (2009) is an example, even though she used a more quantitative type of content analysis. Describing denotative meaning will usually be your first step when you conduct a semiotic analysis, and you can make this more systematic by applying QCA. This is especially so if you are doing a large-scale study. If you are just analysing ten or so images, applying QCA would not really be worth the effort. Also, like Özcan, you can apply QCA to a full set of your material and then use the results to select a smaller part for a more in-depth analysis of connotative meaning.

Example of combining QCA and semiotics

In a study of the representation of the genders in mobile phone advertisements, Döring and Pöschl (2006) drew upon the semiotic categories used by Goffman (1979) in his groundbreaking study of the representation of the genders in advertisements. Döring and Pöschl turned semiotic categories such as *Feminine touch* or *Ritualisation of subordination* into categories in QCA. In order to make them accessible to QCA, complex categories such as *Ritualisation of subordination* were decomposed into simpler categories that were more easily coded. In this way, the authors carried out a semiotic analysis through using QCA.

When it comes to analysing connotative meaning, combining the two methods becomes more difficult. Whether you can combine them ultimately depends on which of the tools provided by semiotics you are planning to use. If you want to do a paradigmatic analysis, for instance, looking for hidden opposites, a combination would be next to impossible. But if you are making use of the building blocks of the 'grammar' of visuals suggested in social semiotics, you can turn semiotic categories into QCA categories, come up with a definition, and categorise each of your segments accordingly. In this case, you would be using QCA as a tool towards semiotic analysis. This is feasible if you focus on semiotic categories that lend themselves to proceeding in this way, such as the distinction between close, medium, and long camera shots, or the differentiation between narrative, classificational, analytical, and symbolic representations suggested by Kress and van Leeuwen (1996).

================================ SUMMARY ================================

Semiotics is concerned with signs, i.e. with anything that meaningfully stands for something else and acquires its meaning by the way in which it is related to other signs. Important concepts in semiotic analysis are denotation, i.e. the literal and descriptive meaning of a sign, and connotation, i.e. the figurative, culturally ascribed meaning of a sign. Both semiotics and QCA are concerned with the description of denotative meaning, but semiotics goes into depth and focuses on the individual case more than QCA. Semiotics is also different from QCA in that agreement between researchers is not a criterion for evaluating the analysis, by taking into account what is not said explicitly in the material, and by letting you analyse multiple simultaneous connotative meanings. Semiotics is especially suitable for analysing material that is intended for a wider audience and material that simultaneously conveys different meanings. Semiotics and QCA can be combined in two ways: by using QCA for describing the denotative meaning of your material, and by turning certain semiotic categories into QCA categories and classifying your material accordingly.

Frequently asked questions

What about qualitative methods for data collection – can I combine those with QCA?

With QCA, it does not matter how you collect your data – as long as it consists of symbolic material requiring some degree of interpretation. So yes, you can definitely combine QCA with all qualitative methods for data collection, such as different kinds of interview, focus groups, observation, or eliciting verbal or visual material from your participants (essays, diary entries, photographs, etc.).

Can I combine QCA with other methods for analysing qualitative data?

There are so many different methods for qualitative data analysis out there that it is hard to tell. But coding, discourse analysis, and semiotics – i.e. the methods described in this chapter – are definitely the methods that are easiest to combine with QCA. With other methods such as hermeneutics, conversation analysis, or narrative analysis, it is difficult to see how combining the methods would work. But this is not to say that it cannot be done. If you are thinking of combining QCA with another qualitative method for data analysis, the key question to ask yourself is whether you can conceptualise part of what you want to find out in terms of categories. Narrative analysis, for example, is difficult to combine with QCA in general. But if you have identified specific narrative trajectories in your material, you can turn these into QCA-type categories.

What about using QCA *after* I have used another method for qualitative data analysis?

Using two methods simultaneously is not the only way to combine them. You can also combine methods by using one after the other. There are no rules for how to do this. It is best to let your research question guide you. For example, you can use a method such as semiotics or discourse analysis first and then use QCA to systematise your findings. Or else you can start out by QCA and then use another method to have a more in-depth look at a part of your material that strikes you as especially interesting or relevant.

End-of-chapter questions

- Name four or more differences between coding and QCA.
- Which research questions are suitable for QCA and coding, respectively?
- What are the most important differences between discourse analysis and QCA?
- How can discourse analysis and QCA be combined despite these differences?
- Name three or more differences between semiotics and QCA.
- What kind of material is especially suitable for doing a semiotic analysis?

4

THE CODING FRAME

Chapter guide

QCA allows you to develop a systematic description of your material, by assigning segments of the material to the categories of your coding frame. The coding frame is therefore at the heart of the method. Before you can get started on building your own coding frame, it is important that you know about coding frames in general. This is what this chapter is about. We will look at:

- what exactly a coding frame is;
- coding frames of varying complexity;
- requirements a coding frame should meet.

What is a coding frame?

The starting point: a wealth of material

In qualitative research, when starting upon data analysis, you can easily end up feeling overwhelmed by your data. If you have conducted one-hour interviews, for instance, you will typically have around 15 pages of transcript per interview. If you conduct 15 interviews, this will make for approximately 225 pages of transcript – a huge amount of material! Even if you have a clear research question, you will most likely discover numerous additional aspects in your material that would be worth looking at. In this situation, it is easy to get carried away, trying to include it all. But when trying to keep track of everything all at once, most likely you will find yourself in a state of mind that has been called 'getting lost in the data'.

— Example of finding additional interesting aspects in the material —

In our study about prioritising in health care, we presented the participants with vignettes and asked them for their opinion. According to our research question, the focus of the analysis was on that opinion and the underlying reasons. But the interviews contained much more than this: the participants added further considerations; they spoke about criteria that, as far as they were concerned, should not play a role in medical decision making at all, and they told us about their own experiences of having been ill and seeking medical treatment.

Main categories

It is one of the great advantages of QCA that it helps you avoid this state of confusion. Instead of trying to keep track of everything all at once and becoming confused in the process, the method forces you to select certain key aspects of your material and to focus on those.

It is these aspects around which you build your coding frame. In the literature, these are called the *dimensions* or the *main categories* of the coding frame (the terms 'main categories' and 'dimensions' are synonymous and will be used interchangeably in the following). Typically, some of these aspects will already be part of your research question (Früh, 2007).

DEFINITION

The main categories (also called 'dimensions') of your coding frame are the aspects on which you want to focus your analysis.

These are the aspects about which you would like to know more. Specifying such aspects involves making choices, but making choices is inevitable: You can never include everything in your analysis.

--------- **Example of focusing research on main categories** ---------

In our prioritising study, when presenting our participants with the case of Terri Schiavo (the young woman suffering from an eating disorder who had fallen into a coma and whose artificial life support was terminated after 15 years, allowing her to die: see Chapter 2). In line with our research question, we focused our analysis on the following key aspects:

- whether the participants were of the opinion that terminating the life support was morally right or wrong;
- whether their decision was clear (or whether they repeatedly weighed the pros and cons);
- the reasons and considerations they mentioned why it was justified to terminate Terri Schiavo's life support;
- the reasons and considerations they mentioned why this was not justified;
- any additional information they would have liked about the case before giving their opinion;
- any considerations which should not play a role in making such a decision.

By focusing on these issues, we did not, for instance, take it into account if a participant mentioned that she had recently discussed just such an issue with a friend whose father was lying in a coma and who would never have wanted to be kept alive on artificial life support. But we had to make choices, considering that we had conducted 45 interviews, and that the case of Terri Schiavo concerned only one interview question out of about 35.

Subcategories

Once you have specified the aspects which constitute your main categories, the next step is to identify what is said in your material about these aspects. In this, you can either draw upon things that you already know before even looking at your material, i.e. work in a *concept-driven* way (deductively), or by looking at what is there in the material, i.e. work in a *data-driven* way (inductively), or both (for more detail, see below and Chapters 5 and 6).

DEFINITION

Subcategories specify what is said about the aspects that interest you, i.e. your main categories.

While the aspects function as dimensions or main categories of your coding frame, the specifications serve as your *subcategories*. Here it becomes apparent how QCA helps you reduce and summarise your material (see Chapter 1): you reduce the many different things that are said in your material about a particular topic to these subcategories.

— Example of specifying subcategories concerning a main category —

In analysing participants' opinions concerning the case of Terri Schiavo, we specified subcategories for each of the above main categories, using a mixed strategy that was part concept-driven and part data-driven. Concerning participants' opinions on the case of Terri Schiavo, we came up with the following subcategories: *morally justified, long overdue, morally wrong, refusal to take any decision, unclear*. In this way, the many different things that participants said were reduced to these five options (and, of course, the other main categories mentioned above), and in the following analysis, anything that a participant said about the topic was assigned to one of these subcategories.

Making choices

The structure of the coding frame, and which main categories and subcategories it contains, is a decision that is mostly up to the researcher, i.e. you, and the research questions you are asking. There is little in the material that requires a particular structure (cf. Kuckartz, 2009, Chapter 11, on different structures of coding frames). Where main categories are concerned, the research questions point the way.

The decision of how many subcategories to include is likewise up to you and what you consider to be important information *vis-à-vis* your research question. One structure is not in and of itself better than another, and the final decision will always depend on what you find relevant and on how many distinctions (in terms of subcategories) you and any other coders can handle in the analysis.

────── **Example of deciding which main categories to include** ──────

The main research question informing our prioritising study was priority setting in medical decision making and underlying criteria in different stakeholder groups. Considering this research question, it was obvious that we would have to include the participants' opinion on the case of Terri Schiavo and the underlying reasons as main categories in our coding frame. The remaining dimensions – whether their decision was clear, additional information they would have liked, criteria that should not play a role in taking such decisions – could also have been left out. We included them partly because we considered this to be important information with respect to our more general research question, partly because of more general considerations in structuring the coding frame (see Chapter 6).

Coding frames as structures

After this long detour it is now time to return to the question at the beginning of this section: what is a coding frame? Ultimately, a coding frame is a way of structuring your material, a way of differentiating between different meanings *vis-à-vis* your research questions. It consists of main categories or dimensions and a number of subcategories for each dimension which specify the meanings in your material with respect to these main categories (Früh, 2007; Holsti, 1969).

─────────── DEFINITION ───────────

A coding frame is a way of structuring your material. It consists of main categories specifying relevant aspects and of subcategories for each main category specifying relevant meanings concerning this aspect.

In the terminology of quantitative research, one might compare the main categories to variables, and the subcategories to the levels of these variables. The coding frame acts like a filter: material that is not covered by the main categories will no longer be visible once you have conducted your analysis, nor will distinctions in the material that are not covered by your subcategories.

— Example of how subcategories structure your view of your material —

Instead of the five subcategories we specified for the dimension *Opinions concerning the case of Terri Schiavo*, we might have specified only three: *morally justified, morally wrong, miscellaneous*. In this case, *morally justified* and *long overdue* would have been combined into *morally justified*, and the distinction between the two positions would have been lost. Likewise, *refusal to take any decision* and *unclear* would have been collapsed into the subcategory *miscellaneous*, and the distinction between not wanting to take any position and trying to arrive at a position, but failing to do so, would also have been lost.

In the following, reference will be made to *main categories* and *subcategories* whenever this distinction is important, i.e. whenever a statement applies either to main categories/dimensions or to subcategories in particular. Where this distinction is not important, i.e. whenever a consideration equally applies to main categories and subcategories, the term *categories* will be used.

A useful analogy would be to think of a coding frame as a system you use when tidying. Imagine that you have just moved to a new apartment, and were in a hurry when leaving the old one, so you just stuffed all your clothes into one large box. Now you empty this box onto your bedroom floor and think about how to put all the clothes into your new closet. One way to do this would be by colour, to have all your purple things hanging together, followed by all the blues and greens. Another way might be to distinguish between types of clothes, putting all your trousers next to each other, followed by your skirts, and then your blouses. Or else you might decide to go by length, starting with the long overcoats, followed by long trousers and skirts, followed by short trousers and skirts.

Let us suppose that you decide to go by colour, i.e. you have decided on this 'dimension' for structuring the 'coding frame' for your clothes. On this basis, it would be easy to group together the blues and greens, for instance. Now what about those blouses with a paisley pattern? Should the patterns go into a separate group? Or should you go by the dominant colour in the pattern and hang up your patterned clothes accordingly? If you do so, the distinction between patterned and single-coloured garments will be lost. Probably your decision will depend on how many items of clothing with a pattern you have, how often you wear them and how important it is to you that you can find them quickly (i.e. on your 'research interest'). If you like patterns and wear them often, you will probably have a 'subcategory' of patterned clothes.

████████████████████████ SUMMARY ████████████████████████

A coding frame is a structure, a kind of filter through which you view your material. It consists of main categories (dimensions) specifying relevant aspects of the material and a set of subcategories for each main category specifying the meaning of the material with respect to the main categories. The structure should be appropriate for answering the research question. In building a coding frame, you reduce the variety of meanings in your material to the distinctions specified by these categories. On the one hand, this helps with handling a large amount of material; on the other hand, distinctions that are not covered by your coding frame are no longer visible and will be lost for further analysis.

Coding frames of varying complexity

Complexity of coding frames

Coding frames can vary considerably in complexity. In *conceptual* terms, the complexity of your coding frame will depend on your research question. Your research question affects the number of dimensions that you will use to structure your material and the extent to which you will subdivide these dimensions. In *practical* terms, complexity depends on the following two aspects: on how many *dimensions* and how many *hierarchical levels* (subdivisions) there are in your coding frame. *Dimensions* in a coding frame have already been introduced in the previous section. They are based on relevant aspects in your material, with each aspect constituting a main category. Coding frames range from one dimension to any number of dimensions, and their complexity increases with the number of dimensions.

████████████████████████ KEY POINT ████████████████████████

In conceptual terms, the complexity of a coding frame depends on your research question. In practical terms, it depends on the number of dimensions and hierarchical levels contained in the coding frame.

In terms of the hierarchical levels in your coding frame, your main categories constitute a first, higher level, your subcategories a second, lower level. Because a coding frame contains by definition at least one main category and its subcategories, each coding frame has at least two levels. But depending on how many conceptual distinctions you make, the number of levels can be considerably increased (Früh, 2007; Kuckartz, 2009, Chapter 11).

Example of the structure of a coding frame with ───── several hierarchical levels ─────

In the previous section, the dimension *Opinions on the case of Terri Schiavo* with the subcategories *morally justified, long overdue, morally wrong, refusal to take any decision, unclear* was used to illustrate main categories und subcategories in a coding frame. *Opinions on the case of Terri Schiavo*, however, is only one of the main categories applied to what participants said about the case, next to reasons underlying these opinions, additional aspects on which they would want information before arriving at a decision, and others; and these can all be conceptualised as subcategories to the main category of *The case of Terri Schiavo*. And *The case of Terri Schiavo*, in turn, is only one of the many aspects covered during the interviews and considered in building the coding frame. Other aspects include: changes for the better in the public health care system, changes for the worse, areas in health care that should be prioritised, patient groups who should receive preferential treatment, and many more. All of these can be thought of as subcategories of the general research topic *Priority setting in health care*. The resulting multi-level structure is shown in Figure 4.1.

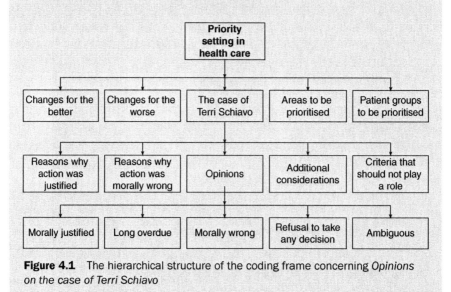

Figure 4.1 The hierarchical structure of the coding frame concerning *Opinions on the case of Terri Schiavo*

It follows that coding frames range from simple frames that comprise only one dimension and two levels; through frames of medium complexity comprising only one dimension but more than two hierarchical levels, or several dimensions but only two hierarchical levels; to highly complex frames consisting of several dimensions and more than two levels. In the following, simple, medium, and highly complex frames will be described in more detail.

Before we will look at the structure of coding frames of varying complexity, it is worth noting that by introducing the distinction between different hierarchical levels, an important aspect of the structure of coding frames is highlighted: Main categories and subcategories are not 'absolutes'. A dimension may be a main category with respect to its subcategories, *and* also a subcategory with respect to yet other dimensions in the coding frame. Because of this, Figure 4.1 shows that *Opinions* simultaneously serves as a subcategory with respect to *The case of Terri Schiavo* and as a main category *vis-à-vis* the subcategories *morally justified*, etc.

Simple coding frames

Simple coding frames consisting only of one dimension and two levels are rare in QCA. Because in qualitative research you are usually concerned with giving an in-depth description of your material, a simple coding frame will not provide enough detail and depth so as to be useful. Nevertheless, more complex coding frames can be composed of a number of such simple coding frames, 'strung together'. In this way, simple coding frames can serve as 'building blocks' of more complex ones. To illustrate, an example will be given which at the same time describes an early, classic study employing the method.

In their study of the representation of Stalin in the Soviet press, Nathan Leites, Elsa Bernaut and Raymond Garthoff (1951) examined articles and speeches on the occasion of Stalin's 70th birthday in 1949 by Politburo members. For their analysis of the images of Stalin presented in this material, they identified statements about Stalin and assigned these to one of three subcategories:

- statements putting the emphasis on the Bolshevik characteristics of Stalin as the party leader;
- statements putting the emphasis on Stalin as the people's leader, focusing on his more popular characteristics;
- ambiguous statements.

Here, the research question immediately translates into the one dimension or main category, i.e. the image of Stalin conveyed by the Soviet press; the Bolshevik image, the popular image, and the ambiguous image are the three subcategories.

The study also illustrates the thin dividing line between QCA and quantitative content analysis. The categories are found inductively, in the material, by grouping statements together, and they are illustrated by many quotations; however, coding frequencies serving to compare the different members of the Politburo in their descriptions of Stalin are also provided.

Coding frames of medium complexity

Coding frames of medium complexity consist either of one dimension that 'reaches down' more than one level or of several simple coding frames 'strung together'.

Coding frames consisting of one dimension and several levels

The coding frame that was developed by David McClelland and his collaborators for analysing evidence of the achievement motive consists of one dimension that reaches down several levels (McClelland et al., 2008). It is one of several coding frames developed for scoring the results of the Thematic Apperception Test. This is an instrument for identifying personality characteristics. The participants are presented with a series of images and are asked to tell the story of what is shown there. These stories are then examined for evidence of different motives, among them the achievement motive. For each motive, a separate coding frame has been developed (cf. Smith, 2008; see also Chapter 1).

The one dimension of the coding frame for the achievement motive concerns the question whether achievement imagery is present in the story. On the first level, this dimension comprises the following subcategories: achievement imagery, doubtful achievement imagery, unrelated imagery. This first level serves to clarify whether the story contains any achievement imagery at all.

The following analysis on the second level is carried out only for those stories that were previously identified as containing achievement imagery. It serves to differentiate between three different kinds of achievement imagery: competition with a standard of excellence, unique accomplishment, and long-term involvement. The structure of the coding frame is shown in Figure 4.2. In their definition of the *subcategory competition with a standard of excellence*, McClelland et al. (2008) further distinguish between different standards of excellence. The authors might have turned these into subcategories, but did not do so, subsuming them all under the general idea of competing against a standard, whatever this standard might be. This shows that there is no right or wrong way to structure your material; the decision about which structure to use depends on the research question and is up to you, the researcher.

Coding frames consisting of several dimensions and two levels

A coding frame of medium complexity that consists of a number of categories, but does not reach down beyond one level of subcategories, is used by a PhD student who is examining broadcasts on German television for their depiction of family life (Viertel, 2010). The coding frame contains a total of 86 different main categories, each with their respective subcategories, among them the following:

- marital status of the parents – subcategories: married and living together; married and living separately; living together and not married; not married and not living together; formerly married, now divorced; formerly married, father is widowed, now single; formerly married, mother is widowed, now single; other; marital status not evident;
- family composition – single mother; single father; parents with child/children; multigenerational family; other; family composition not evident;

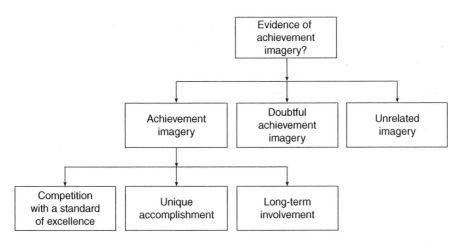

Figure 4.2 The hierarchical structure of the coding frame for the achievement motive (McClelland et al., 2008)

- dominant parenting style – authoritarian; democratic; egalitarian; laissez-faire; negating; no dominant parenting style; other; parenting style not evident;
- organisation of child care – father; mother; both parents jointly; both parents taking turns; grandfather; grandmother; other; organisation of child care not evident.

Coding frames of high complexity

Coding frames of high complexity comprise several dimensions and more than two hierarchical levels. Such a highly complex coding frame was used by Odağ (2007) in her analysis of reading protocols collected from readers of four different narrative texts. Her coding frame for analysing these protocols comprises four dimensions: the quality of the reading experience; topics and points of reference; facets; and emotions.

The first dimension, *Quality of the reading experience*, contains two subcategories, *positive* and *negative*, and each of these is further subdivided into *present* and *not present*. In this way, each protocol was analysed in terms of whether it did or did not contain evidence of a positive and evidence of a negative reading experience:

- Positive quality of the reading experience

  o Present
  o Not present

- Negative quality of the reading experience

  o Present
  o Not present.

The second dimension, *Topics and points of reference*, consists of two subcategories, *point of reference* and *topics of the reading experience;* for each of these, additional subcategories are specified. They are grouped together into one dimension because both topics and points of reference can activate a certain type of reading experience.

- *Point of reference* serves to identify whether the reading experience was activated by something within the text or whether the text was merely the starting point for something else, a memory for instance, which then gave rise to the experience described in the reading protocol. Three subcategories are distinguished:
  - exclusive reference to the text;
  - reference going beyond the text,
  - miscellaneous.
- *For Topics*, seven subcategories are distinguished. For each of these, it is specified whether a reading protocol does (present) or does not (not present) refer to them:
  - character
    - present
      - female
      - male
    - not present
  - story world
    - present
    - not present
  - plot
    - present
    - not present
  - language
    - present
    - not present
  - plausibility
    - present
    - not present
  - author
    - present
    - not present
  - other aspects of the narrative (miscellaneous)
    - present
    - not present.

The third dimension, *Facets*, serves to describe the reading experience in the protocols in terms of the following qualities (subcategories): *closeness to the text; reasons; familiarity;* and *imagination.*

  - *Closeness* in turn comprises two subcategories:

o *degree of closeness* captures the degree of closeness to the textual world which is experienced by the reader:

  o closeness
  o medium closeness
  o distance
  o miscellaneous.

o *type of world* describes whether the readers, during their experience, felt immersed into the world of the narrative or remained focused on their own world:
  o immersion into the world of the narrative
  o immersion into the reader's own world
  o immersion into both worlds
  o immersion into neither of the two worlds.

o *Reasons* specifies what it was about the narrative that gave rise to a reading experience. It contains five subcategories; for each of these it was coded whether the respective reason was mentioned (*present*) or not mentioned (*not present*) in a given reading protocol.

  o similarity
    o present
    o not present

  o plausibility
    o present
    o not present

  o desire
    o present
    o not present

  o unexpected aspects of the narrative
    o present
    o not present

  o miscellaneous
    o present
    o not present.

o *Familiarity* captures whether the readers have ever encountered this specific experience prior to reading the narrative. It comprises the following subcategories:

  o memory of previous experience
  o new or anticipated experience
  o experience without further specification.

o *Imagination* refers to the way in which the readers imagined or experienced the various aspects of the narrative. It was coded whether a reading protocol did (*present*) or did not (*not present*) contain evidence of these different types of experience:

- o visually
  - o present
  - o not present

- o physiologically
  - o present
  - o not present

- o mentally
  - o present
  - o not present.

The last dimension captures which *emotions* were experienced by the readers. For each subcategory, it was noted whether it was or was not present in a given reading protocol:

- o suspense
  - o present
  - o not present

- o enjoyment
  - o present
  - o not present

- o surprise
  - o present
  - o not present

- o sadness
  - o present
  - o not present

- o anger
  - o present
  - o not present

- o disgust
  - o present
  - o not present

- o fear
  - o present
  - o not present

- o shame
  - o present
  - o not present

- o fascination
  - o present
  - o not present

- o relief

- o present
- o not present

- o pride
  - o present
  - o not present

- o affection
  - o present
  - o not present

- o rejection
  - o present
  - o not present

- o boredom
  - o present
  - o not present.

SUMMARY

Coding frames can vary in complexity. Conceptually, the complexity of a coding frame depends on your research question. In practical terms, it depends on the number of dimensions and the number of hierarchical levels. Simple coding frames contain one dimension with its subcategories (i.e. two levels). Coding frames of medium complexity comprise either one dimension reaching down more than one level, or several dimensions, each with its own set of subcategories. Coding frames of high complexity contain several dimensions, of which at least one reaches down more than one level.

Requirements for coding frames

Coding frames are supposed to meet a number of requirements. You can only assess the majority of these, most importantly reliability and validity, once you have carried out a first trial coding; and reliability and validity will be presented and discussed in this context (see Chapter 9). But you should keep the following requirements already in mind as you are building your coding frame: unidimensionality, mutual exclusiveness, exhaustiveness, and saturation.

Unidimensionality

A first requirement states that coding frames should consist of one dimension only (Früh, 2007). Stated in such absolute terms, this requirement is somewhat misleading: most coding frames, especially in qualitative research, will contain several dimensions (compare the coding frames of medium and high complexity above). So how can coding frames that consist of several dimensions meet the requirement of being unidimensional at the same time?

Strictly speaking, the requirement does not refer to entire coding frames, but to each dimension in a frame. Essentially it means that each dimension in your coding frame should capture only one aspect of your material. You should therefore set up your coding frame so as to avoid 'mixing' dimensions.

DEFINITION

Unidimensionality means that each dimension in your coding frame should capture only one aspect of your material.

'Mixing' dimensions is an especially frequent mistake with beginners in QCA. This happened to an MA student who was doing a follow-up study on priority setting in health care, this time with a focus on health care in cancer treatment. She was looking at who, according to various stakeholder groups, should or should not be involved in decision making in this sector, and the reasons why. The first version of her coding frame looked somewhat like this:

- Politicians
  - Should be involved
    - In charge of the state finances
  - Should not be involved
    - Own interests
    - Lack of expert knowledge
- Members of health insurance companies
  - Should be involved
    - In charge of financing treatments
  - Should not be involved
    - Own interests
    - Exclusive concern with saving money
- Scientists
  - Should be involved
    - Expert knowledge
  - Should not be involved
    - Own interests.

In this version, the coding frame 'mixes' two dimensions: the participants' opinions about who should or should not be involved in medical decision making in oncology, and their reasons.

Two signs can help you spot whether you have been mixing your dimensions in setting up your coding frame. One way is to check whether the sub-categories can count as examples or 'values' of the main categories. In the above coding frame, this is clearly not the case: *Should be involved* or *Should not be involved* is not an instance, a type of politician (or member of a health insurance company or scientist), and representing one's own interests is not a way of *Should not be involved*. This is a first sign that something is wrong here. A second and more easily spotted telltale sign is the repetition of category names throughout the coding frame. *Should be involved* and *Should not be involved* recur several times, as does the reason *Own interests* for why a certain group of persons should not be involved in decision making.

BEGINNER'S MISTAKE

'Mixing' dimensions is an especially frequent mistake with beginners in QCA. Two signs can help you recognise whether you are 'mixing dimensions':

- your subcategories cannot be considered instances of the main categories;
- the names of subcategories recur throughout the coding frame (in an identical function).

The student revised the coding frame as follows:
- Involvement
  - Groups who should be involved
    - Medical personnel
    - ...
  - Groups who should not be involved
    - Politicians
    - Members of health insurance companies
    - Scientists
    - ...
- Reasons why a given group should be involved in decision making
  - In charge of finances
  - Expert knowledge
  - ...
- Reasons why a given group should not be involved in decision making
  - Own interests
  - Lack of expert knowledge
  - Exclusive concern with saving money
  - ...

In this revised version, subcategories constitute examples, specifications of main categories; politicians, for instance, are an example of a group who should not be involved in decision making (according to the interviewees), and lack of expert knowledge is one example of a reason why this is so. Likewise, category names no longer recur, but each name appears only once. But be aware that in theory it is still possible for category names to recur. In the above example this would be the case if some interviewees mention that they believe that members of health insurance companies should be involved in the decision making process, whereas others say that in their opinion members of health insurance companies should not be involved. In the revised version of the coding frame, this would not present a problem, because category names would recur in a *different function* each time. In the one case members of a health insurance company would be an instance of a group who *should* be involved, whereas in the other case they would be an instance of a group who *should not* be involved. Confusing though this may sound at first, this is different from the first version of the coding frame, where category names recur in an *identical function*; it is always to say, for instance, that a given group should or should not be involved: politicians, members of health insurance companies, and scientists.

Unidimensionality of coding frames is important for two reasons. In the first place, unidimensional coding frames are more parsimonious and provide a more concise description of the material. With only a few dimensions (as in the above example), this effect may not be very noticeable – but imagine a coding frame employing 80 dimensions or more, where the dimensions overlap. This would be very confusing! The second reason is closely linked to the requirement that subcategories be mutually exclusive (see below): it is more difficult to make subcategories mutually exclusive if a coding frame is not unidimensional.

KEY POINT

Unidimensionality of coding frames is important for two reasons:

- unidimensional coding frames are more parsimonious;
- unidimensionality helps with building coding frames where the categories are mutually exclusive.

Beginners especially often make the mistake of 'mixing' categories because they want to capture information about how two dimensions are related, and 'mixing' seems the only way to do this. The MA student in the above example, for instance, had a hunch that the participants would give different reasons with respect to the different potential decision makers. The concern that persons might be partial in their decision making, for instance, seemed to be especially important when it comes to members of health insurance companies as well as politicians. The student attempted to capture this relationship between the categories by coding the reasons given with respect to the various decision makers, thereby mixing the two dimensions. When I suggested a revised version of the frame, she was concerned that this relationship between the categories would elude her. It is correct that in disentangling main categories, you cannot directly capture how they relate to each other. But you can capture this in a subsequent step of data processing, following upon the actual content analysis. With software, for instance, you can check for co-occurrences of the various reasons and the various types of persons whom the interviewees would like to see included or excluded (see Chapter 12); and the same can be achieved by doing a cross-tabulation of the (sub)categories by hand (see Chapter 11).

BEGINNER'S MISTAKE

Beginners often mix dimensions because they want to capture how the dimensions relate to each other. But there are better ways of finding out about this, after you have done the coding, especially if you are using software.

Mutual exclusiveness

The second requirement of coding frames is that the subcategories in your coding frame mutually exclude each other, i.e. that you can assign each segment of your material to one subcategory only (Krippendorff, 2004; Rustemeyer, 1992). Again, this may be confusing in absolute terms: why should not one data segment convey different kinds of information? Cannot a sentence (to stay with the above example) say (a) that politicians should not be included in the decision about cancer treatment and (b) that this should be so because they do not have the requisite expertise?

DEFINITION

Mutual exclusiveness refers to the subcategories within one dimension. It means that a unit of coding can be assigned to one of these subcategories only.

But like unidimensionality, mutual exclusiveness also does not refer to the entire coding frame, but only to one dimension and its subcategories. It translates into the requirement that the same unit of coding should be assigned to only one subcategory *within a given dimension*. The rationale underlying this requirement is immediately obvious when you are dealing with subcategories for describing opinions on a given issue. When classifying participants' opinions about turning off the life support for Terri Schiavo, for instance, it would not make much sense to code the same passage as both *morally justified* and *morally wrong*. Perhaps a participant is uncertain concerning the issue – in this case it would be better to introduce another subcategory *ambivalent* or *unclear* (which we did) which is in turn different from *morally justified* and *morally wrong*.

The rationale is less obvious when you are dealing with categories that do not by definition exclude each other. The reasons participants give why they consider it morally justified that Terri Schiavo's life support was turned off would be a case in point. It is perfectly possible that a participant, in one sentence, says that a patient lying in a coma for 15 years is a huge strain on the relatives and that this patient would have died of her own accord several years ago, if it were not for the recent technological advances in medicine. In this case the requirement that categories be mutually exclusive relates to the fit between:

- units of coding, i.e. those parts of the material that can be meaningfully interpreted with a view to the respective dimension (see Chapter 7);
- and the definitions of the subcategories (see Chapter 5).

You can meet this requirement if you choose your units of coding such that each unit fits only within one subcategory. When you are dealing with subcategories which are not mutually exclusive by definition, this requirement is important when assessing the reliability of your coding frame. This is much easier if you are dealing with subcategories that mutually exclude each other (see Chapter 9). In any case, the requirement does not prevent you from coding a given passage for several dimensions of meaning; it does not apply to main categories/dimensions, but only to the subcategories comprising the 'values' of one category.

Exhaustiveness

Another requirement to keep in mind as you are building your coding frame is exhaustiveness. A coding frame is said to be exhaustive if you are able to assign each unit of coding in your material to at least one subcategory in your coding frame. This is to say that all that is relevant in your material must be captured by one of the subcategories in your coding frame (Holsti, 1969; Rustemeyer, 1992).

DEFINITION

A coding frame is said to be exhaustive if you are able to assign each unit of coding in your material to at least one subcategory in your coding frame.

This is an important concern, because with QCA you have to take into account each unit of coding, examine it, and determine what it means with respect to your research question. And the only way to make sure that you have really considered the meaning of every single unit is to assign each unit to one of your subcategories. You can easily satisfy this criterion by introducing a residual subcategory within each dimension (and code this whenever the unit does not fit one of the other subcategories). The criterion of exhaustiveness is in fact the reason why each dimension in a coding frame will usually contain a *miscellaneous* subcategory. At the same time, introducing such a residual subcategory makes the criterion of exhaustiveness look almost meaningless. Because of this, exhaustiveness becomes truly meaningful only when you consider it together with validity (see Chapter 9): if your (data-driven) coding frame is to be valid, you should code the residual categories sparingly. In this way, the criterion of exhaustiveness translates into the requirement that you can indeed classify all relevant segments in substantive terms. Exhaustiveness and validity are therefore closely related.

Saturation

The criterion of saturation requires that you construct your coding frame in such a way that the coding frequency for all categories and subcategories equals 1 or higher – or, to put it differently, that in conducting QCA, you use each subcategory at least once and that no subcategory remains 'empty' (Rustemeyer, 1992).

DEFINITION

The criterion of saturation requires that each subcategory is used at least once during the analysis, i.e. that no subcategory remains 'empty'.

This criterion applies differently to data-driven and to concept-driven coding frames. If you are dealing with a data-driven coding frame, this requirement is met by definition: if you had not come across something in your material that you would want to classify under a given category, you would not have created that category to begin with.

If you have created your coding frame in a concept-driven way, it is perfectly possible that you will not use some of these conceptual categories in coding your material, that the categories remain 'empty'. But in this case the criterion of saturation is not applicable: it may be an important finding that some categories are not covered by your material (Rustemeyer, 1992). But in order to arrive at this result, the categories must be part of your coding frame to start with – otherwise you would not have the chance to find out that nothing in your material corresponds to them.

──── **Example of how non-saturated coding frames can be useful** ────

In her analysis of the presentation of family life on German television, one of the concept-driven categories used by Viertel (2010) referred to parenting style, with the following subcategories: *authoritarian; democratic; egalitarian; laissez-faire;*

negating; no dominant parenting style; other; parenting style not evident. It turned out that during an average programme week, parenting style was typically either not evident or it was authoritarian; no families practising a democratic or a laissez-faire style were shown. This is an important finding – but in order to obtain this finding, the empty subcategories had to be retained in the coding frame and had to be taken into consideration in describing the programmes and in calculating overall frequencies.

Therefore, the criterion of saturation is ultimately meaningless: in the case of a data-driven coding frame, it is met by definition; in the case of a concept-driven coding frame, it is not applicable in the first place.

SUMMARY

Coding frames should be unidimensional, subcategories should mutually exclude each other, and coding frames should be exhaustive. Unidimensionality means that each dimension in your coding frame should capture only one aspect of your material. Mutual exclusiveness means that you should design the coding frame so that each unit of coding can only be assigned to one subcategory within a given dimension; it does not rule out assigning one unit of coding to subcategories belonging to different dimensions of your coding frame. A coding frame is exhaustive if you can assign each unit of coding to at least one subcategory. Data-driven coding frames are also saturated by definition, i.e. each subcategory is used at least once during the analysis.

Frequently asked questions

How do I come up with a structure for my coding frame?

Unfortunately there is no clear-cut answer to this question. It is best to start out with your research question in mind and to identify aspects of the material that are necessary for answering this question. You can then turn each aspect into a main category/dimension. In a next step, you should create subcategories for each dimension by going through your material. In doing so, you should keep the three requirements of unidimensionality, mutual exclusiveness, and exhaustiveness in mind. But usually the problem is not to come up with dimensions in the first place, but to cut down on the number that you have come up with. In this, you should again be guided by your research question. You can always go back to the same material at a later stage and analyse it again from a different perspective.

How many categories should there be in my coding frame?

This is yet another question to which there is no clear answer. Experience has shown that coders have difficulty handling more than approximately 40 categories (including subcategories) at the same time (MacQueen et al., 2009). But this is not to say that you should limit your entire coding frame to 40 categories. This is just a good number to keep in mind when you are coming up with a set of (sub)categories that will be applied to the same part of your material. Often, a coding frame will comprise several such sets of categories. In studies using an interview guide, for instance, you will usually apply one set of categories to the replies to one interview question, including follow-up questions. This set of categories should not contain more than around 40 categories. But there is no limit to the number of such sets of categories.

———————————— **End-of-chapter questions** ————————————

- What is the difference between main categories and subcategories in a coding frame?
- In what sense does one have to make choices when building a coding frame?
- What does the complexity of a coding frame depend on?
- Describe the structure of a coding frame of medium complexity.
- What are the requirements that you should keep in mind when building your coding frame?

5

BUILDING A CODING FRAME

Chapter guide

Now you can get started on building your own coding frame, and how to do so will be the focus of this chapter. The process of building a frame can be broken down into the following steps: selecting, structuring, generating, defining, revising, and expanding. We will look at each of these in turn:

- selecting;
- structuring and generating (which are closely related);
- defining;
- revising and expanding (which are also closely related).

Selecting

When you build your coding frame, selection is important in two ways:

1. If you have data from different sources, you have to decide where to start.
2. You have to decide which part of your material is relevant and which part is not. In building your coding frame, you want to focus on what is relevant to your research question.

Deciding where to start

QCA is a method that helps you *reduce* your material. You will therefore use QCA when you are dealing with a lot of data that needs reducing. And because there is such a lot of material, chances are that you will not be able to build a coding frame in one go that covers it all. That would be like trying to build a mansion with several wings all at once. Instead of trying to do it all at once, it is better to break down the task – to do the east wing first, before moving on to the west wing, and so on. If you have a lot of material, it is therefore best to start by building a coding frame that covers only a part of your data. There are two strategies for selecting a part of your material on which to start:

1. breaking down your data according to source;
2. breaking down your data according to topic.

The first strategy is useful if you have data from different sources. This may be data from different types of cases, groups of persons, from different cultures, or from different time periods. If you have data from different sources, it would be a good idea to select one source to start with. You would then create a coding frame that fits this one source, adding to it, so as to make it fit other sources, at a later stage.

The second strategy is helpful if you have long documents. In this case, it is best to begin by selecting only a part of the documents, a part that addresses one particular topic, one aspect of your research question. Replies to an interview question would be an example.

You can also combine the two strategies.

——— Example of breaking data down according to source and topic ———

In our study about priority setting in health care, our material came from interviews with members of different stakeholder groups: healthy persons, patients, nursing staff, physicians, administrators, and politicians. In a first step, we focused on interviews with healthy persons. But these interviews were still too long, covering many different interview questions. We therefore added a second selection step, focusing on the replies to our first interview question (about perceived changes in health care now compared to the past). Thus, the first categories in our coding frame described the changes healthy persons perceived in the health care system.

But perhaps your material is not so diverse. Perhaps you are building a tree house, not a mansion. In this case, you can skip this first selection step – if you are building a simple coding frame that has only one dimension, for example. Ultimately, the decision whether to build the coding frame step by step, or in one go, is up to you and your feeling of how much material you can handle simultaneously.

Distinguishing between relevant and irrelevant material

Once you have decided where to start, you have to make choices again. Chances are that some of your material will not be relevant. And because you will most likely have too much data anyway, you should leave out irrelevant material from your analysis. Because of this, you have to distinguish between relevant and irrelevant parts of your data and focus on the relevant parts only (MacQueen et al., 2009). In a way, the distinction between relevant and irrelevant material is very simple: all material that has a bearing upon your research question counts as relevant, and all material that does not can be considered irrelevant. But in practice, matters are rarely so simple. Chances are that some parts of your material will have more bearing on your research question than other parts – and you are now faced with the decision as to which parts of your material have so much less bearing that, for all practical purposes, you can consider them to be irrelevant. This can be a very difficult choice to make, especially if you are faced with a lot of data that all seems equally fascinating. Nevertheless it is a choice you have to make, or else you risk getting lost in the data.

This choice is difficult not only because there may be so much in your data that you find interesting, but also because it involves a lot of interpretation. Selecting some parts of your material as relevant and other parts as irrelevant can introduce a substantial bias into your analysis. An extreme case would be the researcher who decides to disregard everything that does not fit her pre-conceived notions!

There are two strategies that help you avoid creating bias when selecting material:

1. using a coding frame to select relevant material;
2. selecting relevant material in a research team.

Using a coding frame to select relevant material

The first strategy comes down to using QCA itself for deciding what is and what is not relevant. One way of doing this is to conduct your analysis in two steps. In a first step, you create a coding frame to differentiate between relevant and irrelevant parts of your material. In a second step, you create a substantive coding frame that applies only to the relevant parts of your material. Alternatively, you might build only one coding frame that contains a category for irrelevant material in addition to the categories for describing the relevant material (see the example below).

───── **Example of using a coding frame to select relevant material** ─────

In their analysis of Thematic Apperception Test stories for presence of achievement-related imagery, McClelland et al. (2008) combine the distinction between relevant and irrelevant parts of their material and the description of achievement-related imagery into one single coding frame. They distinguish between the following main categories: *achievement imagery, doubtful achievement imagery, unrelated imagery.* Only passages coded as *achievement imagery* are considered relevant, and only these passages are then coded for the type of achievement-related imagery. Incidentally, McClelland et al. are pursuing a different strategy here from what is suggested below. If in doubt, they prefer to *exclude* material from the analysis. This has to do with the purpose of their coding frame which is used in a clinical context.

If you are new to QCA, it is strongly recommended that you use two steps to distinguish between relevant and irrelevant parts of your material. This two-step analysis requires that you create a coding frame that consists of only two categories: *relevant* and *irrelevant*. You must then define both of these, i.e. you have to make it explicit what you mean by *relevant* and *irrelevant* (category definitions are described in more detail below). In doing so, you will want to err on the safe side. If you classify material as relevant that is really irrelevant, this may be annoying because it disrupts the process of your analysis; but no great harm is done. But if you mistakenly classify material as irrelevant that is really relevant, this material will be lost; you will simply not come back to it in the course of your analysis. Because you want to make sure that all relevant material is included, it is usually best to say: if in doubt, consider it relevant! The category *relevant* should therefore be a broad category. It should contain those parts of your data that are definitely relevant – *and* those parts that may be relevant, where you are not certain. Conversely, the category *irrelevant* should be narrowly defined. To code a part of your material as *irrelevant*, you should be certain that it really does not have a bearing on your research question.

KEY POINT

When distinguishing between relevant and irrelevant data, it is better to err on the safe side. If in doubt, it is better to code irrelevant material as relevant than to code relevant material as irrelevant. Therefore, make the category *relevant* more inclusive than the category *irrelevant*.

Selecting relevant material in a research team

If you are working in a research team, there is a second way to help you prevent bias when selecting the relevant parts of your material. The most parsimonious way to do this is for you (as the researcher) to read your material and to mark any passages that you consider irrelevant or of doubtful relevance. In a next step, you bring in others to supplement your own perspective. This can be one other person who double-checks any passages that you have marked as irrelevant or doubtful. A passage is excluded from further analysis only if the other person also considers it irrelevant. You may also bring in an entire research team, with all of you making a joint decision about those passages that you have marked as *irrelevant* or *doubtful*. The underlying rationale is that you may be biased towards your material, that you may overlook (and consider irrelevant) aspects that do not fit your preconceived notions. Bringing in other, unprejudiced perspectives can help you correct this bias.

Selecting relevant material in a team is less time-consuming than doing it through QCA, because the selection process is focused on the doubtful passages. But there is also a certain danger that your notion of relevance remains vague or that your understanding of relevance changes during the research process. It is therefore a good idea to write down what you mean by *relevant* before beginning the selection process, even if you do not use this as a category in QCA.

If you are working in a research team, you can also combine the two strategies for selecting relevant material. In this case, you would carry out a QCA to distinguish between relevant and irrelevant material, and you would have a part of the material double-coded, by yourself and another coder (see Chapters 8–10 for details).

================================ SUMMARY ================================

When building a coding frame, selection is important in two ways: in deciding where to start and in distinguishing between relevant and irrelevant parts of your material. Deciding where to start is important if you have a lot of material and at least a medium complex coding frame. In this case it is a good idea to start with material from one source, and possibly with one out of a number of topics. Distinguishing between relevant and irrelevant parts of your material can be integrated into QCA, or it can be done in a research team, focusing only on passages of doubtful relevance. In either case you should write down what you mean by *relevant*. These two strategies for selecting relevant material can also be combined.

Structuring and generating

Once you have selected the material to start with, the second step is to decide about the *structure* of your coding frame. This means that you will have to decide which dimensions you will use to describe your data, and you will have to *generate* subcategories for each dimension (see Chapter 4). These two steps of structuring and generating are closely related. There are three ways in which you can go about this task:

1. in a *concept-driven* way, i.e. based on what you already know;
2. in a *data-driven* way, i.e. by letting the categories emerge from your material;
3. by *combining* the two strategies.

These strategies are described below. Following this description, we will also look at the process of structuring and generating in more general terms, and at some considerations to keep in mind when you decide about a structure.

Concept-driven strategies

If you are using a concept-driven, deductive strategy for building your coding frame, you are making use of things that you already know, without even looking at your data. This knowledge can come from different sources: from a theory, from previous research, from everyday experience, or from logic.

DEFINITION

Using a concept-driven, deductive strategy means basing your work on previous knowledge. This can come from different sources: a theory, prior research, everyday experience, or logic.

Drawing upon theory

A first type of conceptual knowledge you can draw upon in building your coding frame is theory. In fact, this is precisely what *deductive* means in a narrow sense of the term. A lot has been written about what exactly a theory is (for an overview see French, 2008). For the present purpose we will ignore these debates and simply assume that a theory consists of concepts and relations between these concepts.

Example of a concept-driven coding frame based on theory

The coding frame developed by McClelland et al. (2008) for assessing achievement-related imagery in stories created during the application of the Thematic Apperception Test would be an example of such a theory-driven coding frame (see Chapter 4). The types of achievement imagery that are distinguished in the frame (competition with a standard of excellence, unique accomplishment, and long-term involvement) and their definitions are all based on concepts from the theory of achievement that was likewise put forward by McClelland.

Such theory-driven coding frames are especially useful for hypothesis testing. This is why they are comparatively rare in qualitative research, which is more often exploratory or descriptive. It is more common for qualitative coding frames to contain only a few theory-driven dimensions or subcategories. Other parts of the coding frame may be based on other kinds of prior knowledge or may be derived from the data.

Drawing upon prior research

Another way of working in a concept-driven way is to make use of research conducted by others, especially research that also involved QCA and coding frames. In this way, you can adapt categories that were used by other researchers when building your coding frame. This is especially useful if you want to compare your results with theirs, thereby comparing across time, cultures, or different kinds of data.

The procedure is as follows (see Boyatzis, 1998, Chapter 2):

- You look at each of the main categories and subcategories in the coding frame that was used in previous research, and you check whether the category definitions fit your material. It may be that you have to adapt the definitions somewhat. This is because, after all, your data is of necessity different from the other researchers' data.
- You look at your material to check whether it contains any other important aspects that are not covered by the original coding frame. If so, you have to add more inductive categories or subcategories.

Drawing upon everyday knowledge

Sometimes it is also possible to base some dimensions and subcategories – though not entire coding frames – on a less formalised, everyday kind of knowledge. You may not be able to draw on a theory or on research, but nevertheless you vaguely know what to expect. Such aspects of 'what to expect' can be turned into dimensions and subcategories. Nevertheless, you would not want to rely on your intuition and everyday knowledge alone. Therefore, when making use of everyday knowledge in building parts of a coding frame, it is essential that you add a second, inductive step where you make use of one of the inductive strategies described below.

Example of drawing on everyday knowledge
—— when building a coding frame ——

In our study about prioritising in medicine, we asked participants whether any areas in health care should, in their opinion, receive more or less financial support than is presently the case. No definitive list of areas in health care exists that could have been used as a deductive category frame. But some areas constitute common knowledge, and we used these as subcategories. These included research and development, diagnostics, and rehabilitation.

Drawing upon logic

There is yet another situation where you will also know what to expect – not because of what you know about your field of research, but simply as a matter of logic (in a loose, everyday sense of the term). This is the case whenever you are assessing the expression of opinions or attitudes. Opinions can be favourable, unfavourable, or something in between – regardless of what the opinion is about. Similarly, if you want to assess agreement, the data can indicate agreement, disagreement, or something in between, again regardless of the specific issue at hand.

—— **Example of drawing upon logic when building a coding frame** ——

As part of a questionnaire study about the experience and the effects of the London bombings in July 2005, Bux and Coyne (2009) asked participants to describe their experience in their own words. QCA was used to analyse these responses. In assessing the experiences described by the participants, three main categories are immediately obvious: *negative emotional responses, positive emotional responses,* and *neutral emotions.* In fact, if the researchers had not drawn upon 'logic', they might haven chosen not to include *positive emotional responses.* But whether any positive responses are present is an empirical question, and it can only be answered by including the respective subcategory in the coding frame. If the participants do not mention any positive responses, the category will remain empty. In fact, two types of positive emotional responses were found: *thankfulness and relief* (for their own safety and that of important others) and *pride* (about how the UK handled the terrorist attack).

Coding for the presence or absence of a phenomenon would be another example of drawing upon logic in this loose sense of the term (see Chapter 4 for the coding frame developed by Odağ, 2007, for an example).

Drawing upon an interview guide

If you used a topic guide for collecting your data, you can then use this guide as a deductive framework for building part of your coding frame. The topics provide you with the dimensions; the subcategories for these dimensions are best generated inductively, using one of the strategies described below (see Chapter 4 for examples taken from our study about prioritising in health care).

Data-driven strategies

Another way of building a coding frame is to do so inductively, creating categories and subcategories based on your data. A data-driven strategy for building a coding frame is especially appropriate if your research goal is to describe your material in detail. In QCA, at least a part of your coding frame will typically be data-driven. This is so because qualitative data is usually so rich, containing much more than you would have anticipated. Nevertheless entire data-driven coding frames are rare, simply because your research question already specifies certain dimensions which you can turn into main categories during the analysis. What is said in your material with respect to these main categories, however, is precisely the detail that you cannot anticipate – you will need a data-driven strategy to capture this.

DEFINITION

To work inductively is to create categories and subcategories in a data-driven way. This is especially useful if you want to describe your material in depth.

Even though a data-driven strategy is important in building coding frames, only few authors have made concrete suggestions for how exactly to go about this. In this chapter, I will describe these strategies only in brief; they are presented in more detail in Chapter 6.

A first strategy is to successively *summarise* your material (Mayring, 2010, Section 5.5):

- paraphrasing relevant passages;
- deleting from the paraphrases anything that strikes you as superfluous;
- summarising similar paraphrases as one paraphrase;
- using the paraphrases to generate category names.

The second strategy involves *subsumption* (Mayring, 2010, Section 5.5). This strategy is especially useful if you have already decided upon your main categories and now want to generate the subcategories. The strategy consists of the following steps:

- Examine relevant passages for pertinent concepts;
- Decide whether the concept is new:
  - o if it is new, it is turned into a category;
  - o if you have already generated a (sub)category that covers it, you simply pass it over;
- Continue with the next pertinent concept.

Boyatzis (1998) developed a data-driven strategy for generating categories that is useful for *contrasting* material from two different sources. He suggests proceeding as follows:

- generating categories which capture the similarity within the material from the first source;
- adding more categories so as to capture the differences between the two sources.

A final data-driven strategy is to adapt the steps of data analysis in *grounded theory* to generating inductive categories. This strategy is especially helpful for creating entire inductive coding frames, comprising both main categories and subcategories:

- Open coding: identifying relevant concepts;
- Selective coding:

o determining which concepts make suitable main categories or subcategories;
o structuring the concepts accordingly;
o adding more categories and subcategories if necessary.

———— **Example of generating subcategories in a data-driven way** ————

In our study about priority setting in health care, we made use of subsumption for generating subcategories in a data-driven way. This seemed the most appropriate way to proceed, considering that the interview guide already provided us with many of our main categories. In looking at the reasons why participants considered it morally right or wrong to turn off the life support for Terri Schiavo, we went through every participant's answer, creating a new subcategory whenever a new reason was mentioned. Because we wanted to both summarise and describe the material, we then, in a final step, again had to cut down on the resulting subcategories: those that occurred for only one participant were not retained, because they served the purpose of detailed description, but not the purpose of summarising the material. We either aggregated such subcategories with other small subcategories or we subsumed them under the residual subcategory of *miscellaneous* reasons.

Combining concept-driven and data-driven strategies

As mentioned above, it is rare in QCA to create a coding frame that is purely concept-driven or purely data-driven. Most of the time, you will mix both strategies (see also Früh, 2007). A typical 'mix' would be to come up with important topics based on what you already know and to turn these into main categories; this first step would be the concept-driven part of the procedure. In a second step, you then specify what is said about these topics by creating subcategories based on your material; this is the data-driven part of the strategy.

But it is not always the case that main categories are concept-driven and subcategories are data-driven. You can also combine concept-driven and data-driven subcategories, or concept-driven and data-driven main categories.

Example of combining concept-driven and
———————————— **data-driven main categories** ————————————

Concerning the case of Terri Schiavo, we had asked participants in our prioritising study for their opinion about turning off her life support and the reasons for their opinions. Opinions and reasons in favour of and against turning off her life support were our concept-driven categories. When looking at our data for the exact reasons (data-driven subcategories), it turned out that some participants said that in order to give an informed opinion they would need information about other aspects of the case, for instance about the exact diagnosis or whether there existed a living will; others explicitly mentioned that some considerations must *not* enter into the decision about turning off the life support of a patient lying in a coma, such as the duration of the coma or the costs of keeping the patient alive. We therefore added the data-driven main categories *Additional considerations* and *Rejected criteria* with their respective (and likewise data-driven) subcategories.

The relation between concept-driven and data-driven categories can be whatever seems appropriate. In some mixed coding frames the majority of categories will be data-driven, with only a few concept-driven ones added. In others, the majority of categories will be concept-driven, supplemented by only a few data-driven ones. And yet other mixed frames will consist in equal parts of concept-driven and data-driven considerations. There is no 'right mix'. What matters most is that the categories in your coding frame allow you to capture what is important about your material. It does not matter whether you get there one way or another.

Additional considerations in generating categories

In the following, we will look in more detail at the actual process of structuring and generating (procedural considerations) and at some useful considerations concerning the structure of your coding frame (structural considerations).

Procedural considerations

If you are using a concept-driven strategy for generating your categories, there is not really any question about which main categories and subcategories to include: deductive categories emerge directly from what you already know. But to the extent that you are using a data-driven strategy, it can be quite difficult to decide which categories to include. And the decision is an important one and has important consequences: because your categories are the 'filter' through which you view your data, anything that you do not include in your coding frame will be lost from view following your analysis.

Working with others can help you with these important decisions. In the first place, another person can help you overcome your own preconceptions and potential biases. You cannot help but read the data through the filter of your own world view, your own preconceptions, and your own motives – and wanting to find evidence of certain events or processes in the data can be a very powerful motive, clouding your perceptions, although you may not be aware of this. The various perspectives that different people bring to the material can complement each other, highlighting different aspects of the data. If several people – or at least two, you and someone else – read your material, chances are that you will discover more and come up with more categories than you would have done on your own. It may even happen that more aspects emerge than you can accommodate in your coding frame. But it is always easier to cut down on a coding frame that is too extensive than to add to a coding frame that is too narrow to start with. The other person to whom you show your material need not be another formally trained researcher. It can be anyone willing to have a look and to tell you what they think. Also, they do not need to read all your material – it will be helpful to get a different perspective on any part of it, however small. If you are working on your MA thesis or your PhD, chances are that you will know others who are doing the same and who are also doing qualitative research, maybe even QCA. Why not help each other?

KEY POINT

Bring in someone else to help you build your coding frame. This will help you overcome any preconceptions and will help you see more in the data.

Another procedural concern is how much of your material you should use for building your coding frame. In quantitative content analysis, you are supposed to base your coding frame on material other than the data for your main study (Früh, 2007, Part II, Chapter 1; Weber, 1990, p. 23). This is because in quantitative content analysis, the coding frame is often used to test a hypothesis. And to use the same material for generating the coding frame and for testing the hypothesis would be to prejudge the results in favour of the hypothesis.

In QCA, the situation is different. Hypothesis testing is less of an issue; additional material on which to base and try out a coding frame is often not available. And if your main concern is with describing your material, it would even be a bad idea to use different data for the trial and the main coding: perhaps the materials differ, and this would adversely affect the quality of your coding frame. Therefore, in QCA it is usually best to build your coding frame using the same material that you want to analyse.

How much of this material to use in building the frame depends on how much your data sources differ. If your material is very diverse and different for each case, building your coding frame will take a long time – chances are that you will have to look at *all* your material before you can finalise the frame. If your material is not that diverse and key points recur over and over again, you can stop much sooner – perhaps after having looked at 40% or even only at 15% of your data. You know that you can stop looking at more material and leave the frame as it is when looking at more material does not produce any new insights, and does not make you want to add more categories. This is called the criterion of *saturation* (Strauss & Corbin, 1998, p. 136).

━━━━━━━━━━━━━━━━━━━━━ KEY POINT ━━━━━━━━━━━━━━━━━━━━━

You should base your coding frame on the same material that you want to ana-lyse. Use more of the material to generate categories as long as new aspects continue to emerge.

Structural considerations

As mentioned before, in principle no one structure is better than any other structure. This is especially the case when you are building your coding frame in a data-driven way. Nevertheless, even when using an inductive strategy, some general considerations concerning structure can be useful. One point to keep in mind even with data-driven coding frames is the relation between main categories and subcategories. If you can come up with one subcategory only for a main category, it is not worth introducing subcategories in the first place. In other words, if you want to make use of subcategories, there should always be at least two of them. If there is only one, it is better to just have the main category and not to differentiate it any further.

─────── **Example of a coding frame with a suboptimal structure** ───────

In an MA thesis about medical decision making, a student conducted focus groups where she presented the participants with vignettes of patients who had been diagnosed with cancer and were now discussing different treatment options with their physician. One main category in her coding frame was *Additional information*. This was meant to capture any additional information that the focus group members felt they needed in order to decide between the different treat-ment options. As a subcategory of this main category, the student came up with *Additional information about treatment options*, and this was further subdivided into the subcategories *success rate, tumour growth rate, risk of dying*, and a residual subcategory. This is not the best possible structure because *Additional information about treatment options* remains the only subcategory on this middle level. There is no other subcategory to distinguish it from, such as *Additional information about the patient*. A better solution in structural terms would be to delete the main category, i.e. to make *Additional information about treatment options* the main category, with *success rate*, etc. as the subcategories.

When building a concept-driven coding frame, structural considerations gain in importance. The main concern in this case is to build coding frames that are structurally complete. Structural completeness refers to a set of categories that are mutually exclusive. This applies, for instance, to subcategories such as *agree, disagree, unclear*. When using (sub)categories that are mutually exclu-sive, they are structurally complete if all of these categories are included in the coding frame. Conversely, if only some of them are included, the frame is incomplete.

When building a concept-driven coding frame, you should make sure that your coding frame is structurally complete, i.e. includes all subcategories that are mutually exclusive.

Usually, the reason why you would want to include only part of such a set of categories in your coding frame is that you are coming from a data-driven perspective. If your material includes only cases of *agree* and *unclear*, it might seem like an obvious choice to include only those two subcategories in your coding frame. But this is to forget that if your material contains no cases of *disagree*, this is also important information, and you can only capture this information if you include the respective subcategory in your coding frame.

Another structural consideration concerns including residual categories in your coding frame. Residual categories are important for two reasons. In the first place, as has been mentioned many times before, qualitative data is usually rich and full of surprises. You may be convinced that you have included substantive categories that cover every piece of information that you may possibly encounter in your material – but chances are that you have not, and that you will find something that you have not anticipated. In this situation you will need residual categories, also termed *miscellaneous* categories. They function as containers for all unanticipated information that is relevant to your research question, but does not fit into any of your substantive categories. In the second place, if you are working with a data-driven coding frame, chances are that some information will be mentioned only once throughout your material. Because QCA is for summarising your material, such aspects would not normally be turned into categories; instead, they would either be subsumed under an already existing category or they would be classified as *miscellaneous*.

Usually, you will need a residual category at every hierarchical level of your coding frame, at the level of the main categories as well as at the level of your subcategories – and at the level of any subcategories of your subcategories, and so on, depending on how far 'down' your coding frame reaches (see Chapter 4).

When building a coding frame, you should make sure to include residual categories at all levels of your coding frame.

You may wonder at this point why you are supposed to include residual categories in your coding frame instead of adding more substantive categories whenever you encounter information that is not yet covered by the categories in your coding frame. Sometimes, indeed, adding another substantive category is the best way to proceed. This is the case when your coding frame is data-driven, when you are still building it, and when you repeatedly encounter this aspect in your material (for details on building a data-driven coding frame, see Chapter 6). But if you are working with a concept-driven coding frame, additional information that is not covered by your substantive categories may not be of interest to you; in this case you should classify it as *miscellaneous*. With a data-driven coding frame, you will eventually get to the point where you finalise the frame and try it out (see Chapter 8). In this case, chances are that your material will contain occasional pieces of information that are not yet covered by your categories. Again, this is where you will need your *miscellaneous* categories. If this happens a lot, however, it is a sign that you should go back and revise your frame (see Chapter 6). Finally, as mentioned before, even with a data-driven coding frame, QCA aims to reduce and summarise your material. Aspects that are only mentioned once throughout your material would usually be classified as *miscellaneous*.

████████████████████████ SUMMARY ████████████████████████

To build a coding frame, you can use one of three strategies: a concept-driven strategy, i.e. drawing on previous knowledge; a data-driven strategy, i.e. basing the categories on your material; and combining concept-driven and data-driven strategies. In QCA, the combined strategy is the one that is most frequently used. Concept-driven categories can be based on theory, on prior research, on logic, on everyday knowledge, or on an interview guide. Data-driven strategies include aggregation, subsumption, contrasting, and making use of open and selective coding adapted from grounded theory.

When building a coding frame, especially in a data-driven way, it is useful to bring in a second person to alert you to additional aspects in the material that may have escaped your notice. It is best to base the coding frame on the material that you want to analyse and to keep on adding categories to the point of saturation. When using a concept-driven strategy, your coding frame should be structurally complete. You should also include residual categories at all levels of your coding frame.

Defining

Once you have decided what your coding frame will look like, what the dimensions/main categories and what the subcategories are, the next step is to define what exactly you mean by your categories. Category definitions are the rules for assigning data segments to categories, i.e. the rules you use for coding your material. This is a crucial step in QCA: unless you make it explicit what you mean by a given category, you yourself may not remember, using a category name sometimes in one way and sometimes in another. Also, chances are that others will understand a category name differently from you. Making the meaning of your categories explicit is therefore a prerequisite for using categories consistently and for making your analysis reliable. Moreover, unless you make it clear what you mean by a given category name, the meaning of this category may subtly shift and change during the analysis. As a result, your analysis would no longer be valid (see Chapter 9 on reliability and validity in QCA).

KEY POINT

Defining your categories is important so that both you and others (coders and readers) know what you mean and use category names consistently.

A category definition has four parts (see also Boyatzis, 1998; Rustemeyer, 1992):

1. a name;
2. a description of what you mean by that name;
3. examples;
4. decision rules (if needed).

A name, description, and examples are 'must-haves', whereas decision rules are optional; they are needed only if categories overlap.

Naming your categories

Category names are labels that should be chosen to provide a concise description of what the category refers to. This is important when using the coding frame in the actual coding process. Here, coders will typically work with a list of the category names, referring to the definitions only to refresh their memory of a category or when in doubt about how exactly it is defined. When coding, coders should therefore be able to use the coding frame based on the category names only (of course they will have familiarised themselves with the category definitions during the coder training; see Chapter 8).

Chances are that you will have already come up with names during the previous step of building your coding frame, as you generated categories. When you generate a category, you have to somehow refer to it, and you will do so by calling it something.

On the one hand, finding names for your categories and subcategories is pretty straightforward. On the other hand, beginners in QCA especially make certain typical mistakes in naming their categories.

BEGINNER'S MISTAKE

The first of these mistakes comes from wanting to be overly precise, and as a result coming up with a name that is too long. Names should be convenient labels for referring to a category, not a description or a definition. Overly long category names can also be the result of taking an expression verbatim from the data and turning it into a category name (which in grounded theory is called *in vivo coding*). One way of avoiding overly long category names is to remind yourself that categories are concepts – so what is the concept that you are turning into a category here? It is usually possible to come up with a pithy, concise label for referring to a category. But how do you recognise overly long category names? There are no rules concerning the length of a category name. But a good rule of thumb is to reconsider the name if it does not fit on a single line on your computer screen.

Example of overly long category names

The MA student who conducted focus groups on deciding between different treatment options for cancer also looked at the reasons participants gave for favouring one treatment over another. In this, she generated category names such as *The therapy may not be able to relieve the pain* or *When given morphine to alleviate the pain, the patient may lose consciousness*. These names are not suitable because they describe the respective category instead of labelling it. One telltale sign is the fact that the names are provided as sentences. Sentences belong in the description, not in the category name. More suitable names would be *No pain relief* and *Potential loss of consciousness*.

BEGINNER'S MISTAKE

Another typical beginner's mistake is to go to the opposite extreme, making labels too short. If a label is too short, it is not sufficiently descriptive, it does not capture the essence of a category, or it may be too general. When a reader or a second coder encounters a category name that is too short, a typical reaction would be: So what about …? In what context, to what purpose does it feature in the frame?

In finding names for your categories, you should therefore aim for the middle ground, making them neither overly long and descriptive, nor overly short and cryptic.

Describing your categories

Next, you have to say what exactly you mean by a given category name. There are two ways of doing this: describing the features of the category, and providing indicators of the category. In the process of coding, category descriptions serve as rules, telling you and the other coders whether a data segment should be coded under a given category.

KEY POINT

Categories are described by describing the features of that category and by providing indicators, i.e. aspects of the data that point you to the category.

Describing the category features

Let us suppose that you wanted to describe QCA. You might say that QCA is a systematic procedure for describing symbolic material by assigning data segments to the categories of a coding frame. This would be to describe the features of QCA. And in determining whether a given study has employed QCA (i.e. in coding empirical studies), the coders would have to decide whether the method used in the study referred to symbolic material, whether it was carried out systematically, whether a coding frame was used, and whether data segments were assigned to the categories in this coding frame. In order to do so, you might want to know a bit more about what exactly a systematic method entails, what is meant by 'symbolic material' (and what data would *not* qualify as such), and what a coding frame is. In describing a concept via its attributes you should therefore do more than provide only the 'bare bones'. At the same time, you need not go into every detail; for instance, in describing the characteristics of QCA you need not spell out what a 'method' is. In writing your descriptions, imagine that you are writing them for someone who studied your research topic a few years ago, but has not gone back to it since. Such a person would be familiar with the basic technical terms, but would need some reminding where everything else is concerned.

The main difficulty with describing category features is to know when to go into more detail. You are familiar with your own research topic, and the meaning of the words you are using in describing a category will seem obvious to you – but they may be much less obvious to others or to yourself in a year's time.

Example

The MA student who conducted interviews about priority setting in providing medical care for cancer patients had asked her participants who should be involved in decision making about treatment. In her QCA, she generated subcategories

---

specifying different groups of people, such as the patient herself, physicians, or relatives. Her initial description of the subcategory *physicians* read as follows: 'A unit of coding belongs with this category if an interviewee expresses the opinion that physicians should be involved in making decisions about the treatment of cancer patients. It does not matter whether the interviewee refers to physicians in general, the physician treating the patient, a general practitioner, one physician or a group of physicians, the ward physician, or the physicians on the tumour board of the respective hospital.'

At first sight, this description seems perhaps a little too obvious, and perhaps a little too detailed concerning the various physicians who might be involved, but quite straightforward in general. But when looking more closely at the interviews, it quickly became obvious that the student had forgotten to go into detail concerning the most crucial part of the description: she does not say what it means to be involved in decision making. Some interviewees said that physicians were the experts, that their advice was therefore essential, but that only the patient or the relatives could make the final decision concerning treatment. Other interviewees were of the opinion that the physicians knew better than anyone else and should therefore be the ones to make the decision. So what does 'involved in decision making' refer to? Does it include all those who are heard, regardless of who makes the final decision? Or does it apply only to those who make the decision? A better description would be: 'A unit of coding belongs with this category if an interviewee expresses the opinion that physicians should be involved in making decisions about the treatment of cancer patients. A physician is considered to be involved in the decision process if an interviewee would want to hear his or her advice, i.e. it does not matter how much of a say the interviewee would want the physician to have in actually making the decision. The category applies regardless of the kind of physician to be involved; i.e. it does not matter whether the interviewee is referring to a GP, an oncologist, a ward physician, etc.'

BEGINNER'S MISTAKE

Another typical mistake that beginners make is to stay too close to the data they are analysing when describing category features. The mistake consists of focusing too much on features that are specific to the text, i.e. purely incidental and not really relevant as category features.

Example

This example goes back to the same student doing interviews about priority setting in providing medical care for cancer patients. In her first interview question, she asked participants about any changes in medical care for cancer patients during the past years. One of her subcategories related to the lack of sufficient funds for providing high-quality medical care to all patients. Her initial definition of the subcategory read: 'The category applies if the medical personnel feel that, because of today's economic situation in the country, they cannot always administer the best therapy, due to the high costs.' This definition (while too short in general) is too specific in two respects. What if the best therapy is considered too expensive for reasons other than the general economic situation in the country? What if certain hospitals or oncology wards in a hospital are under financial pressure? Surely the category would also apply – but the case would not fit this specific definition. And what if a patient feels that she is not receiving the best therapy because she cannot pay for it? This might again be a case where the category in general would apply, but it would also be ruled out because the category is explicitly limited to medical personnel expressing this opinion. A better way to phrase this would have been: 'The category applies if an interviewee expresses the opinion that cancer patients do not always receive the therapy that would be best for them because this therapy would be too expensive.'

In describing the features of your categories, finding the middle ground is again important. If your descriptions are too abstract, you and any other coders will find it difficult to decide whether a segment really fits the category. But if your descriptions are too specific, this will exclude many segments that may fit the category in general, but not the specific combination of features that you have specified in your description.

Providing indicators to categories

Another way to describe a category is to provide the coders with some indicators. An indicator is a sign that points to the presence of a phenomenon, something by which you recognise the phenomenon; high fever, for instance, indicates that someone has the flu (although this is by no means the only indicator, and not a very specific one at that).

Indicators have been very important in computer-aided quantitative content analysis. Here, the idea is to describe categories by building a so-called dictionary. This dictionary contains all the words that indicate the presence of what the category is about. Whenever the software encounters one of these words in a unit of coding, the unit is assigned to the category that is indicated by the respective word (Neuendorf, 2002, Chapter 6).

Using only indicators to describe categories can be problematic for a number of reasons. But the idea underlying indicators as pointers is useful and can be very helpful in QCA. This is because indicators are more concrete than descriptions of features (and concreteness always helps), yet not as specific as actual examples (which by their very specificity can be misleading: see below). In this way, indicators serve as a bridge between the concept underlying the category and actual examples in the data. Indicators can be specific words, or else they can be descriptions of the ways in which a phenomenon manifests itself in the data.

──────────────────── **Example** ────────────────────

In her analysis of reading protocols, Odağ (2007) includes as one category the readers' *point of reference*: what is it about the text that has evoked a particular type of reading experience? This may, for instance, be one of the characters, the narrative world, the plot, the language. Odağ describes the subcategory *characters* as follows: 'This category applies if a reading protocol contains at least one reference to one of the characters in the narrative. Thus, the category applies if any of the character's actions, experiences, motives, thoughts, or characteristics motivates the reader to reflect or to empathise. ... The category only applies if the focus is on something that is happening inside the character from the narrative' (Odağ, 2007, pp. 303ff.). In this description, references to 'any of the character's actions, experiences, motives, thoughts, or characteristics' (including their external appearance) serve as indicators: if the coders encounter any of these, they are pointed to using this subcategory.

While indicators should be included in category definitions where possible, you may find yourself dealing with category descriptions where no suitable indicators come to mind. In this case it is better to have no indicators at all than to have unsuitable indicators that lead the coders astray. Having some sort of category description, however, is mandatory. This can consist of the features and indicators (the best case), or of features only, or of indicators only.

Providing examples

Category descriptions, even if they contain indicators, nevertheless remain somewhat abstract. Because of this, it is helpful to have some examples that illustrate the category. Some authors, when discussing examples, write of positive and negative examples, with *positive examples* illustrating what the category is and *negative examples* illustrating what the category is not meant to cover (Boyatzis, 1998; Mayring, 2010). This section will focus on positive examples only (and negative examples will be discussed in the following subsection, in the context of decision rules).

Typically, such examples are taken from the data that are used for developing the coding frame. If possible, you should quote entire units of coding and provide the reader with enough context to understand the meaning of the quote and how it exemplifies the category. If your units of coding are large, comprising several pages or entire works (books, scientific articles, TV programmes), you cannot include the actual examples in your coding frame. In this case, the relevant page numbers, paragraph numbers, or the title of a book or programme should be given. Examples usually follow the category description.

If you build your coding frame in a data-driven way, you will of necessity come across examples in your data that you can use to illustrate your categories. But sometimes, especially when you are dealing with concept-driven categories, suitable examples may not be available. In this case it is legitimate to come up with *hypothetical examples*. If the data contained a reference to this, the category would apply; if the interviewee talked about this particular aspect, this would constitute an example of the category. Hypothetical examples allow you to illustrate a category where actual examples are missing altogether or where the available examples cover only certain aspects of your categories.

BEGINNER'S MISTAKE

Beginners often make the mistake of assuming that quotes from their data are invariably preferable to hypothetical examples. But this is not the case. Actual examples from the data can be misleading if they emphasise only selected aspects of a category. Examples should therefore be *typical* examples. If no typical examples are available, it is better to construct a hypothetical example.

—— Example of using an atypical example to illustrate a category ——

In her study about decision making in medical care of cancer patients, one of the MA student's interview questions referred to what the interviewees considered to be especially important during the final, terminal phase of a cancer patient's life. One aspect that was mentioned by the participants was that patients should not suffer any pain. The student used the following quote to illustrate the category: 'And as for my husband, they asked me: So how come you do not agree that we implant a pacemaker? And I asked them: Do you really want him to be conscious through all of this? Just let him be, let him go. And then the senior physician asked me: Do you want to kill your husband? And I said: No, I want to release him. And this is so very, very awful. ... Maybe you see this differently if you haven't lived through it yourself. But I feel that it is so very, very important that the patient is not in pain.' There is no doubt that this unit of coding has been assigned to the right category: That the patient should not suffer any pain is indeed a key issue here. But this issue is somewhat obscured until the very end of the quote; overall, the question whether the patient should be kept alive at all costs seems to be of equal or even greater importance. Because of this, this unit of coding is not a good choice for illustrating the category.

In this case, the student did not need to construct a hypothetical example because a more suitable unit of coding was available that focused only on the issue of pain: 'And, maybe, at the very end, having it end without pain. It is over. Therapy cannot really do anything for you any more. To then say: Make sure that she is free from pain for those last remaining days or hours or whatever.'

Another frequent mistake beginners make is to believe that many examples are preferable to few examples. Again, this is not the case. Examples cannot possibly capture the full range of a category; they can illustrate only what is most characteristic, most typical. Moreover, a coding frame is a tool that is used in the process of coding the data. But the more examples you use, the more this tool increases in size – until it becomes so unwieldy that coders prefer to do without it and never look at the many examples you have compiled!

Including decision rules

Coding frames should be built so that subcategories relating to the same main category mutually exclude each other (see Chapter 4). But sometimes this is difficult to achieve because there is some conceptual overlap between subcategories. If this is the case, coders do not really have sufficient grounds for saying that a unit of coding fits the one subcategory better than the other. Deciding between the overlapping subcategories becomes arbitrary, and the meaning of the respective unit of coding is left unclear.

To prevent such uncertainty on the part of the coders, you should include decision rules in your definitions of the overlapping subcategories. Decision rules tell the coders which of two overlapping categories to use. They are not a mandatory part of your category definitions, but should be used only if your subcategories overlap.

Decision rules tell the coders which of two overlapping categories to use. They should specify what is not to be included in a category and which category to apply instead.

Example of using decision rules in dealing with conceptual overlaps between categories

The MA student who conducted interviews about priority setting in the medical care of cancer patients asked her interviewees who should be involved in making decisions about treatment. Looking at the participants' replies, she generated subcategories such as: *physicians, patients, relatives, patient advocacy groups,* and *others*. But there was some conceptual overlap between the two subcategories *patients* and *patient advocacy groups*, especially because the category *patients* had been defined so as to apply to both individual cancer patients and to organisations representing the interests of patients. What about units of coding such as: 'Well, patients maybe, something along the lines of a patient advisory board. Yes, it would be a good idea to include patients'? Should this go into the category *patients* or into the category *patient advocacy groups*? This issue can only be resolved by means of a decision rule that specifies how coders can differentiate between the two subcategories. I advised the student to reconceptualise the subcategory *patients* to apply only to individual patients, excluding organisations, and to rename *patient advocacy groups* as *patient organisations*. Then, the following decision rule can be added to *patients*: 'If an interviewee suggests that patient organisations such as advocacy groups, patient lobbies, etc., be included in the decision making process, this category does not apply. This category applies only to individual patients. Suggestions that groups of patients with an organisational structure should be included in the decision-making process should be coded under *patient organisations*.' A corresponding decision rule should also be added to *patient organisations*.

When specifying a decision rule, you should always include it with both the categories that it helps to differentiate. Content-wise, it is up to you how to distinguish between the two categories. There is no right or wrong way of doing this, of pulling apart two categories that share some of their meaning – if there was, chances are that no decision rule would be necessary in the first place. The only rule of thumb is to stay relatively close to conventional meanings, if such meanings are available.

In your decision rules you should always specify which meanings are excluded from the respective category and which category applies instead. In addition, some authors also include negative examples in their decision rules (e.g. Boyatzis, 1998), illustrating where the category does not apply (for the use of positive examples see above). Negative examples are optional, i.e. it is up to you whether you would like to include them or not.

Just like positive examples, decision rules can be useful, but too many decision rules make your coding frame unwieldy. I still remember the student who added a decision rule to every single subcategory… You should add them where they are necessary, i.e. where there is conceptual overlap between subcategories. But if there is no overlap, there is no need for decision rules!

SUMMARY

A category definition has four parts: a name, a description, examples, and decision rules. Names should be labels that are both concise and descriptive and capture the essence of what a category is about. Category descriptions can contain a description of important features and/or indicators; they should be neither too abstract nor too specific. Positive examples illustrate your categories. They can be actual examples from your material or hypothetical examples; in either case, they should be typical. Decision rules are needed only if two subcategories overlap.

In this case you should specify how material that falls into this overlap is to be coded. Decision rules can also contain negative examples which illustrate material that does not fall within the range of a category.

Revising and expanding

Revising your coding frame

When you have generated all the categories you want to include and have defined them all, it is time to take a step back and to revise your coding frame. To revise your coding frame means to go over the main categories and the subcategories that you have created in structural terms (Mayring, 2010, Section 5.4). Have you 'mixed' dimensions anywhere, for instance? Have you always included the full set of (concept-driven) categories that are mutually exclusive? This is also the time to check whether there are any substantial overlaps between your categories. If there are, and two (sub)categories are quite similar, perhaps it would be better to collapse them into one category. If you meant the two similar categories to refer to the same kind of phenomenon and had simply forgotten about the first category when generating the second, it is most likely a good idea to combine them into one. But if there is a conceptual difference between the two categories that you want to capture, you should definitely retain the two categories. In this case it would be a good idea to highlight the difference between the categories by including a decision rule. To revise your coding frame means to 'tidy' it and to remove any loose ends.

Example of how to revise a coding frame

The MA student who conducted focus groups on comparing treatment options in cancer therapy included in her coding frame the main category *additional information desired by the participants*. Subcategories were: *information about the healing rate; information about life expectancy in case of metastases developing; risk of dying because of the therapy; information on how far the tumour had spread; whether the patient was already in need of care; probabilities;* and *miscellaneous*. Among the subcategories, *probabilities* presents some structural problems, considering that a number of other subcategories have already been generated that refer to probabilities, such as the healing rate, life expectancy, and others. It is quite likely that at first *probabilities* was generated so as to capture the desire to know more about various kinds of risks and rates. As the coding frame grew, it became obvious that various participants asked for more specific rates and risks, and to capture these, the more specific subcategories were introduced. In this case, the more general subcategory *probabilities* can be deleted.

Expanding your coding frame

If you started out by selecting only a part of your material, you have carried out the previous steps of building a coding frame for that part only. Now that your coding frame for that part of your material has been finalised, it is time to include the next part of your material and to expand the frame to fit this material as well. If you have material from different sources, you will now want to include the next type of source (e.g. material from a different time period or interviews conducted with a different group of participants). For this set of material, you now have to go through the previous steps yet again: you will have to generate new main categories and subcategories if necessary, define them, and finally go over the resulting coding frame again to check for any structural inconsistencies. You will have to repeat this cycle as many times as you have sets of material. Once you have gone through the final set of materials, the first version of your coding frame has been completed and you are ready to try it out.

SUMMARY

When you have generated all the categories that you want to include in your coding frame, you should revise your frame, checking for any 'loose ends'. If you have used only a selected part of your material for generating your coding frame, you have to repeat all previous steps (selecting, structuring, generating, defining, and revising) as many times as there are parts of your material, until you arrive at a coding frame that covers all the variation in your data.

Frequently asked questions

How do I know whether to include decision rules?

Decision rules are only required if two subcategories overlap, that is if they share some of their meaning. In the best case you spot this as you are building the coding frame. But chances are that you will not spot many of these overlaps initially. This is not a problem – it is one reason why you should leave time for a pilot phase where you and other coders try out the coding frame (see Chapter 8). Following the trial coding, you and any other coders will have a closer look at those units that you assigned to different categories. This is when overlaps and the need to add decision rules will become apparent.

Should I use a concept-driven or a data-driven strategy for building my coding frame?

A concept-driven strategy is most appropriate for hypothesis testing or for doing a comparison with prior research. A data-driven strategy is best for describing your material in detail. But as mentioned above, the two strategies are not mutually exclusive and are in fact frequently combined. This is because a purely deductive coding frame runs the danger of disregarding part of the material (as in conducting a comparison over time if things have changed); it is therefore often necessary to add data-driven categories in order to satisfy the requirement of exhaustiveness (see Chapter 4). And a purely data-driven coding frame will often not be feasible in the first place because the research question (and even more so an interview guide) already specifies relevant dimensions.

Do I have to define main categories as well as subcategories?

Defining subcategories is most important, because the subcategories for one dimension are usually the categories to choose from during coding. These definitions should be as precise as possible. Definitions of main categories can be more general; they are often limited to descriptions of category features, but do not include examples and only occasionally decision rules. Any information that applies to all the subcategories under one main category should also be mentioned in the definition of the main category. If you do so, you do not need to repeat this piece of information in each of the subcategories.

--- **End-of-chapter questions** ---

- Which strategies are available for distinguishing between relevant and irrelevant parts of your material?
- What is meant by using concept-driven and data-driven strategies for building a coding frame?
- Name three strategies that are useful when building a data-driven coding frame.
- What are the four parts of a category definition? Which of these are mandatory, and which are optional?
- What is a decision rule, and what information should it contain?
- Why is it necessary to revise your coding frame? How often do you have to do this?

6

STRATEGIES FOR BUILDING A DATA-DRIVEN CODING FRAME

Chapter guide

In the previous chapter you saw that data-driven strategies, i.e. strategies for generating categories based on your material, are an important part of building a coding frame. In this chapter, we will look in more detail at the strategies already mentioned in Chapter 5 and at research examples where these strategies are applied:

- progressively summarising your material;
- adapting coding from grounded theory;
- subsumption;
- contrasting.

Progressively summarising your material

The strategy

The first strategy makes use of progressively more abstract paraphrases of your material (Mayring, 2010). In a first step, you paraphrase all those parts of your material that strike you as relevant to your research question. In a second step, you 'streamline' each paraphrase, deleting anything that distracts from the main statement. The third step requires you to go beyond the individual paraphrases and to look at the paraphrases in comparison. Those that refer to similar content are paraphrased yet again, focusing on what they all have in common. In principle, the third step can be repeated several times. In practice, you will most likely perform it only once or twice. After all, the idea behind generating data-based categories is to make your categories concrete and to have them reflect your material. And if you repeat this step too often, you will lose that very closeness to the data. Once you have reached your desired level of paraphrasing and abstraction, the final step is to generate a category name and definition. The easiest way of doing this is to use the paraphrase to generate a category name (see Chapter 5 on category names and labels).

An example

This strategy was used by Hermann (2010) in her study about constructive ageing and developing projects aiming to improve psychological health in old age in Switzerland. For data collection, she first conducted search conferences and then collected additional data to find out about participants' impressions of the search conferences and whether they believed that such conferences were useful for project development. The following example is taken from her analysis of group discussions using QCA.

As is often the case in QCA, Hermann's coding frame combined concept-driven and data-driven elements (see Chapter 5). Some very general main categories resulted from the research question: she was interested in participants' impressions of the search conference, in what ways they believed that such conferences could contribute to the development of projects aimed at improving emotional well-being in old age, and what they considered to be the difficulties and problems of this type of forum. This resulted in *Impressions*, *Constructive features* of search conferences, and *Difficulties* in applying search conferences as her main categories. The category *Impressions* was subdivided further, on 'logical' grounds (see Chapter 5), into *positive*, *critical*, and *neutral impressions* of the search conferences and the way in which they were conducted.

In parallel to generating these concept-driven categories, Hermann applied progressive summarising to relevant passages in her focus group discussions. The following are two original passages taken from one of the focus group discussions and the paraphrases she created to summarise the main ideas in these passages:

- I was actually quite surprised after two days, what you can do in such a short – and I believe that this was really because of the structure, the structure the moderators had prepared, that within two days really important projects were initiated. *Paraphrase*: Surprise: Structure allows for important project in a matter of two days.
- No matter what will become of this, but that there was so much material, discussion, and the procedure, the way the moderators had prepared for this. I found this quite impressive, what was achieved in a matter of two days. They pointed to the time constraints a few times, but then this was the only way to do it.
- *Paraphrase*: Impressive procedure despite time constraints.[1]

By creating these paraphrases, Hermann combined the first two steps of progressive summarising, namely generating a paraphrase and deleting anything superfluous. A more detailed paraphrase of the second passage might have read: 'Impressive material, discussion, procedure, and preparation despite time constraints.' The second step would then have been to summarise all the different aspects which the participants found impressive – i.e. the material, discussion, procedure, and preparation – under the more general term 'procedure', and to arrive at the above paraphrase in this way. 'Procedure' is the most suitable term here: It is more abstract than 'material', 'discussion', and 'preparation' (by the moderators), which name specific features of the overall procedure.

---

1   I would like to thank Dr. Hermann for letting me access and quote her original material and analysis here.

Once she had paraphrased all the relevant passages in her material in this way, she read through them and compared them all, eventually grouping them according to similarity. In this way, she found two additional paraphrases which expressed a similar idea as the two paraphrases given above. This resulted in the following group of four paraphrases which all express a similar idea:

- Surprise: Structure allows for important project in a matter of two days;
- Impressive procedure despite time constraints;
- Fascinating dynamics in a short period of time;
- Well prepared, so something had to come of it.

Hermann summarised these four paraphrases under the label *impressive proce-dure*, and together they make up one of her data-driven subcategories under the main category *Impressions – positive*. Hermann classified all her paraphrases into groups in this way, generating data-driven subcategories for all her main categories. Those paraphrases containing an important concept or idea that was found in this one paraphrase only were left to stand on their own, i.e. each of these paraphrases formed a separate group (see Table 6.1).

This procedure resulted in 1,034 data-driven subcategories – a very large number. Although this already entails a considerable reduction of the more than 4,000 paraphrases which she had generated in her first step of progressive summarising, this reduction was not enough. With 1,000 and more subcatego-ries, it is almost impossible to gain a clear idea of what the results of the study are. To achieve a greater degree of reduction, she therefore repeated the step of grouping and paraphrasing, applying it not to the paraphrases, but to the category labels she had created in the previous step. As a result of this process, the subcategory *impressive procedure* was grouped together with several other subcategories (such as *variable group composition, experienced moderators*) under the more general label *execution*. In this way, *execution* functions as a second-level data-based subcategory in Hermann's coding frame. The para-phrases which are summarised into first-level data-based subcategories and their labels (which together make up the second-level data-based subcategory *execution*) are shown in Table 6.1.

Execution, in its turn, was conceptualised as a subcategory of the main cat-egory *Impressions – positive*. Other more general labels which she arrived at by grouping her first-level data-based subcategories included *method* and *general impression*; these were also conceptualised as subcategories of *Impressions – positive*. In total, this resulted in a hierarchical coding frame with four levels (see Figure 6.1).

By progressively summarising her material on those levels, Hermann was able to create a coding frame that allowed her to reduce her material to a manageable degree. At the same time, by showing the paraphrases which are grouped into first-level data-based categories, her categories always remain

Table 6.1 Paraphrases and first-level data-based subcategories of *Impressions, positive – execution*

Surprise: Structure allows for important project in a matter of two days	Impressive procedure
Impressive procedure despite time constraints	Impressive procedure
Fascinating dynamics in a short period of time	Impressive procedure
Well prepared, so something had to come of it	Impressive procedure
Impressed: Easy interaction between professionals and volunteers	Positive atmosphere of solidarity
Very good: All equals sitting around one table	Positive atmosphere of solidarity
Found solidarity in open, pleasant conversation	Positive atmosphere of solidarity
Attempted to create a relaxed atmosphere of solidarity	Positive atmosphere of solidarity
Impressed by bringing together such different people	Variety of group composition
Participants: Great variety across all professional and age groups	Variety of group composition
Representatives of different disciplines make for a lively discussion	Variety of group composition
Preliminary meeting already showed expertise and initiative of the moderators	Experienced moderators
Positively surprised by the turnaround at the end	Experienced moderators
Participants showed initiative and enthusiasm	Participants highly motivated
Impressed by the motivation of participants who were very different	Participants highly motivated
Valuable: new contacts which will last	New contacts
Made new contacts because of the way the participants were selected	New contacts
Many good, impressive speakers	Impressive speakers
Euphoria and pioneer spirit were great	Euphoria and pioneer spirit

close to the data. The example also demonstrates how concept-driven and data-driven elements of creating a coding frame can be combined in research practice.

SUMMARY

Progressive summarising consists of four steps: (1) paraphrasing all relevant parts of your material; (2) 'streamlining' each paraphrase by deleting anything that distracts from the main statement; (3) comparing paraphrases and creating a more general paraphrase based on similarity; (4) creating a category name and definition. You can repeat the third step as needed, but it is important not to lose touch with the data.

– Impressions
  • Positive
    ○ Execution
      ▪ Impressive procedure
      ▪ Positive atmosphere of solidarity
      ▪ Variety of group composition
      ▪ Experienced moderators
      ▪ Participants highly motivated
      ▪ New contacts
      ▪ Impressive speakers
      ▪ Euphoria and pioneer spirit
    ○ Method
    ○ General impression
  • Critical
  • Neutral

– Constructive features
– Difficulties

Figure 6.1 Four-level structure of Hermann's coding frame

Adapting coding from grounded theory

The strategy

Another strategy that is helpful for generating data-driven categories and sub-categories is to adapt part of the coding procedure used in grounded theory (GT). In GT, coding consists of three steps: open, axial, and selective coding. Among these, open coding is especially suitable for developing inductive categories in QCA. GT is an approach for building theory from data, and open coding is the first step in this process. Open coding is a strategy for discovering concepts in your data.

KEY POINT

Coding in GT consists of three steps: open, axial, and selective coding. Among these, open coding can be adapted to developing data-based categories in QCA. Open coding is a strategy for discovering concepts in data.

Strauss and Corbin (1998) have divided the process of open coding into three steps: conceptualizing, defining categories, and developing categories:

• *Conceptualising.* In conceptualising, you go through your material with a view to: What is happening here? How is it happening? Who is involved? You do so by looking at your data from up close, trying to take different perspectives, and pinpointing any concepts that strike you as relevant. Over time, you will find the same concept coming up again, or you will be struck by different descriptions, different events or happenings. So, over time, you will increasingly make use of similarities and differences which you notice in your material.

- *Defining categories.* In a second step, similar concepts are grouped together into categories. Categories are defined according to what the concepts have in common. In GT, the idea is to come up with concepts that are able to explain and predict the phenomena that you are studying. QCA is different in this respect. QCA does not aim to generate theory; it is primarily descriptive. In making use of open coding for generating categories, you therefore have to adapt this step taken from GT. You would simply be looking for similarities between concepts, not for categories which have the power to explain these similarities.
- *Developing categories.* The goal of developing your categories in GT is to identify the ways in which these categories vary. In QCA, this has been described as introducing structure into your coding frame (see Chapter 5), i.e. deciding upon your main categories and your subcategories and arranging these in a hierarchical structure. Again, the idea of doing this in GT is with a view to generating theory, and you will have to adapt this to the descriptive perspective of QCA.

KEY POINT

Open coding in GT consists of three steps: conceptualizing, defining, and developing categories. In GT, defining and developing categories are done with a view to arriving at categories with explanatory power. In QCA, these steps are only descriptive.

Axial and selective coding, the next steps in the GT coding process, focus on the explanatory goal of GT and are not helpful for developing a coding frame in QCA. In axial coding, the focus is on continuing the process of relating the different categories to each other, and selective coding is about further refining and integrating the theory that is beginning to take shape.

An example

The following is a fictitious example, making use of an excerpt from the focus group conducted by an MA student about how the participants evaluate various cancer therapies (see Chapter 5).

Conceptualising

To start with, let us have a look at the concepts that emerge from the passage where the participants in the first focus group discuss a first scenario describing the decision a cancer patient is faced with: whether or not to have a certain

Table 6.2 A focus group discussion on cancer treatment: Conceptualisation

C: Well, in this case, I would say that I would do the chemotherapy,	Doing the chemotherapy
Including the potential side effects.	Side effects
Just to make sure,	Making sure
just to have tried everything.	Trying everything
A: Normally I would also have asked about the age,	Age
because that's a critical question really for deciding on a treatment plan.	Treatment plan
But with an outpatient treatment	Outpatient treatment
for half a year,	Half a year
if the patient is able to live at home, this is definitely OK, I would say.	Living at home Doing the chemotherapy
No matter whether the patient is 17 or 70 years old.	Irrelevance of age
And the restrictions, I would expect them to be minor.	Side effects/restrictions
This sounds like a bit like a cold that is dragging on, the way it is described in the scenario.	Side effects: minor, like a cold dragging on
In the end, I would say this is about how proportionate the quality of life is that is lost at each point in time, and also over time. ...	Proportionate to? Loss of quality of life: at one point in time; over time
I: And what do you think of the side effects?	Side effects
B: Well, I was a bit surprised, actually. Because I have heard that people who get chemo, that they also suffer from nausea and hair loss and whatever.	Side effects: nausea, hair loss
But maybe side effects can be of varying degrees.	Side effects: varying degrees

type of chemotherapy (see Table 6.2). The participants in the focus group are referred to as 'A', 'B', and 'C'; 'I' refers to the interviewer.

Defining categories

The next step is to define your categories, i.e. group the concepts that have emerged during the first step according to similarity, and think about the variation in these concepts and underlying reasons for variation.

A first concept that emerges from the contribution of participant C is 'Doing the chemotherapy'; this also emerges from the contribution of participant A ('this is definitely OK, I would say'). Thinking about potential variation points to different opinions, such as not wanting to have the chemotherapy or wanting to have it only under certain conditions. In fact, a closer look at the contributions of these two participants reveals that they are not unconditionally in favour of chemotherapy. Participant C says that 'in this case' she would have the chemotherapy, and participant A states that she would have it considering that the patient is able to live at home. Underlying all these concepts is the overarching category *Decision about chemotherapy*. Potential subcategories emerging from the excerpt are *unconditionally in favour of chemotherapy* and *conditionally in favour of chemotherapy*. To this we could add on conceptual grounds, even though these subcategories are not relevant to the excerpt we are looking at here, *unconditionally against chemotherapy* and *conditionally against chemotherapy*.

Another concept that comes up repeatedly, and is in fact brought up by all three participants, relates to the *Side effects*. Participant B points out that side effects can be of varying kind and intensity. Participant A explicitly calls the side effects mentioned in the scenario minor (these are: damage to the mucous membranes, the fingers becoming especially sensitive to cold, sensation of numbness in the fingers). A similar opinion is implied in the statement made by participant C that she would go through with the chemotherapy in this case, considering the side effects – i.e. the side effects are not so severe that they would make her reconsider. Participants A and B also mention a number of concrete side effects and compare them to the side effects described in the scenario. Participant A says that they sound like a cold that is dragging on; he clearly considers side effects like a cold to be minor. Participant B mentions side effects which (this is only implied) she considers to be more severe: nausea and hair loss. This results in the following categories: *Side effects* with the subcategories *minor side effects* (subcategories: *damage to the mucous membranes, sensitivity to cold of the fingers sensation of numbness in the fingers; cold symptoms*) and *severe side effects* (subcategories: *nausea; hair loss*).

Two additional concepts appear twice in the contributions of participant A: patient age, which may be relevant or irrelevant, contrasting the young age of 17 with the older age of 70, and outpatient treatment. Outpatient treatment points to an underlying category, namely treatment location, which may be inpatient or outpatient. This results in the following categories: *Patient age*, with the subcategories *young* and *old*, and *Treatment location*, with the subcategories *inpatient* and *outpatient*. These categories, as well as side effects, are all mentioned as reasons for deciding in favour of (or potentially against) having chemotherapy; *Reasons* therefore emerges as an additional main category. Other such reasons that appear in the above excerpt are 'half a year', pointing to the category *duration of chemotherapy*; *trying all options* ('trying everything', 'making sure'); and *quality of life* ('at one point in time', 'over time'). Another concept which can be turned into a category is *Treatment plan*.

Strictly speaking, this second step of creating a coding frame by adapting open coding also includes coming up with category definitions. This will not be covered here, since it has already been discussed and illustrated in the previous chapter.

Developing categories

The third step in adapting open coding to creating a coding frame consists in developing categories. This amounts to creating a structure around the categories that were identified in the previous step. In part, the second and third steps overlap: wherever it was obvious how categories relate to each other and which ones function as main categories or as subcategories, this has already been pointed out. Figure 6.2 shows the resulting structure of the coding frame.

- Decision about chemotherapy
  - ○ Unconditionally in favour
  - ○ Conditionally in favour
  - ○ Conditionally against
  - ○ Unconditionally against
- Reasons
  - ○ Side effects
    - ▪ Minor side effects
    - ▪ Major side effects
  - ○ Patient age
    - ▪ Young
    - ▪ Older
  - ○ Treatment location
    - ▪ Inpatient
    - ▪ Outpatient
  - ○ Duration of treatment
  - ○ Trying all options
  - ○ Quality of life
    - ▪ At one point in time
    - ▪ Over time
- Treatment plan

Figure 6.2 A focus group discussion on cancer treatment: Structure of the coding frame

Note that, based on the short initial excerpt to which this analysis refers, the reasons have not yet been differentiated according to whether they are reasons in favour of or against chemotherapy for the patient described in the scenario. This would be a further step in building the coding frame as more and more differentiated concepts are identified and categories are created.

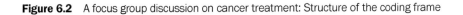
SUMMARY

Open coding from grounded theory can be adapted to build entire data-based coding frames for QCA. Open coding consists of three steps: conceptualising, defining categories, and developing categories. Conceptualising involves identifying categories in your material; in defining categories, you group the concepts according to similarity into categories; and by developing categories, categories are arranged in a hierarchical structure.

Subsumption

The strategy

When using subsumption (Mayring, 2010), you also build your categories from the data, but not to the same extent as you do when using progressive summarising or when you are adapting coding from grounded theory. You can use subsumption only if you have already decided on a main category, i.e. if you already have some idea of what you are looking for. Once you have decided on this perspective for looking at your data, in a first step you go through your material, examining it for concepts related to that perspective. When you first come across such a concept, you create a provisional name or label. This marks your first subcategory under the main category that you are focusing on. You then continue going through your material until you next come across a relevant passage. Now that you already have a first subcategory, you have to check whether or not this new passage fits into the subcategory you have already created. In other words, you check whether the meaning of this new passage is highly similar to the meaning of the other passage you have already looked at. If it is very similar, the main idea in the passage is covered by the first subcategory you have already created. It therefore does not add anything to your coding frame, and you mentally *subsume* it to the already existing subcategory. If the passage is different and points to a new concept, you create a new subcategory. You then repeat the previous steps:

- You look at your material until you reach a part that is pertinent to your present main category.
- You check whether it is similar to or different from the parts you have already looked at.
- If it is similar, you mentally subsume it to one of your already existing subcategories.
- If it suggests a new concept, you create a new subcategory.

You continue doing this until you have reached the end of the material you wanted to use for building your coding frame or until the next parts of your material no longer bring up anything new, i.e. until you have reached the point of saturation.

KEY POINT

You can use subsumption only if you have already decided on a main category, i.e. if you already have some idea of what you are looking for.

In using this strategy, you are constantly faced with the question of whether to subsume a segment of your material under the subcategories you have already created or whether to create a new subcategory. If you are too quick to subsume a segment under an already existing subcategory, you run the danger of losing sight of something important. But if you are too reluctant to subsume segments and keep on creating new subcategories, you are in danger of getting lost in the data. It will take you a bit of time to find a proper balance between these two extremes. This is perfectly normal!

The more subcategories you create, the harder it will be to keep track of them all. And the more subcategories you are looking at, the more difficult you will find it to decide whether to create a new subcategory or to subsume a segment under an already existing subcategory. Chances are that the first version of your coding frame will contain some subcategories which overlap. This is why it is so important to have a revision phase for doing some 'cleaning up' and some 'streamlining' of this first version of your coding frame, before you move on to the pilot phase (for revising your coding frame, see Chapter 5).

KEY POINT

Subsumption can be 'messy', and chances are that some subcategories will overlap in the first version of your coding frame. Make sure to leave sufficient time for revising the frame before you get started on your pilot phase.

An example

We used subsumption to create categories and subcategories in our prioritising study. In the following we will look at a few excerpts concerning the case of Terri Schiavo where we looked for reasons and considerations why participants believed that it was morally justified or not justified that her life support had been turned off. We will go through the passages one segment after another. Let us start with the first participant (from the stakeholder group of healthy persons) and let us assume that this is the first segment from all the interviews we are looking at:

> [1.1] 'I would say that this is for the relatives to decide, whether to turn off the life support.'

For this first segment, we created the subcategory *relatives' consent*. We then moved on to the next segment.

> [1.2] 'But, really, I would say that this wasn't such a bad decision, because her brain was already destroyed, so you don't really know whether she was still alive, in the proper sense, whether she was still aware of what was going on around her.'

To start with, we checked whether the information contained in this statement was similar to the information expressed in the first segment. But this is not the case: in the first segment, the participant is talking about the relatives' consent, and here she is making a very different point, wondering whether Terri Schiavo was at all aware of her surroundings and assuming that probably she was not. For this second segment, we therefore created a new subcategory, *lacking awareness. Brain damage* might have been another option, but this struck us as too specific. Other participants might also mention lack of awareness, but they might attribute this to other causes or not mention any cause at all. Because of this, *lacking awareness* seemed like a more comprehensive and therefore promising subcategory. Note that the segment also contains explicit information about this participant's opinion about the case of Terri Schiavo. By stating 'I would say that this wasn't such a bad decision', she expresses the opinion that it was morally justified that the life support was turned off. But because we were looking at our material from the perspective of the reasons participants give, we ignored this information for the time being and moved on to the next segment.

[1.3] 'And, after all, this had been going on for 15 years, and nothing really changed during all that time.'

Again we checked for similarities with the preceding statements, and again we came to the conclusion that we could not subsume the segment under one of the subcategories we had already created. We therefore generated yet another new subcategory, *duration of the coma*.

[1.4] 'But on the other hand, this is – well, it means to take someone's life. It means to kill someone, and that is really bad.'

Again, the information contained in segment [1.4] cannot be subsumed to one of the existing subcategories. So far the participant had been giving reasons why she believed it was justified that the life support for Terri Schiavo was turned off. Now she gives a reason why she considers this course of action to have been morally wrong: it constitutes murder. We therefore generated yet another new subcategory, *murder*, this time as a subcategory of *Reasons for considering it morally wrong to turn off the life support*.

You may wonder at this point why, if we had started out by focusing on the main category *Reasons for considering it morally justified to turn off the life support*, we did not ignore this information for the moment and come back to it later. After all, this is what we did concerning segment [1.2], when the participant gave her opinion about the case of Terri Schiavo. But we proceeded differently here and decided to create subcategories for both types of reasons – for and against turning off the life support for Terri Schiavo – on two accounts. First, the participants frequently mixed the two types of reasons, as the participant is doing here. Second, segment size is the same for reasons for and against. Because of this, in any one segment we might either come across a reason for or against the case of action described in the scenario. Under these circumstances, we considered it more efficient and time-saving to generate subcategories for both these main categories simultaneously.

The situation concerning participants' opinions about the case of Terri Schiavo (see segment [1.2]) is different. Segment size for expressing an opinion corresponds to everything a participant says about the case. Segments for expressing an opinion are therefore larger than segments for giving reasons. Because of this, it would not have been efficient to create categories for both types of segments simultaneously (on segmenting and how this relates to building your coding frame, see Chapter 7).

[1.5] 'But if this is what her relatives decided on, it is OK. If it is OK for the relatives.'

This time, when we checked whether the statement could be subsumed under already existing categories, we did find a suitable category. What the participant is saying here seems very similar to what she said in segment [1.1], and the subcategory we created there, *relatives' consent*, also covers what is said in segment [1.5]. We therefore subsumed the segment to the already existing category and moved on to the next segment. In the following segments, the participant repeats several of the points she already made, and many more segments can be subsumed under the already existing subcategories.

Let us now have a brief look at what another participant (from the same stakeholder group of healthy persons) says about the case of Terri Schiavo, leaving out the first two segments where the participant states that she considers it morally justified that the life support was turned off.

[2.3] 'If there is really no chance that someone will again be able to participate in life, it should be possible to let them die, and to let them die sooner.'

This segment is slightly similar to what the first participant says about potential brain damage and that Terri Schiavo may not be aware of what is happening around her. But ultimately we found that this segment focuses a different aspect: that there is little chance for Terri Schiavo to lead a normal life in the future. We therefore generated a new subcategory, *unlikely to lead a normal life*.

[2.4] 'And in the end – I am glad that they were all redeemed [Terri Schiavo and her relatives].'

This passage also points to a new aspect: that Terri Schiavo's being in a coma puts a burden on her relatives, and that turning off her life support puts an end to that burden. Accordingly, we generated the subcategory *ending the burden on her relatives*.

[2.5] 'And the husband, he knew what his wife wanted. He knew that his wife would not have wanted to live like this. And because of this, it was the right decision.'

This segment can be interpreted in different ways. It can be read as saying that turning off the life support is what Terri Schiavo herself would have wanted; this would require a new subcategory. Alternatively, it can be read as saying

Table 6.3 Data-driven subcategories on Terri Schiavo generated through subsumption

Reasons in favour	Reasons against
Relatives' consent	Murder
Lacking awareness	
Duration of the coma	
Unlikely to lead a normal life	
Ending the burden on her relatives	

that turning off her life support was justified because her husband agreed; in this case a suitable subcategory already exists, namely *relatives' consent*. We interpreted the passage as focusing on the husband's consent and mentally subsumed it under the already existing subcategory.

The subcategories generated through subsumption, based on the responses by these two participants, are summarised in Table 6.3.

After we had read what other participants had to say about the case of Terri Schiavo, we made several changes to these subcategories (and of course we added others). *Lacking awareness*, for instance, became part of a more comprehensive subcategory *prolongation of life as a prolongation of suffering*, and *murder* was subsumed under the more comprehensive subcategory *criminal offence*.

SUMMARY

> Subsumption is a strategy for generating data-driven subcategories to an already existing main category. For each relevant segment, you first check whether it fits an already existing subcategory. If it does, you mentally subsume it to this subcategory and move on to the next segment. If it does not, you generate a new subcategory. These steps are repeated until you reach the end of your material or until the point of saturation. It is important to revise this first version of the coding frame, collapsing subcategories which overlap.

Contrasting

The strategy

Contrasting is a strategy for developing data-based categories that is especially suitable for comparing two types of material (Boyatzis, 1998). This can be material from different sources (men and women, persons from two different stakeholder groups, etc.), different time periods, or material varying on any other criterion that informed your data collection process. Like subsumption, you can only use the strategy if you already have an idea of what you are looking for, i.e. if you already have some main categories in mind. Contrasting involves the following three steps:

- *Identifying similarities within the first source.* In this first step, you read through your material from the first source with an eye on similarities between your cases from this first source. You create a subcategory for each similarity that you identify.
- *Identifying similarities within the second source.* Here you proceed just as you did with respect to your first source, again looking for similarities between your cases. It is important that you look for similarities only between your cases from this second source and not for any similarities between your first and your second source.
- *Identifying differences between the two sources.* You now look at the categories you have identified in the first two steps with an eye on how the cases in your first and your second source differ. Your goal is to develop a coding frame that allows you to differentiate as clearly as possible between the two sources, and you modify your categories so that they capture these differences. It is unlikely that you will be able to do this based only on your category names. Most likely you will have to go back to your material and read this again.

KEY POINT

Contrasting is best for developing a coding frame that compares two sources. It cannot be used if there is no variation or too much variation between sources.

In principle, you can also use the strategy to compare more than two sources. But in practice, this tends to become overwhelming very quickly, as you try to mentally keep track of all the comparisons simultaneously. Try to imagine that you are comparing four sources. This would mean keeping track of the comparison between sources 1 and 2, 1 and 3, 1 and 4, 2 and 3, 2 and 4, and 3 and 4 all at once! Contrasting is not a suitable strategy if you are either dealing with material from only one source or if your material is very heterogeneous, varying on a number of dimensions simultaneously.

An example

To illustrate, I will again use excerpts concerning the case of Terri Schiavo, contrasting the opinions of some of the physicians in our sample with the opinions of representatives of the public health insurance system, examining both the decisions they take and the reasons they give. Note that the creation of categories that is described in the following is fictitious and only presented for illustration purposes; in fact, we used the strategy of subsumption (see the previous section). Also, the cases are deliberately chosen so as to illustrate the strategy.

The first step of the strategy involves looking at similarities between the cases in the first subsample. This is what three of the physicians in our sample say about the case of Terri Schiavo:

A: 'The machines were turned off too late. Because – even 15 years ago there were ways of telling whether she would be able to return to a normal life or not. And the decision should have been made then, based on those tests. Evading this, this wasn't good. [...] And keeping someone alive in the long run, while this isn't doing the patient any good whatsoever – I would say that (a) we can no longer afford this, and (b) isn't humane for the patient concerned.'

B: 'The decision should have been made sooner, during the transition period, during the first years. [...] I would ask myself earlier. If I have the impression that a patient is in a vigil coma, definitely in a vigil coma, after half a year or a year, I would definitely consider initiating such steps.'

C: 'Why only after a period of 15 years? Well, I would say it was a good decision to turn off the machines, but too late. I would say that no one should have to stay alive as a patient lying in a vigil coma. Because, if there is no longer any brain function, and there are ways these days of making sure, I don't understand why a patient would be kept alive. If the relatives say so, and if this is what the patient would have wanted – why shouldn't one let the patient go.'

There are a number of similarities between these three passages from the interviews with physicians. In the first place, they are all of the opinion that not only was it justified to turn off the life support for Terri Schiavo, but that it should in fact have been turned off earlier. This results in a first category, *Decision – justified, but long overdue*. Second, all three physicians seem to agree on their main reason for this opinion, namely that Terri Schiavo would not be able to return from her coma to lead a normal life. Participant A explicitly mentions this; with participant B it is implicit in the definition of the vigil coma to which he refers; and participant C specifies what it is about a vigil coma that prevents the patient from returning to lead a normal life, namely the loss of brain function. This results in the category *Reasons in favour – irreversible brain damage*. Finally, participants A and C both raise the consideration that keeping a patient alive in a vigil coma for such an extended time period may be a degrading way of treating this person. This leads to the category *Reasons in favour – degrading*.

The second step consists of looking at the similarities among the cases in the second subsample, i.e. the representatives of public health insurance companies.

D: 'Well, I don't remember who made the decision. And I believe – in these cases, no matter how you decide, this way or that, you never know whether you made the right decision. I would think that there is a 99.99 per cent chance that by turning off her life support, you didn't deprive her of a single day of being alive and aware of it. But you cannot be 100 per cent certain.'

E: 'That's very difficult. Because – even with a patient who is in a vigil coma, you cannot be sure that they are really brain dead. Patients in a vigil coma are most likely aware of what is going on around them, and chances are that they are able to enjoy life. So it is really difficult, difficult from a moral point of view, to let a patient starve who is in a vigil coma. I don't know – perhaps it can be justified. But I don't have a final, conclusive opinion. It is difficult.'

F: 'Difficult to say. Who is responsible? Did the relatives make the decision? In this case it is perfectly OK. Did the relatives take the decision in consultation with the physician, was it a medical decision? If so, it is also beyond question. And because of this I cannot really take any kind of position. The costs have arisen for 15 years, and they have been paid. And they would have been paid in the future, if this had been the medical advice. I can't really say, as long as I don't know on what basis the decision was taken.'

One striking similarity between these three representatives of public health insurance stands out: All three do not take a clear stand. This leads to the category *Decision – unclear*. In terms of their reasoning, however, the three participants differ considerably. Participant D raises the issue of brain function, assuming that probably there was no brain function left, and implying that in this case he considers it justified that Terri Schiavo's life support was turned off. Participant E is also concerned about brain function, but he thinks it likely that Terri Schiavo was aware of her surroundings and may even have enjoyed life. So he tends towards the position that it was wrong to have turned off her life support. And participant F raises all kinds of considerations, including the medical diagnosis, the relatives' consent, and the costs. Because of these diverging considerations, no further similarities between the three representatives of public health insurance can be identified, and no additional categories are generated on this basis.

In the third step, the strategy of contrasting requires a comparison between the two subgroups. Categories should be designed in such a way that they capture the differences between the two groups. As far as the opinions of the participants are concerned, the categories created in the two previous steps succeed very well in capturing the differences (*Decision – justified, but long overdue* versus *Decision – unclear*). When it comes to the reasoning of the participants, one issue that comes up in nearly all the excerpts concerns the question of brain function. The physicians are very clear in saying that a patient like Terri Schiavo has no (higher) brain functions left; if there is any doubt, medical tests exist for making sure. Two representatives of public health insurance companies, on the other hand, are of a different opinion: they either believe that higher brain functions are still intact in a vigil coma patient or that one cannot be certain. To capture this important difference between the two subgroups, the following categories seem suitable: *Reasons in favour – irreversible brain damage* and *Reasons against – brain functions may still be present*.

Based on the physicians, we had also generated the category *Reasons in favour – degrading*. But this issue does not come up among the representatives of public health insurance companies, i.e. the category does not differentiate between the two stakeholder groups. If you are faced with this kind of situation after comparing two subgroups, one way of proceeding would be to simply drop the category. Alternatively, you might consider it an important piece of information that a certain consideration is raised by the members of one subgroup, but not by members of the other subgroup. In this case you could create a coding frame where you register the presence or absence of the reason: *Reasons in favour – degrading – present* versus *Reasons in favour – degrading – not present*.

Note that in this latter case you would be dealing with two types of correspondences in your coding frame. A first type of correspondence concerns *Reasons in favour* versus *Reasons against* (turning off the life support): the subcategories *Reasons in favour – irreversible brain damage* versus *Reasons against – brain functions may still be present* correspond to each other. The second type of correspondence occurs among the subcategories for *Reasons in favour*: *Reasons in favour – degrading – mentioned* versus *Reasons in favour – degrading – not mentioned* correspond to each other. Creating such correspondences in your coding frame is what the strategy of contrasting ultimately is about. If you have a (sub)category in your coding frame that does not correspond to some other (sub)category, chances are that something is wrong somewhere and that your categories do not sufficiently differentiate between the groups you are comparing.

SUMMARY

The strategy of contrasting is best for creating data-driven categories when you are comparing two sources. Using the strategy requires that you already have a main category in mind. The strategy consists of three steps: identifying similarities within the first source; identifying similarities within the second source; and identifying differences between the two sources. The resulting coding frame contains categories which correspond to each other.

Frequently asked questions

Are these the only strategies for generating data-driven categories?

Probably not, but they are the only ones that I have come across. Some authors have made other suggestions (Bilandzic et al., 2001; Früh, 2001), but they all strike me as very similar to one of the strategies described here (in this case progressive summarising). If you have any other ideas for how to go about this, I would like to hear from you!

Can I combine these strategies with concept-driven categories?

You definitely can. In fact this is the idea behind combining concept-driven and data-driven strategies for creating a coding frame described in the previous chapter. You usually start out with your concept-driven categories, and then you add data-driven ones, using one of the strategies described here. In case of subsumption and contrasting, you actually have to combine these with a concept-driven strategy: both subsumption and contrasting require that you already have your main category in mind, and most likely this main category will be concept-based.

Can I combine different data-driven strategies?

I have never done so, and I would imagine that it could become rather confusing. But why not give it a try?

What do I do if I want to contrast and compare more than two sources?

I would suggest that you start out by creating a coding frame for your first source, then add to it to cover the material in your second source, then add to it to cover your material in your third source, and so on – the way we did for our six different stakeholder groups in our prioritising study (see Chapter 5). In generating the coding frame, I would not pay much attention to contrasting these sources. I would generate the coding frame to describe the material and would do the contrasting in a later step. I would not make the contrasting part of QCA (as Boyatzis does when comparing two sources), but would leave it for the interpretation that follows upon QCA (see Chapters 11 and 12).

───────────── **End-of-chapter questions** ─────────────

- What are the steps in generating data-driven categories through progressive summarising?
- Which steps in open coding can be adapted to create a data-based coding frame? What does each step involve?
- What are the steps in generating categories by subsumption?
- What are the steps in generating categories by contrasting?
- Which of the four strategies are especially suitable for creating an entire coding frame the data-driven way, including both main categories and subcategories?

7
SEGMENTATION AND UNITS OF CODING

Chapter guide

Before you can get started on trying out your coding frame, you first have to divide your material up into smaller units, which you will then code using your coding frame. This is called *segmentation*. To help you do so, we will look at:

- what segmentation is and why it is important;
- different kinds of segments – units of analysis, of coding, and context units;
- criteria to use in the process of segmentation – formal and thematic;
- how to go about segmentation.

Segmentation and why it is important

Introduction to segmentation

In the last two chapters we have looked at the process of constructing categories that help you describe selected aspects of your material. But what exactly are the parts of your material to which you apply these categories? You could of course take all the material that you have previously selected as relevant to a given theme, read through it, and assign all the categories that apply. But this can become quite messy – imagine that the relevant material is around three pages long and that you are dealing with about four main and altogether around 40 subcategories!

─────── **Example of why coding long passages is not feasible** ───────

Take the example of the case of Terri Schiavo from our prioritising study. We developed six main categories – opinion about turning off the life support, reasons why this was considered morally right, and so on – and quite a number of subcategories. What participants said about the case ranged from around one to around three pages of interview transcript. It would have been impossible to keep track of all subcategories simultaneously. We might have tried reading through the transcript once for each of the dimensions and applying only the subcategories for one dimension at a time. But this would have been very time-consuming. It would also have been misleading: coding one, two, or three pages as an instance of one subcategory (e.g. turning off her life support was justified because Terri Schiavo would already have died a natural death if the machines had not been keeping her alive) would be to suggest that the entire passage meant that it was justified for that reason. But the entire passage has many other meanings besides, and it is difficult to pinpoint these various meanings when coding long passages.

This is where segmentation comes in: instead of coding longer passages using a large number of categories, it is much more economical to divide these passages into smaller bits and pieces, in such a way that each piece is small enough to fit into one of the categories of your coding frame. In this way it is clear which part of the passage has what meaning.

DEFINITION

Segmenting your material means dividing it into units such that each segment/unit fits into one category of the coding frame.

In earlier times, before computers came into existence, this was typically referred to as 'cut and paste' in the literature. In those days, dividing your material up into smaller units literally involved cutting it up into small snippets – and all those snippets that went into the same category would then be placed in one pile and pasted on index cards (hence the 'paste'). But putting together these piles is already taking us ahead to the actual coding. In the present chapter the concern is with segmentation.

Why segmentation is important

Although segmentation is helpful in the research process, it is also quite a time-consuming additional step. Because of this, beginners in QCA are sometimes tempted to leave it out. But segmentation is not only helpful, it is also an important part of QCA for three reasons:

1. it helps to make sure that you really take all your material into account;
2. it helps you implement a clear research focus;
3. it allows you to compare the coding by different persons or your own coding at different points in time, i.e. it helps with assessing consistency (see Chapter 9).

Let us take a closer look at each of these reasons in turn.

Taking all material into account

Take a moment to think back. Why did you decide to use QCA in the first place? Why not just read through your material and paraphrase it? (It might be a good idea to go back to Chapter 1 for this.) One reason why just reading through your material is not enough is that we invariably perceive the world selectively. Once we have an idea in mind, we cannot but perceive our material through the filter of this idea: if I have read in a few interviews about the importance of collective decision making in a case like that of Terri Schiavo, any references to collective decision making in any of the other interviews will 'jump out' at me. I will notice them immediately, whereas other considerations, such as the role played by Terri Schiavo's husband, might elude me altogether. Of course there is nothing wrong with discovering relevant concepts in your material, exploring them further, and having them guide your analysis – but there is something wrong with overlooking other concepts and the role they might play for your phenomenon under study. QCA prevents you from falling into this trap by requiring you to analyse all relevant material, segment by segment. By dividing the material into segments, you are forced to look at every piece and to assess it according to the coding frame. When you do this, you have to pay equal attention to all that is said and make sure that you do not overlook anything. This is one of the great strengths of QCA compared to other qualitative methods for data analysis, and it rests upon going through with segmentation.

Implementing a clear research focus

The size of your units of coding will depend on your coding frame and what you are looking for in the material. This forces you to be very clear about your objectives. Of course you can still adapt your research question so as to include additional aspects that you discover in your material as you go along. But once you have finalised your coding frame, you cannot suddenly change direction.

Segmenting your material is informed by a clear research focus. At the same time it helps you maintain this focus by directing your attention to those issues in the material that fit the size of your units of coding. This is especially important in qualitative analysis, where the sheer amount of material and number of interesting aspects can be quite overwhelming.

Facilitating comparison

Every qualitative method for data analysis entails some procedure to make sure that the researcher's interpretation is not just a subjective and partial reading of the material. The idea behind using a method in the first place is to transcend an everyday way of understanding. In QCA, this procedure involves – among others – checking for the consistency of the coding. This is done either by having different persons code the material independently of each other ('blind' coding), or by you coding the material at two different points in time, and then comparing the results (see Chapter 9). But such a consistency check only makes sense if the coding refers to the same pieces of text. And this is what segmentation is all about: by dividing your material into segments, you specify which parts of the material are to be coded.

Example of why it is important that double-coding refer to the same text segments

Take the following excerpt, again referring to the case of Terri Schiavo: 'And, well, there have always been cases where someone in a coma came back and where one can say that it was worthwhile to make it through those difficult times.' If someone were to code this segment in terms of whether it was justified to turn off the life support for Terri Schiavo, they would probably code it as *Opinion: morally wrong*. But what if this was only part of what this interviewee is saying, and the excerpt continued for more than one page, concluding: 'And I would not want to cause such a patient any more pain. But, well, one has to consider both the pros and the cons, and I would say that this should always be done under threat of punishment, to make sure that this is done responsibly and that people don't start saying: Oh well, it is cheaper to turn off these machines. Let's say that it is necessary to turn them off, that it is in the interest of the patient. To make sure that this doesn't turn into the normal case, that such issues are dealt with in a very responsible manner.' If you were coding the interviewee's entire reply, you would probably conclude that the interviewee considers it justified to turn off a patient's life support under certain conditions. In this way, the coding of the smaller section and the full reply to the interview question would differ, not necessarily because the interpretations are different, but because the coding referred to segments of different size. In order to meaningfully compare coding for consistency, it is therefore imperative that the same segments have been coded.

SUMMARY

Segmenting your material means dividing it into units such that each segment/unit fits into one category of your coding frame. This is important for three reasons. First, segmentation forces you to take all relevant material into account. Second, because the size of the units is made to fit the coding frame, you are forced to be explicit about your objectives. Finally, segmentation ensures that coders are interpreting and referring to the same parts of your material. This is a precondition for comparing their coding at a later stage.

Types of units

When reading about content analysis, you will find references to many different kinds of units: context units, units of sampling, enumeration, recording, analysis, coding. In QCA, three types of units are particularly important: units of analysis, units of coding, and context units.

Units of analysis

The *unit of analysis* (which is largely synonymous with the unit of sampling, enumeration, and recording) refers to that unit which you have selected for QCA, each unit yielding one text; often, the unit of analysis will be identical to the 'case' (see Boyatzis, 1998, Chapter 3). When conducting interviews, each interview serves as the unit of analysis.

DEFINITION

Each case on which QCA is carried out constitutes a unit of analysis.

Examples of units of analysis

In a study about the motives attributed to terrorists in German newspapers, an MA student used articles in two newspapers as his units of analysis. Another MA student focused on the kinds of feminist issues addressed by feminist NGOs in three Central American countries; she used documents issued by the NGOs as her units of analysis. In our prioritising study, each interview was considered a unit of analysis.

In quantitative content analysis, the selection of units of analysis is typically discussed in the context of sampling, and quantitative content analysis is conceptualised as the method of data *collection* (Krippendorff, 2004, Chapter 5; Weber, 1990, pp. 21ff.). Especially in communication studies, appropriate designs and sampling strategies are discussed in great detail. In QCA, by contrast, content analysis is considered the method of data *analysis*: you apply the method to the material that you have generated or selected at an earlier stage in your research. If you are conducting an interview study, for instance, you will decide whom to interview early on, and this decision is not a part of doing QCA. That is to say, in qualitative research, case selection, methods for data collection, and QCA as the method for data analysis are considered separate steps within your overall research design.

KEY POINT

In qualitative research, case selection and QCA are separate steps in your research.

Of course earlier steps will affect later steps, but not vice versa. The decision to carry out a cross-sectional interview study and the decision about whom to interview will therefore have an effect on your units of analysis – the interviews – which you will then subject to QCA. But planning to carry out a QCA will not affect the cases you select or your method of data collection – nor should it: the choice of an appropriate research design and methods depends on your research question. I will therefore assume that you have selected your cases at an earlier stage of your research and independently of doing QCA, and I will not discuss issues concerning case selection here.

Units of coding

Units of coding are those parts of the units of analysis that you can meaningfully interpret with respect to the categories at hand. They are those units that you assign to a category in your coding frame (Boyatzis, 1998, Chapter 3; Krippendorff, 2004, Chapter 5).

DEFINITION

Units of coding are those parts of the units of analysis that can be interpreted in a meaningful way with respect to your categories and that fit within one subcategory of your coding frame.

------ **Example of segmenting a text passage into units of coding** ------

The following excerpt concerning the case of Terri Schiavo was divided into units of coding as follows, with each unit enclosed in brackets. The size of the units was chosen so that each unit fitted into a subcategory of the dimensions *Reasons why it was justified to turn off the life support* or *Reasons why it was morally wrong to turn off the life support.*

'[Of course this is – it's a complete borderline issue, and of course you can never tell whether someone might not wake up again after 20 years or so.] [This is not, it is not just about the costs, but, well]… [You have to, and this always applies where medical issues are concerned: have another very close look at the medical parameters. This is a very decisive factor.] [And when it comes to breaking off treatment, maybe this is something one shouldn't decide on one's own, this should always be done by a board, if at all possible.]

Sometimes the unit of coding can be identical to the unit of analysis. Imagine that you are coding the articles published in psychology journals over the past ten years for the subfield of psychology to which they belong (e.g. differential, developmental, social, …). In this case you would be conducting a QCA for each article published, i.e. the article would be your unit of analysis. When coding for subfields, you would also be looking at the entire article, i.e. your unit of coding would also be the article. In this case, your unit of analysis and your unit of coding would be identical. But usually the unit of coding will be smaller than the unit of analysis, i.e. each unit of analysis will contain several units of coding. Dividing the unit of analysis up into smaller units of coding is exactly what is meant by segmentation in QCA.

KEY POINT

Units of analysis are usually larger than units of coding, and each unit of analysis will contain several units of coding.

It is important to keep in mind that units of coding are defined not in absolute, but in relative terms: they are those parts of your material that can be interpreted in a meaningful way *with respect to your categories*. Sometimes your unit of coding will be as large as an entire article or even an entire book (especially if you are coding for overall themes; compare the psychology articles above); with other types of categories your unit of coding will be one paragraph or several paragraphs long (e.g. when you are coding someone's opinion); and at other times your unit of coding may consist only of a few words.

Example of using words for units of coding

Gottschalk, Gleser and Hambidge (1957) were interested in the speech of psychotic individuals. Their goal was to identify speech characteristics that would allow them to distinguish between psychotic and non-psychotic persons. Once they had found such speech characteristics, these could then help them identify psychosis and help with treatment. One such speech characteristic in which they were interested was the number of references to the self: they believed that this number would be higher in psychotic persons. In their study, they collected speech samples of both psychotic and non-psychotic persons. For data analysis, they used content analysis in looking for references to the self. Their units of coding were single words, such as *I, my, we, us*.

What would be a suitable unit of coding therefore depends on your categories. Because of this, developing your coding frame and segmenting your material into units of coding are not two separate steps of QCA which follow upon each other, but two steps which are closely interrelated (Rustemeyer, 1992, Chapter 3).

When you decide upon your units of coding, it is important to keep in mind that each unit should fit into one subcategory only (Rustemeyer, 1992, Chapter 3). In terms of your coding frame, this is the equivalent of saying that your subcategories should be mutually exclusive (see Chapters 5 and 9). Of course you can code each part of your material as many times and assign it as many meanings as seems appropriate to you, considering the research question – provided that each 'meaning' refers to a different dimension of your coding frame.

Context units

To understand what *context units* are, it is useful to remember that dividing your units of analysis into units of coding can be thought of as cutting your text into snippets with a pair of scissors. This image shows that segmentation involves *decontextualisation*: in segmentation, you remove the unit of coding from its surrounding context and examine it in comparative isolation. This is where context units come in. Basically, the context unit is that portion of the surrounding material that you need in order to understand the meaning of a given unit of coding (Krippendorff, 2004, Chapter 5; Rustemeyer, 1992, Chapter 3). In an interview, for instance, this will typically be the preceding interview question, the full answer of the interviewee, and maybe earlier portions of the interview.

DEFINITION

The context unit is that portion of the surrounding material that you need to understand the meaning of a given unit of coding.

The idea of the context unit goes back to the quantitative origins of QCA. In qualitative research, it is obvious that context is required in order to interpret meaning. But even so it can be useful to decide in advance how much context you are willing to consider in your analysis. There is no need to mark context units in the material as you would units of coding (see below). But it is a good idea to specify which parts of the context you will look at if the meaning of a unit of coding is not clear and you believe that the context might be of help in clarifying that meaning.

Example of specifying context units

In her examination of the presentation of family life on television, Viertel (2010) specified her context units for coding soaps and other serials like this: when information about the characters and their relation to each other was missing, coders should refer to the information provided on the website of the television station. If this was not sufficient to clarify the relations between the characters, no additional context information was looked for, and these aspects were coded as *unclear*.

SUMMARY

Segmentation means dividing your material into smaller units so that one unit fits exactly one subcategory within a dimension. Units of coding are embedded within units of analysis, i.e. the entire text or case on which QCA is carried out. Context units refer to the part of the material that you need to adequately understand the unit of coding. Only units of coding are marked in the material, whereas the other units are not.

Segmentation criteria

In segmenting your material into units of coding, you need some criterion that helps you decide where one unit ends and another unit begins. Two types of criteria help you with this: formal and thematic criteria (Rustemeyer, 1992, Chapter 3). We will look at each of these in turn.

Using a formal criterion

each unit is a segment

When using a formal criterion to decide where one unit ends and another begins, you make use of a structure that is already inherent in your material. Interviews, for instance, are divided into interviewer questions and 'turns', i.e. everything an interviewee says until the interviewer asks another question. Books are divided into chapters, and each chapter contains a number of paragraphs. A newspaper consists of articles, and each article contains a heading, perhaps several subheadings, at least one paragraph, and perhaps an accompanying visual. All texts – documents, newspaper articles, diaries, etc. – consist of sentences; sentences consist of clauses; clauses consist of words, and words of letters. Any of these can be a formal criterion. You can divide your material up into articles, chapters, paragraphs, sentences, and so on, provided that the units make a good fit with your categories.

If you use a formal criterion for dividing your material into units of coding, you are saving yourself a lot of time and trouble. It is usually pretty obvious where one segment ends and where the next segment begins. But using a formal criterion also has one big disadvantage: formal units of coding do not necessarily provide a good fit with your categories; they often do not fit into only one subcategory.

Example of a lack of fit between categories
and formal units of coding

Consider the following response of an interviewee to the question whether it was justified to turn off the life support for Terri Schiavo (we already looked at this in the previous chapter):

'Of course this is – it's a complete borderline issue, and of course you can never tell whether someone might not wake up again after 20 years or so. This is not, it is not just about the costs, but, well... You have to, and this always applies where medical issues are concerned: have another very close look at the medical parameters. This is a very decisive factor. And when it comes to breaking off treatment, maybe this is something one shouldn't decide on one's own, this should always be done by a board, if at all possible. This should include the relatives, the person concerned, of course, if she is at all capable of participating. This is more important than the relatives. Or else the relatives, and one should try to find out whether the person has written down anything about what is to be done, although this cannot be the only criterion, like if that was twenty years ago, and maybe today she thinks very differently, and several of the doctors who are treating her, and some who are not treating her, to make sure that someone is completely neutral, and someone from the nursing side, they should all constitute a kind of board to take that decision.'

If you want to code this passage for reasons why it was justified or not to discontinue intravenous feeding, you will quickly find that a formal criterion (i.e. taking one turn as the unit of coding) is not very helpful here. A number of reasons and considerations are mentioned throughout the unit: whether the patient can be expected to regain consciousness, that the patient's own wishes should be taken into account, that the decision should be taken by a board representing different types of interest in the well-being of the patient, etc. If you take the entire response as your unit, this unit will be too long.

But what about dividing the turn into sentences? At first sight it seems that this might work. The reply starts out with a sentence ('Of course this is – it's a complete borderline issue, and of course you can never tell whether someone might not wake up again after 20 years or so.'), giving one reason why turning off the life support might not be justified: because one never knows whether the person might regain consciousness. You can code the sentence using one subcategory from the dimension *Reasons why turning off the life support is morally wrong*. But this good fit between formal unit and coding frame soon breaks down. The sentence 'And when it comes to breaking off treatment, maybe this is something one shouldn't decide on one's own, this should always be done by a board, if at all possible' contains only part of what the participant says about the suitability of a board and how this should be composed. Here, the unit should therefore be longer than the sentence. And then you come across 'and one should try to find out whether the person has written down anything about what is to be done'. Here, a reason is mentioned in a clause that is part of a sentence. The segment should therefore be shorter than the sentence so as to fit the coding frame. As you can see, making sentences the units of coding does not work either: sometimes one reason is given in one sentence, sometimes a reason reaches across several sentences, and sometimes a reason is provided in a clause that is part of a longer sentence.

Especially if you have conducted interviews or focus groups, you will often find that 'formal' segments do not fit your coding frame. In an interview, it often happens that at first participants answer an interview question only in part, and come back to the question at a later time. Because of this, it is usually not a good strategy to divide interviews up by turns. If you are considering dividing such material into sentences, it is useful to remember that you actually collected the data in an auditory format and turned it into writing by transcribing it. But transcribing your material involves quite a bit of interpretation. Moreover, spoken language certainly does not contain any punctuation marks. Punctuation marks are therefore not inherent in your material and, for this reason, do not make good segmentation criteria.

But formal criteria are very useful when you are dealing with material that has an inherent structure. A newspaper headline, for instance, will usually capture the main topic of the article; i.e. the headline would be a suitable formal unit to use if you want to code the main topic of a newspaper article. Similarly, when you are examining legal documents that are divided into paragraphs, segmenting by paragraphs will probably be a suitable strategy. But when you are dealing with material that does not have such an inherent structure, thematic criteria will usually be better for deciding where one unit ends and another begins.

KEY POINT

Formal criteria are useful for segmenting material that has an inherent structure (such as newspaper articles). They are less useful for segmenting material such as transcripts from interviews or focus groups.

Using a thematic criterion

When you use a *thematic criterion* for dividing your material into units of coding, you will be looking for changes of topic. Topic changes signal the end of one unit and the beginning of another. In this way, each unit corresponds to mentioning or discussing one theme (the terms 'theme' and 'topic' are used interchangeably here). This sounds deceptively simple – but the devil, as usual, is in the detail. In particular, no one really knows what exactly a theme is. Themes have been conceptualised as assertions about some subject matter (Berelson, 1954, p. 508), as abstract constructs (Ryan & Bernard, 2003, p. 87), or as recurrent patterns (Stone, 1997, p. 36). For the purposes of segmentation, I will adopt the definition suggested by Tesch (1990, p. 119) who distinguishes between theme/topic on the one hand and content on the other hand: 'The topic is what is talked or written about. The content is the substance of the message.' One might say that a theme contains statements or utterances that 'go together' because they have a common point of reference. But this only partially solves the problem, because both 'theme' and 'common reference point' are relative, not absolute terms.

Example of different definitions of a theme, depending on point of reference

In using a thematic criterion, we might have considered the entire excerpt provided above as one segment, because everything that is said concerns the issue of turning off the life support for Terri Schiavo. Alternatively, we might have divided the section into five smaller segments (see below; the segments are enclosed in brackets: [...]), arguing that each segment addresses another consideration (the possibility of regaining consciousness, the costs, the medical parameters, having the decision taken by a board, and the patient's advance directive). Or else we might have subdivided the last unit into even smaller units, arguing that each suggestion concerning the persons who should be on the board constitutes a separate theme (see again below; these smaller segments are enclosed in parentheses: (...)).

'[Of course this is – it's a complete borderline issue, and of course you can never tell whether someone might not wake up again after 20 years or so.] [This is not, it is not just about the costs, but, well]... [You have to, and this always applies where medical issues are concerned: have another very close look at the medical parameters. This is a very decisive factor.] [[And when it comes to breaking off treatment, maybe this is something one shouldn't decide on one's own, this should always be done by a board, if at all possible.) (This should include the relatives), (the person concerned, of course, if she is at all capable of participating. This is more important than the relatives.) (Or else the relatives,) [[and one should try to find out whether the person has written down anything about what is to be done,) (although this cannot be the only criterion, like if that was twenty years ago, and maybe today she thinks very differently,)]] (and several of the doctors who are treating her), (and some who are not treating her, to make sure that someone is completely neutral), (and someone from the nursing side), (they should all constitute a kind of board to take that decision.)]]'

In this way, themes can be very broadly or very narrowly defined. Themes are not 'present' in your material, waiting to be discovered. Instead, if you decide to use a thematic criterion for segmentation, you will typically conceptualise a 'theme' with a view to both your research question and your coding frame. Also, you will define your themes in such a way that one theme will fit exactly one subcategory in your coding frame.

—— **Example of making thematic units of coding fit your categories** ——

If we had wanted to code our interview sections about Terri Schiavo only for the interviewees' general opinion about turning off a patient's life support, the entire excerpt shown above would make a suitable unit of coding. When coding for reasons and considerations justifying (or not) turning off her life support, it would be appropriate to divide the excerpt into five units of coding. And if we were primarily interested in who should be involved in making the decision, the smallest segments shown above would be suitable units, and the first part of the interviewee's reply would actually be irrelevant.

In other words, using a thematic criterion for segmentation requires that you always keep your coding frame in mind. This is much less clear-cut than using a formal criterion, but at the same time it is very much in line with the recommendation that you choose your units of coding to fit only one subcategory; segmenting according to thematic criteria actually helps you to implement this suggestion.

▩▩▩▩▩▩▩▩▩▩▩▩▩▩▩▩▩▩▩ **SUMMARY** ▩▩▩▩▩▩▩▩▩▩▩▩▩▩▩▩▩

In deciding where one unit of coding ends and another begins, you can use either formal or thematic criteria. Formal criteria, such as chapters, paragraphs, or sentences, make use of the structure of your material. If you use a formal criterion, this has the advantage that your criterion is unambiguous; but unless your material has a clear internal structure, formal segments will probably not make a good fit with your coding frame. If you use a thematic criterion, one unit ends and another begins with each topic change. Because you always do this with your coding frame in mind, using thematic criteria will provide you with units of coding that are more likely to fit your coding frame. But thematic criteria are more ambiguous than formal ones, and it is not always easy to decide where one topic ends and another begins.

How to go about segmentation

So far in this chapter we have looked at various aspects of segmentation. But how does it all hang together, how do you actually go about segmenting your material? As mentioned above, to segment your material means to divide your units of analysis into units of coding. In the following, we will take a closer look at the steps this involves and at some strategies that can help you with segmenting your data.

Steps involved in segmentation

Segmentation involves three steps:

1. marking the relevant parts of your material;
2. deciding on your criterion of segmentation;
3. marking your units of coding.

Marking the relevant parts of your material

In a first step, you have to decide which parts of your material you consider to be relevant (we have already looked at this in some detail in Chapter 4) and you mark this. If you are dealing with interviews or group discussions, typically only a few categories will be applicable to a given section of the material. In our interviews about prioritising in medicine, for instance, participants would not spontaneously talk about turning off the life support of severely ill patients at any time during the interview, but they would talk about this topic in reply to our question – and perhaps return to it once or twice during the remainder of the interview. If your material allows for this, it would be a good idea to work through it section by section, with a view to a selected set of categories and their subcategories. The first step therefore involves marking your relevant material and from among that material singling out a section to which only a subset of your categories applies.

Deciding on your criterion of segmentation

In a second step, you have to decide how large your units of coding will be and which criterion you will use for dividing your material into these units. Does your material have an internal structure, suggesting a suitable formal criterion? And do these formal units fit into one subcategory each? If this is the case, you should use a formal criterion to segment your material, because this is much easier to implement. If your material does not have an internal structure, a thematic criterion will be the better choice. In this case, you should consider how large your segments should be so as to fit into your subcategories.

Marking your units of coding

Once you have decided on the material to work with and on your segmentation criterion, you can now go ahead and apply this criterion, clearly indicating the beginning and the end of all the units you have identified. If you are working 'by hand', i.e. without software, it is also a good idea to number your units consecutively – this helps you at a later stage, when comparing the coding for these units (on segmentation when using software, see Chapter 12).

─────── **Example of how to mark and number your units of coding** ───────

'[1][Of course this is – it's a complete borderline issue, and of course you can never tell whether someone might not wake up again after 20 years or so.] [2][This is not, it is not just about the costs, but, well]... [3][You have to, and this always applies where medical issues are concerned: have another very close look at the medical parameters. This is a very decisive factor.] [4][And when it comes to breaking off treatment, maybe this is something one shouldn't decide on one's own, this should always be done by a board, if at all possible. This should include the relatives, the person concerned, of course, if she is at all capable of participating. This is more important than the relatives. Or else the relatives, [5][and one should try to find out whether the person has written down anything about what is to be done, although this cannot be the only criterion, like if that was twenty years ago, and maybe today she thinks very differently,] and several of the doctors who are treating her, and some who are not treating her, to make sure that someone is completely neutral, and someone from the nursing side, they should all constitute a kind of board to take that decision.]'

If you are using a formal criterion, you can simultaneously mark and code your segments (see Chapters 8 and 10). But if you are using a thematic criterion, it may not always be clear where a topic change occurs. Because of this, when it comes to checking coding consistency, you may end up marking and coding units of differing length at different times (if you are working on your own) – and if this happens, you can no longer compare your codes. If you are working together with another coder, it is even more likely to happen that the units of coding identified by you and another coder will differ – and again this will make checking for coding consistency impossible. If you are using a thematic criterion, it is therefore best to first complete the segmentation and then do the coding.

Strategies for segmentation using a thematic criterion

In the following, we will look at two strategies to help you with segmentation if you are using a thematic criterion. I will also touch upon a third strategy which essentially amounts to doing without segmentation, but would definitely advise you against this.

Strategy no. 1: The researcher carries out the segmentation

A first strategy is that you identify and mark the segments before doing the coding. Because you are familiar with your research question, categories, and material, you will be able to do this rather quickly. If you are working on your own, this is in fact the only strategy that is available to you. But if you are working together with another coder, the strategy can have a disadvantage: even though you are familiar with all the aspects of your research, you might sometimes select units which the other coder does not find appropriate. In this case the other coder will either collapse smaller units into a larger one or divide a larger unit into smaller ones. In either case, the result will be that you will code one unit and the other coder will code another unit – and you will no longer be able to compare them. If this happens only occasionally, it is not a problem to discuss these units and decide together on a suitable size and code. But if it happens more often, it can considerably affect the quality of your research.

KEY POINT

A first strategy for segmenting your material according to a thematic criterion is to do the segmentation on your own before starting on the coding. This is the only strategy possible if you are working on your own. If another coder is involved, it can present problems.

To prevent this from happening, it is a good idea to have you and any other coders mark the first units of coding together. You should continue doing this on your own only once all coders agree what constitutes a theme and a suitable unit of coding – in this case you can be reasonably confident that the other coders would divide the material into segments pretty much the same way as you. If you are dealing with a large-scale study, you should get back to the other coders at regular intervals and jointly decide on a few segments, just to make sure that your understanding of what constitutes a theme has not changed. You continue with the coding only once you have completed dividing the material into units of coding.

Strategy no. 2: Several coders are involved in the segmentation

The second strategy is only an option if you are working together with at least one other coder: you and the other coders jointly divide the material into units of coding. There are different ways of doing this.

One way is to have you do this independently of each other, compare the units you have come up with, come to an agreement, and then do the coding. While this is possible in theory, in practice it will often be too time-consuming to have all of you work through all the material twice, once when doing the segmentation and again when doing the coding.

Another way is to do the marking, the coding, and the discussion of the coding simultaneously – in one go, so to speak: in a first step, all coders (including yourself) decide on a suitable unit; in a second step, you all – and independently of each other – write down the code you would use for that unit ('blind coding'); and in a last step, you discuss your coding of this unit. This is a good way to proceed – provided that you can arrange for all coders to work together in the same room at the same time, and provided that the amount of material is such that it can in fact be handled by all coders involved.

If you have a lot of material and will divide it up between coders (so that each coder deals only with a part of the material), there is yet another option for how to go about segmentation: to divide this up between coders as well, thereby reducing the workload for everyone involved. In this case you would also start out by having all coders sit down together and jointly deciding on the first segments. Once you have established that all coders go about this in a similar way and have a shared understanding of what constitutes a theme, the coders can then, in a next step, work separately, continuing with segmenting different parts of the material. But to make sure that coders do not begin to develop their own, idiosyncratic understanding of what constitutes a theme, it would be best to bring them back together again at regular intervals. After having segmented a certain number of units in different parts of the material independently of each other, all coders should again sit down together and jointly decide on a few units, until they again do so in a similar way. This is similar to the procedure described in the first strategy, except that now you are not the only one to do the segmentation; here, this task has been divided between all coders. This is how we proceeded when coding the interviews for our study on prioritising in medicine.

Strategy no. 3: Not recommended!

In practice, researchers sometimes proceed in yet another way – which is much more economical, but goes against the methodological requirements of QCA. They merely mark relevant passages in their material, but do not segment these into units of coding. Coders then proceed – independently of each other – to apply all relevant categories to these passages. This essentially amounts to skipping segmentation altogether! Obviously, this is not recommended, because segmentation constitutes a crucial part of QCA (see above for the reasons).

SUMMARY

Segmenting your material involves three steps: you have to mark the relevant parts of your material, decide on the criterion you will use to decide where one unit ends and another begins, and mark your units of coding.

If you are using a formal criterion, marking the units and doing the coding can go hand in hand. If you are using a thematic criterion, you can either work on your own and do the marking and coding simultaneously, or you can work with others and separate the steps of segmentation and coding.

Frequently asked questions

Can it happen that different categories require different units of coding?

Because you should choose your units of coding so that one unit fits the description of one subcategory only, you always have to keep your categories in mind when deciding on suitable units of coding. This implies that different categories may well require units of coding that differ in length. The more extensive your coding frame is, the more likely this is to happen. But it can happen even if your coding frame is short and contains different dimensions. When looking at the interview material relating to the case of Terri Schiavo, I pointed out that coding for attitudes and opinions will typically require longer units of coding, comprising everything that is said on a given topic – in case an interviewee mentions both pros and cons or changes her mind in the course of replying. Coding for reasons and considerations underlying these opinions, on the other hand, typically requires much shorter units of coding.

This does indeed make the segmentation process more complicated – but it does not make it quite as complicated as it may appear at first sight. Remember that it is a good idea to get to work on a set of categories relating to the same broad topic. The first step of segmentation, marking the relevant portion of your material, will apply to all these categories at once. The second step, deciding on suitable criteria for your units of coding, has to be carried out separately for each dimension/main category. But ultimately this only requires you to sit down, do some thinking, and write down your criteria. When it comes to the actual marking, you do not need to read through your material separately for each main category/dimension. As long as you are dealing with no more than three different dimensions at once, you can easily do the marking for your units of coding simultaneously, even if they differ in length. Moreover, different units of coding will usually be substantially different – if they differ only to a small extent, you are probably carrying differentiation too far and can use the same unit of coding for both dimensions.

For the case of Terri Schiavo, we were using six different main categories: opinion whether turning off the life support was justified or not; whether the interviewee changed her mind; reasons and considerations why it was justified; reasons and considerations why it was not justified; points on which the participants would have liked more information; and criteria that should not play a role under any circumstances. From among these six dimensions, the first two required a unit of coding that contained everything a person said on the topic, while the remaining four required a much shorter unit of coding, each reason or consideration constituting a separate theme. In other words, we were dealing with two thematic units of coding. The first of these – everything a person said on the topic – coincided with the relevant material and therefore did not need to be marked. This left only the smaller units to be marked.

What do I do if a topic is covered in different parts of the material?

Especially with interviews and group discussions it can happen that a participant starts out by replying to a question, goes on to talk about a different topic, and takes up the first topic again at a later point. What that person says on the first topic is therefore spread out over different parts of the material. In this case, when marking the relevant parts of your material, you must mark all of these parts, whether they are continuous or not. Likewise, if you need a large unit of coding that comprises everything a person says on that topic, the unit must contain all that material, minus the material in between that is not relevant to the topic in question. Units of coding are therefore not necessarily continuous.

What is the unit of coding when I am analysing other than linear, textual material?

In the previous discussion of units of coding I have made the implicit assumption that you are looking at textual material with a linear structure, such as newspaper articles, letters, historical documents, interview transcripts, and the like. But QCA is not limited to the printed page. It has also been applied to visuals, artefacts and websites, to name only a few of the additional possibilities. If you are dealing with this type of material, you have to adjust the definition of the various units. With still images, the image can be your unit of analysis and your unit of coding; if you are looking at visuals in newspapers, the caption will typically constitute your context. Alternatively, and depending on your research question, each person shown in an image can be your unit of coding (and the entire image again your unit of analysis). With films, entire films or episodes can serve as the unit of analysis; units of coding would more typically be shots, individual characters, or groups of persons (see Rose, 2007, Chapter 4 on applying content analysis to visuals). Websites are usually to a large extent text-based and are in this respect similar to text on the printed page. But they have a hypertext structure, not a linear structure, and this has to be taken into account in locating all the relevant material on a given topic. Moreover, due to the hypertext structure both the unit of analysis and the context unit can be difficult to determine, as the 'page' seems to branch out in all directions. Adapting content analysis to websites is a field that is still under development (Franzosi, 2008, Part 8; McMillan, 2000).

Is it OK for me to do segmentation on my own, if I do not have anyone to help?

If you are working on your own, you in fact have to do it all on your own. In this situation, segmentation is just as important as when you are working with several coders. Especially if you use a thematic criterion, your interpretation of what constitutes a unit of coding might well change over time. In this case it would be best to do the marking and the coding simultaneously when you tackle it for the first time. But you should make sure that you save a version of your material where the units of coding are marked and no codes are assigned. You can then use this version later when you again assign codes to check for consistency (see Chapters 8–10).

End-of-chapter questions

- What is segmentation?
- What is the difference between units of analysis, units of coding, and context units?
- Give some examples of formal criteria for segmentation.
- When would you use a thematic criterion for segmenting your material?
- What are the three steps involved in segmentation?
- Describe one strategy for segmentation when using a thematic criterion.

8

TRYING IT OUT: THE PILOT PHASE

Chapter guide

Once you have developed your coding frame and divided your material into units of coding, you are ready to try out the coding frame on a part of your material. This is called the pilot phase and will be the focus of the present chapter. More specifically, we will look at:

- why a pilot phase is necessary in the first place;
- how to select your material for the trial coding;
- how to proceed before and during the trial coding;
- how to proceed after trying out the coding frame.

Why a pilot phase is necessary in the first place

What the pilot phase is

Once you have developed your coding frame and have decided on your units of coding, you are all set for the actual data analysis. But before starting to code all your material, it is usually a good idea to try out the coding frame first, i.e. to apply your categories to part of your material, proceeding exactly as you are planning to do during the main analysis phase. This is called the trial coding, and it is the core of the pilot phase (Früh 2007, Part II, Chapter 1; Neuendorf, 2002). If you are working with another coder, both you and the other person should code the material independently of each other ('blind coding'). If you are working on your own, you should recode the material after 10–14 days.

Following the trial coding, the pilot phase continues by comparing the two rounds of coding for consistency. This will show you which categories have been difficult to apply. On this basis, you can then adjust the coding frame, the units of coding, and your procedure. The pilot phase therefore consists of three stages: the trial coding, a consistency check, and an adjustment of your coding frame.

DEFINITION

The pilot phase begins by applying your coding frame to part of your material, proceeding exactly as you would during the main coding. It is followed by a consistency check and an adjustment of your coding frame.

Why a pilot phase is important

It is common in empirical research to have a pilot phase whenever you are dealing with a newly developed instrument – be it an interview guide, a questionnaire, or a coding frame. It is impossible to think of all the pitfalls that may occur in actual research practice – only practice itself will show. Perhaps additional aspects of meaning emerge from your material which are not yet covered by your coding frame; some of your categories may overlap; or the phrasing of some of your categories may be awkward, to mention only some of the most common problems that beset coding frames in their initial versions.

KEY POINT

No coding frame is perfect! A pilot phase is essential for discovering these shortcomings at an early stage.

If other coders work together with you, they will have to familiarise themselves with the coding frame, and they will most likely bring their own individual understanding of the categories and the material to the task. Talking to them about their understanding may help you add more categories, enriching your coding frame. Alternatively, the other coders may have to adjust their understanding of the categories.

Whatever adjustments you decide to make in the end, you cannot make them unless you first realise that there is a need for these adjustments – and it is here that the pilot phase is essential. If you analyse all your material without a pilot phase, you run the risk of discovering such shortcomings only once you have already completed most of the work (or all of it). You then face the choice between settling for partially invalid results and going back and doing the work all over again. And there *will* be such shortcomings – not even the most experienced researcher will be able to think of everything that might go wrong. It makes life much easier to implement a pilot phase, allowing any problems to emerge early on during your research.

SUMMARY

The pilot phase involves trying out your coding frame on part of your material, the trial coding. Following this, you should compare the two rounds of coding for consistency and make adjustments to categories that turned out to be difficult to apply. This allows you to identify the inevitable shortcomings of your coding frame at an early stage, and it allows other coders working together with you to familiarise themselves with the coding frame.

How to select material for the trial coding

Probably the most important decision that you have to take during the pilot phase concerns the selection of the material for trying out the coding frame. In the following, we will first discuss whether the material for the trial coding should be part of the data for your main study. Then we will look at two criteria that can help you select your material. A final subsection deals with the question of how much material to include in the trial coding.

Should the material for the trial coding be part of your main data?

The reason for discussing the question whether you can use some of your material for your main study in the pilot phase goes back to the origins of content analysis in quantitative research. Quantitative research is typically hypothesis-testing research. And if you are testing a hypothesis, it would mean prejudging the results in your favour if you used the same data for testing the hypothesis and for developing the instrument you are using to test this same hypothesis (see also Chapter 4). Because of this, authors in quantitative content analysis will advise you to use another, additional sample of material during the pilot phase, i.e. that you try out the coding frame on material that is not identical to the material you will use for the main coding. If you are testing a hypothesis, it is important that you follow this advice and use different material for trying out your coding frame (Neuendorf, 2002; Rustemeyer, 1992).

But in qualitative research, the situation will usually be different. You will often use QCA to summarise and describe your material. In our study about prioritising in medicine, for instance, we were interested in providing a detailed description of the opinions and underlying criteria of the different stakeholder groups, i.e. we wanted to know about nurses', doctors', politicians', and others' thoughts about the issues at hand as they were expressed in the interviews. In other words, if your goal is to describe, there is nothing to prevent you from using the same material for trying out the coding frame and for doing the main coding at a later stage. Because you are concerned with obtaining an in-depth description, one might even say that it is *better* to try out your coding frame on part of the very material on which you will carry out the main coding. If you used other material, this might differ from the material in your main study in various ways. If you then adjusted your coding frame to this other material, it would no longer be suitable for describing the material on which you are focusing in your analysis.

KEY POINT

> If you are using QCA to test a hypothesis, you should use different material for the trial and the main coding. If you want to describe your material, it is better to try out your material on a subset of the data you will use for the main analysis.

Selection criteria

When trying out your coding frame, you want to make sure (or at least as sure as you reasonably can!) that there are no unpleasant surprises awaiting you down the road once you get to the main coding. This means that you should try out your categories on all the different kinds of material that you may have – if you do not, you may find that your coding frame does not suit the untried parts of your material very well. Likewise, try out all your categories and sub-categories during the pilot phase – if you do not, you cannot spot any short-comings they may have. The most important concern in selecting material for the trial coding is therefore *variability*, concerning both your material and your coding frame.

First criterion: Variability of the material

When selecting material for your trial coding, you should first of all make sure that all the variability, i.e., all the differences in your material, are adequately represented in the subset you select. Your material may be variable in different ways: you may be looking at different groups of persons, at material from different cultures or from different time periods. If this is the case, you have to select the material for your trial coding in such a way that you do your trial coding on data from all the groups of persons, all the cultures, or all the time periods you are examining. Whenever your research involves some sort of comparison, variability plays a role and needs to be taken into account (Neuendorf, 2002, p. 134).

Example of sources of variability in your material

Depending on the design and the research question, variability may also result from other factors. In her study of the role of identification and empathy during reading, Odağ (2007) introduced variability by having different groups of participants (men and women) read different kinds of texts (varying in terms of text type, i.e. fiction/non-fiction, and in terms of perspective, i.e. internal/external). To take this variability into account, she included reading protocols from both men and women relating to all the four texts in her pilot phase.

As a rule of thumb one can say that all those criteria that went into your selection of units of analysis for your study should also go into your selection of material during the pilot phase. Depending on the size of your units of analysis, you should include at least one unit of analysis per criterion or, to be more exact, per value of each criterion (e.g. one interview each with patients, healthy persons, doctors, nursing staff, politicians, administrators for the criterion of stakeholder groups). If the units of analysis are short (e.g. blog entries or jokes), you can use even more material during your pilot phase (for more detail on how much material to include see below).

Second criterion: Trying out the entire coding frame

At the same time you should also select your material for the trial coding so that it allows you to indeed try out your entire coding frame. Unless you try out a category definition at this stage, you cannot tell whether the phrasing is suitable and whether the category overlaps with any other categories. In part this second criterion actually follows from the first criterion, i.e. variability of your material. The more variable the material is that you use in the pilot phase, the more categories you will be able to apply during the trial coding.

But other considerations also play a role here. The simplest among these might seem almost too obvious: when conducting interviews, you should include the entire interview in the trial coding. Other considerations that are closely related are not quite as obvious. When you code the reasons underlying a particular opinion, for instance, the reasons will obviously vary with the direction of the opinion. It is therefore important that the material you use for your trial coding cover the full range of opinions that can be found across your material.

--- **Example of variability of opinions in your material** ---

In our prioritising study, some participants were of the opinion that it was morally justified to turn off the life support of Terri Schiavo, whereas others considered this morally wrong. The reasons these participants gave for their opinions differed substantially: The interviewees who were in favour of turning off her life support referred to considerations such as unduly prolonging the suffering of Terri Schiavo by keeping her alive or that she would already have died a natural death if it were not for the machines. Participants who objected to turning off her life support, on the other hand, would argue that this amounted to letting Terri Schiavo starve or that this constituted a criminal offence. If we had included only interviews with participants who approved of turning off the life support for Terri Schiavo in our pilot phase, we would not have been able to assess the suitability of the part of the coding frame relating to reasons why this course of action was considered wrong.

Such additional aspects to take into account in selecting material for the trial coding will vary with the nature of your research. What you can and should do is pay attention to any sources of variability in your material and take these into consideration when selecting the material for the trial coding.

How much material to include?

If there is a lot of variability in your material, you may soon find yourself getting close to doing a trial coding on all your data! So how much of your material should you include at this stage?

In quantitative content analysis where the pilot phase is used to calculate a coefficient of inter-rater agreement, it has been suggested that the material be selected in such a way that each category will be coded between 30 and 50 times (Früh, 2007, Part II, Chapter 1). But this rule of thumb is not applicable to QCA: quantitative content analysis will usually be more reductive than QCA, i.e. the coding frame will contain fewer categories – and the fewer categories a coding frame contains, the more frequently each category will be applied. In QCA, the researcher is typically looking at fewer units of analysis, which are at the same time described in more detail, than would be the case in quantitative content analysis. Because of this, in QCA some categories may be applicable only twice across the entire material.

Therefore, the criterion for deciding how much material to include in the trial coding must be different for QCA than for quantitative content analysis. Typically, this will entail a trade-off between the criterion of variability, on the one hand, and of practicability, on the other hand.

KEY POINT

In deciding how much material to include in the trial coding, you have to achieve a balance between variability and practicability.

On the one hand, you will want to include as much variability as possible, for the reasons given above. On the other hand, you will usually modify your coding frame based on the results of the trial coding. And all units of coding that you have previously coded with the first version of the coding frame will have to be coded again with the new, modified version. Because this is quite time-consuming, you will want to keep the amount of material that you have to recode to a minimum. As a rule of thumb, including between 10% and 20% of your material in the trial coding will often constitute a reasonable trade-off between variability and practicability. But this is only a suggestion, not a rule cast in stone, and should be adjusted to your specific case.

━━━━━━━━━━━━━━━━━━━━━━━ SUMMARY ━━━━━━━━━━━━━━━━━━━━━━━

Whether you should do your trial coding on a part of the material that you will later use for the main coding depends on the goal of your research. If you want to test a hypothesis, you should use different material; if you want to produce a summary description of your data, you should use a subset of your material during the pilot phase. Your main concern in selecting the material should be variability: the material should be selected in such a way that differences in the material are adequately represented and that as many categories as possible from the coding frame can be used in the trial coding. The decision about how much material to include involves a trade-off between the variability of your material, on the one hand, and practical considerations, on the other hand.

How to proceed before and during the trial coding

Throughout the first part of this chapter I have used the term 'trial coding' as an important part of the pilot phase. But what exactly does the trial coding entail? The following subsections will deal with this question, and we will also look at some of the issues that may arise during this phase of your research.

Familiarising the coders with the research

Before you actually get started on the trial coding, you have to make sure that all the coders are familiar with your research and with your coding frame. If you do the coding all by yourself, this does not require any additional steps. Nor do you have to take any special measures if there are other coders working with you, but they were already involved in constructing the coding frame. If any additional coders come to your research only at the stage of the trial coding, however, you should plan for a phase of familiarising these coders with your work.

━━━━━━━━━━━━━━━━━━━━━━━ KEY POINT ━━━━━━━━━━━━━━━━━━━━━━━

If any coders join your research team only at the stage of the trial coding, you have to allow for a phase of familiarising them with your research in general and the coding frame in particular.

In this case you should inform the coders about the research question, the data collection and the coding frame. They should have time to read the coding frame and to try it out. This involves sitting down with you and going through some of the material. The coders should say how they would interpret and classify each unit of coding, giving their reasons, and all units on which there is any disagreement should be discussed in the group. Sometimes you will be called upon to explain what is meant by a certain category and how it is to be handled, asking the other coders to adjust their understanding of a given category. But the process may also take the opposite direction, with the coders' comments and questions alerting you to unclear passages in the code definitions, to overlaps between categories, and to any other shortcomings of the coding frame. In this case, you should revise the coding frame accordingly. This process of familiarising the coders with the coding frame can therefore be seen as an extension of the earlier phase of code development. It emphasizes how useful it can be to bring several different perspectives to bear on this task.

The phase of familiarising the coders with the coding frame is also found in quantitative content analysis, where it is called 'coder training' (Krippendorff, 2004, Chapter 7; Neuendorf, 2002, pp. 133ff.). But coder training in the quantitative sense differs in one important respect from the procedure suggested here: in quantitative content analysis, it is considered desirable that the coders remain 'blind' to the research question. Because in quantitative content analysis the method is typically used for hypothesis testing, it is assumed that the coders, if they knew about the hypothesis, would work in a biased fashion, coding in accordance with the hypothesis (or in contradiction to it, if they had any reason to be inimical towards the researcher). In QCA, on the other hand, knowledge of the research question and of issues surrounding the research is usually considered to be important context information and therefore an essential prerequisite to the coding. The situation is different, however, if you are using QCA to test a hypothesis. In this case it is advisable that you follow the rules of quantitative content analysis.

Coding simultaneously or consecutively

If your coding frame contains more than one dimension (and a qualitative coding frame most likely will), you have to decide whether to code the material on these dimensions simultaneously or on one dimension after another, i.e. consecutively.

This decision depends on the number of the units of coding for each unit of analysis and on the complexity of your coding frame. If each unit of analysis consists only of a few units of coding, and if the coding frame is easy to learn and to handle, it would simply not be economical to go over those few segments separately for each dimension. If, on the other hand, you are dealing with interviews consisting of 100 or more units of coding each, and if your coding frame contains just as many categories, trying to apply all categories simultaneously would quickly result in cognitive overload and make the entire process highly error-prone. Typically, a person can remember and differentiate around 40 (sub)categories at the same time (MacQueen et al., 2009). If your coding frame contains approximately this number of (sub)categories, you will usually be able to code your material on all dimensions and subcategories simultaneously. If your coding frame is larger, it is better to subdivide the coding task.

KEY POINT

You can apply up to 40 categories, including subcategories, to your material simultaneously. If your coding frame is larger, you should subdivide the coding into smaller coding tasks.

Subdividing the coding task can be done in the following ways:

- One way is to divide the task according to dimensions, i.e. you would code your entire material first on dimensions no. 1 and 2, then in a second round for dimensions no. 3 and 4, and so on.
- Another way is to divide the task according to both units of coding and dimensions, and this would be the usual way to handle this issue when dealing with interview material. If you have conducted semi-standardised interviews, chances are that you have constructed your coding frame around your interview questions. One might also say that you have constructed a separate smaller coding frame for the replies to each interview question, and these smaller frames will often contain no more than around 40 subcategories (and around three to five dimensions/main categories). Moreover, each reply to an interview question (which may well be spread over different sections of the interview; see Chapter 7) can be considered a smaller text on one topic within the overall interview. You can therefore divide the task of trial coding into coding one such smaller text relating to one interview question after another. In this way, only part of your total coding frame will be relevant and applicable at any given time.

Example of subdividing the trial coding by units of coding and dimensions

In our study on prioritising in medicine, we used the second method of subdividing the trial coding. We had constructed the coding frame around the interview questions, and we applied these smaller coding frames one at a time, to the replies the participants had given to the respective interview question. That is to say, two coders classified the relevant segments simultaneously according to the interviewee's attitude towards turning off the life support for Terri Schiavo, how the interviewees arrived at their final opinion (i.e. whether they changed their mind in the course of replying to the interview question), the reasons given in favour of and the reasons given against this course of action, any additional information the participants would have liked to arrive at an opinion, and considerations that in their opinion should not play a role in making this kind of decision.

How to handle repetitions

A problem that typically comes up during the trial coding concerns the question of how to handle repetitions in your material. If the same information occurs more than once within the same unit of analysis, should you code this information again and assign it to the same subcategory that you have already used once before?

Example of repetitions in your material

In response to our question concerning the case of Terri Schiavo one interviewee said: 'Have you ever been to a supermarket, have you ever had a look at how much we spend on feeding our pets, our favourite pets? ... Surely we can afford keeping alive the people who are loved by someone!' The interviewer responded by challenging this statement, asking whether the money might not be better spent on financing campaigns informing the public about eating disorders. The participant now continued: 'How much does it cost to maintain a yacht or a racing horse? I always consider these questions in relation to society as a whole. ... Can a society afford to treat itself in this manner?' These passages were considered different units of coding, and each unit would have to be assigned to the same subcategory under the dimension *Reasons why it is considered wrong to cut off the life support for Terri Schiavo*, namely *irrelevance of the costs*. It being the same interviewee who mentions this aspect, the question arises whether the subcategory should be coded twice.

There are two aspects to this question, the first of a substantive, the second of a more practical nature. The substantive question is what exactly the repetition means, what information it conveys (and whether it conveys any information in the first place). Unfortunately, there is no clear-cut answer to this. Depending on your research question, you might simply want to know whether a certain aspect features in the material at all. In this case the fact that a certain aspect is mentioned repeatedly does not really add any information.

Alternatively, you might be interested in how strongly an opinion is expressed, arguing that information that is repeated indicates a stronger opinion than information that is only given once. If a participant mentions twice that the costs are irrelevant for deciding about the treatment of a coma patient, whereas another participant mentions this only once, the reasoning would be that the first participant is more concerned with ignoring treatment costs in such a situation than the second participant. In quantitative content analysis especially, frequency has often been considered to convey information about importance. At the same time, the issue has generated much discussion (Stewart, 1943; see also Holsti, 1969, Chapter 5; Krippendorff, 2004, Chapter 3) – but this lies beyond the scope of this book.

KEY POINT

If you are interested in how strongly an opinion is expressed, you can use repetition of information as one indicator of importance. In this case, repetitions in your material are meaningful and should be coded.

If you do not find repetitions meaningful in the context of your research question, you have two options for how to proceed during the trial coding. The first option is to choose larger units of coding (possibly as large as the entire unit of analysis) and to simply code for the presence or absence of subcategories. This procedure has been termed *synthetic* because it allows you to synthesise information about the presence of various pieces of information, a bit like putting together a number of building blocks (Früh, 2001, Part II, Chapter 2). The disadvantage of this procedure is that it is very time-consuming.

The second procedure involves using smaller units of coding and assigning each unit to a category, disregarding whether this constitutes a repetition or not. At a later stage, following the main coding, you then assemble the data for each of your units of analysis. At this point, a change of perspective takes place. Up to now, the unit of coding has been your focus. After the main coding, your focus changes and becomes the unit of analysis (see Chapter 10). At the early stage of the trial coding, you can simply disregard any repetitions. While this might sound complicated, it is actually easier than any other way of doing this. It is less time-consuming than the first option, and it is less error-prone than constantly checking whether you have already used a certain category or subcategory in coding a given unit of analysis.

--- **Example of handling repetitions** ---

In the prioritising study, we simply wanted to know which reasons and considerations were mentioned by the participants in favour of or against turning off the life support for Terri Schiavo; we were not interested in how strongly our interviewees made any of their points. We therefore chose the second option: we used smaller units of coding and assigned each of these to a subcategory, regardless of any repetitions. After the main coding, we created a table for each interviewee. In this table, we entered all the reasons and considerations mentioned by this person. In this, we disregarded the frequency of mentioning a particular consideration. If an interviewee said once that maintaining the life support was equivalent to prolonging Terri Schiavo's suffering, the category name would be entered into the table as a consideration mentioned by this interviewee. If the same person came back three times to the point that Terri Schiavo would already have died a natural death if the machines had not been keeping her alive, the category name would also be entered (once) into the table as a consideration that was mentioned.

Keeping a record of codes

For the actual trial coding, the coders should, independently of each other, assign each segment to a (sub)category. 'Independently' means that one coder should not be aware of how the other coders interpret each segment and what meaning they assign to it ('blind' coding). If you are the only coder, you should let a time period of 10–14 days pass between the time of the first and the second coding. Considering the amount of material that is usually involved, it is unlikely that you will be able to recall how you interpreted all these units of coding. Overall, your procedure during the trial coding should be as similar as possible to how you will proceed during the main phase of coding. Moreover, all coders should make a note of any difficulties they experience during the trial coding. These may relate to problems coding certain units because they seemed too long or too short; that they found it difficult to decide between certain subcategories; that they found a category definition difficult to understand; or anything else that comes up during this phase.

KEY POINT

During the trial coding, the coders should make a note of any difficulties they encounter in applying the coding frame to the material.

To facilitate the comparison of categories assigned to the units of coding by the different coders, coders should enter their codes on a coding sheet. A coding sheet is essentially a spreadsheet, where each line represents one unit of coding (see Table 8.1). Entering the codes becomes easier if you have consecutively numbered both the units of coding and the categories in your coding frame. The best way to number the units of coding is to identify each unit by a first digit that refers to the unit of analysis and subsequent digits referring to the position of the unit of coding within the unit of analysis. If you are working on your own, you should use a separate coding sheet at each of the two points in time when you are coding.

--- **Example of numbering units of coding** ---

In our study, the interviews (units of analysis) were numbered from 1 to 45, and within each interview the units of coding were numbered from 1 to n, depending on how many units of coding there were (up to around 250). The first unit of coding in the first interview would be referred to as 1.1, the 15th unit of coding in the third interview as 3.15, the 123rd unit of coding in interview no. 40 as 40.123, etc.

Table 8.1 Coding sheet

Name of coder/Point in time:_____

Unit no.	Category for dim. 1	Category for dim. 2	Category for dim. 3
1.1	1.3	2.5	3.2
1.2	1.2	2.4	3.1
...	...	...	...
2.1	1.3	2.5	3.7
...	...	...	...
3.1	1.5	2.2	3.2
...	...	...	...
n.n	...	...	...

The unit identification should be entered in the first column of the spreadsheet. In the second column the coder should enter the name or the number of the subcategory to which she assigned this unit of coding. The category name is more descriptive, but in the long run entering category names can become rather cumbersome. If there are many units of coding to enter, it is generally easier to refer to the categories by number, simply numbering them from 1 to however many categories there are. If the coding frame is complex, comprising more than one dimension, with each unit of coding being assessed on several dimensions, there should be additional columns in the spreadsheet for entering categories for the various dimensions, with one column for each dimension in the coding frame (see Table 8.1).

========================= SUMMARY =========================

If any coders join your research team only at the stage of the trial coding, you have to allow for time to let them familiarise themselves with your research and your coding frame. An important decision before the trial coding concerns the question whether to code your material on several dimensions simultaneously or consecutively. If your coding frame contains more than 40 (sub)categories, it is best to subdivide this task. A second decision concerns the question of how to handle repetitions. It is usually easier to code them at this stage, regardless of whether you will make use of this information at a later stage. The trial coding should be as similar as possible to the main coding, i.e. coders should code the segments independently of each other and enter their decisions into a coding sheet. They should also make a note of any problems they encounter at this stage.

How to proceed after trying out the coding frame

Once you have completed the trial coding, you will take a closer look at those units that you assigned to different categories. If you are working together with

Table 8.2 Comparative coding sheet for dimension 1

Unit no	First coder	Second coder
1.1	1.3	1.3
1.2	1.5	1.5
...	...	...
2.1	1.3	1.7
...	...	...
3.1	1.5	1.5
...	...	
n.n	...	...

other coders, you will sit down and discuss these units with them. We will look at how this is done, at the various outcomes of this discussion between the coders, and how to proceed in each case, including the situation where you are the only coder.

Discussion between the coders

Following the trial coding, you should sit down with any other coders and discuss those units of coding which you interpreted differently, i.e. those units to which you assigned different codes. Obviously, this step comes in only if you are working together with other coders (see below if you are working on your own). At this point the coding sheet prepared by each of the coders comes in useful: to prepare this discussion, it is helpful that you sit down with the sheets, comparing the categories to which each unit of coding was assigned, highlighting all differences between coders, and examining any notes concerning problems experienced during the coding process. When doing so, it is helpful to create a comparative coding sheet, where the rows again represent the units of coding, and the columns represent the codes assigned by each coder (or by yourself at different points in time; see Table 8.2). This helps you identify the controversial units of coding and highlight the differences between the coders.

Following this preparation, you and any other coders should sit down together and discuss the interpretation of all units where you disagreed. An important part of this process is that you all explain your reasons for interpreting a unit of coding in a given way and choosing a particular category. There are three possible outcomes of this discussion:

1. Sometimes it will turn out that you do not in fact disagree, but that one of you has simply made a mistake. This can easily happen, especially if there has been a lot of material to code, and you become tired. In this case the issue is easily resolved, the mistake corrected, and no further action is necessary.

2. It may also be the case that you agree on how you understand a given unit of coding, but disagree about the appropriate category. In this case, you differ in your understanding of the relevant categories. How to proceed in this case is described below.

3. You may also have used different categories because you differ in your interpretation of the respective unit of coding. How to proceed in this case is also described below.

Typically, this discussion following the trial coding will help clarify both your and the other coders' understanding of the different categories and the coding frame, and it will help you eliminate any overlaps between categories.

How to proceed if coders differ in their interpretation of categories

If you and any other coders agree about what a certain passage in your material means, but have nevertheless assigned it to different categories, you differ in your interpretation of the categories. Typically, this kind of disagreement is due to one of the following reasons:

- One of you understands the category in a way that is different from the definition of that category, and is guided by this understanding in her coding. Putting it differently, one might also say that this coder is wrong in her interpretation of the category and has to adjust her understanding.
- The category definition is not sufficiently clear. This is especially likely to lead to disagreement if there are overlaps between categories. In this case, the coding frame does not specify to which category these 'overlaps' should be assigned. And as a result, one of you chooses one category, and another one of you chooses another category. In this case, the category definitions have to be revised and a decision rule must be specified.

Let us look at examples of each of these two situations.

One coder is guided by a mistaken understanding

To illustrate the situation where one of you misinterprets a category definition, let us take the following passage from an interview concerning the case of Terri Schiavo as an example:

'I would say that it is high time to have the discussion ... surrounding euthanasia change direction, instead of letting someone starve and die of thirst. From an ethical perspective I find it more acceptable to give someone an overdose of morphine than to let that someone die of hunger and thirst, for days, it took a couple of days before she died.'

According to our understanding as the researchers, this unit is to be classified as *Manner of death* (one of the *Reasons why turning off the life support for Terri Schiavo is considered wrong*). According to the definition in the coding frame, this category is to be applied if an interviewee considers Terri Schiavo's manner of death to have been cruel to an unacceptable degree. Let us further assume that one of the coders did use this category, whereas another classified it as *Unethical procedure* (another of the *Reasons why turning off the life support for Terri Schiavo is considered wrong*). *Unethical procedure* is to be applied if a participant considers it morally unacceptable to turn off the life support of a coma patient, regardless of the underlying reasons. It further contains a decision rule to the effect that if an interviewee does not consider turning off the life support as such to be morally unacceptable, but feels that Terri Schiavo's manner of death was unacceptable (namely to die of starvation and thirst), the category *Manner of death* applies.

The coder who used *Unethical procedure* might now argue that the participant explicitly uses the phrase 'from an ethical perspective' which to her clearly indicates that the participant considers this a case of *Unethical procedure*. She also points out that it says in the definition that the category is to be applied regardless of the reasons underlying this judgement. Now we as researchers might argue that the coder is not applying the category as it was meant to be applied. According to the definition, *Unethical procedure* refers specifically to turning off the life support, whereas *Manner of death* refers to the fact that Terri Schiavo ultimately died of starvation and thirst. We would explain to the coder that if she understands the relevant passage in the sense that the interviewee considers it morally wrong to let someone die of starvation and thirst, this meaning is covered by the category *Manner of death* and not by *Unethical procedure*. We would therefore ask the coder to adjust her understanding of the two categories in question.

The category definitions are not sufficiently clear

If the category *Unethical procedure* in the above example did not contain a decision rule, however, the situation would be different. In this case the coder might justifiably argue that this is exactly what she took the segment to mean, but that she had been uncertain whether to choose the category *Unethical procedure* or *Manner of death*. In this case, the coder's reasoning would have alerted us to the fact that the two categories overlap and that the definitions should therefore be clarified. This can be done by collapsing the two categories into one (if the distinction between the two does not seem worth preserving) or by highlighting the differences between them and adding a decision rule. In the present case it should be clarified, for instance, that *Unethical procedure* refers to turning off the life support only, not to Terri Schiavo's manner of death.

How to proceed if coders differ in their interpretation of the material

But it can also happen that you all disagree concerning the interpretation of the material. The coder who classified the passage above as *Unethical procedure* might argue, for instance, that the way in which Terri Schiavo died was a necessary consequence of her life support having been turned off, at least for as long as assisted suicide was considered a criminal offence – whereas the other coder might uphold the distinction. In this case each coder would interpret the passage differently and would be able to provide reasons supporting her interpretation. This example is somewhat artificial, but in practice this situation can easily arise: communication frequently is open to different interpretations, each of them equally feasible. If this happens, the difference cannot be resolved and the passage cannot be assigned a single meaning. During the pilot phase this is not a problem, but it does become an issue when it comes to the point of describing and interpreting the results (see Chapter 11). During the pilot phase, you just leave it at that; no further action is needed.

How to proceed if there is only one coder

For obvious reasons, you can discuss the results of the trial coding with the other coders only if more than one coder is involved. If you are the only coder, applying the coding frame to the material twice, you have to adjust the procedure that is described here. But even though you are only dealing with yourself, it is still useful to take a closer look at those units that you coded differently at the two points in time. Usually, you will be able to at least vaguely recall the reasons why you chose one category at one time and a different category at another time. This does not allow you to adjust your understanding of the categories. But this is not really a problem, because you will of necessity be familiar with your own understandings. You will, however, still be able to identify overlaps between categories and unclear phrasings, and this will help you to modify the coding frame and improve it.

████████████████████ SUMMARY ████████████████████

After the trial coding, you should sit down with any other coders and discuss those units of coding that you assigned to different categories. There are several reasons why coders assign segments to different categories: because one of them has made a mistake; because categories overlap; because one coder was guided by a mistaken understanding of a category; or else because the coders differ in their understanding of the material. As a result of the discussion, coders should adjust their understanding of the categories, and you as the researcher should modify the coding frame so as to eliminate any overlaps between categories. If you are the only coder, thinking about your reasons for assigning segments to different categories can still help you to identify overlaps between categories.

Frequently asked questions

What if one coder misinterprets the coding frame more often than another?

Coders invariably bring their own individual understanding of key terms and concepts to the research – and ideally this will contribute to the construction of the coding frame at an earlier stage of the research (see Chapter 5). But category definitions specify a particular usage of relevant terms, and the success of your content analysis depends on the willingness of the coders to adopt these specifications in going through the material. If one of you understands some of these key terms in ways that differ from the specifications in the coding frame – for instance, because she has very strong opinions on the issue in question which simply override the specifications – this endangers the research. If this happens, you might even consider working with another coder.

Does this not mean that I force coders to adopt my understanding of the texts?

The above suggestion may give you the impression that the coding frame and the definitions it contains are used to 'indoctrinate' the coders, forcing them to adopt a very specific usage of key terms and thereby limiting their understanding of the material. But this is to confuse the process of interpretation and the process of using the coding frame, i.e. the process of coming to interpret the unit of coding in a particular way on the one hand and classifying this interpretation under recourse to the coding frame on the other hand (see also Früh, 2007, Part I, Chapter 3). In a first step, the coders are of course free to interpret the material, trying to understand the meaning that is being conveyed. But once they have done so, in a second step their task is to locate this meaning within the coding frame, i.e. to identify the (sub)category that comes closest to the meaning they have identified in the material and to assign the respective unit of coding to that category. The definitions in the coding frame specify the rules according to which this process takes place, and the coders are indeed required to follow these rules. A coder is, for instance, free to interpret a participant as saying that she considers it utterly immoral and an act of murder to turn off the life support of a coma patient. But once the coder has read the segment in this way, she is then no longer free to assign this to any category she pleases, but is required to identify the segment as an instance of the category *Unethical procedure*. QCA regulates how a previously identified meaning is classified, but it does not regulate the process of identifying this meaning.

What if the coders are different for the trial and the main coding?

The trial coding serves a double purpose: it serves to try out the coding frame, but of course it also helps to familiarise the coders with the research and the coding frame and to discuss their understanding of the categories. Anyone who has not participated in this 'initiation' phase will lack important background information and will therefore be likely to make mistakes. For this reason you should involve the same coders in the trial and in the main coding phase. If this is not possible, you should carry out another trial coding with the new coders.

Is one trial coding enough?

This depends on how many adjustments you had to make following the discussion after the trial coding. If only a few adjustments were necessary, one trial coding is enough, and you can move on to the main coding phase. If you had to make a lot of adjustments, perhaps even involving changes to the structure of the coding frame, it would be best to conduct a second trial coding if there is time and if coders are available.

How many times can one repeat a trial coding?

A rule of thumb in the literature is to do a trial coding twice, but no more (Rustemeyer, 1992). If your first trial coding shows that you have to substantively revise your coding frame, it certainly makes sense to do a second trial coding. This way you can find out whether the adjustments have made the coding frame easier to understand and to handle. It may of course happen that the second trial coding shows that this is not the case, that the coders find the coding frame just as difficult to handle as they did before, and that considerable overlaps between categories still exist. In this case something fundamental must be wrong, something that goes beyond what you can remedy by yet another trial coding and yet another revision of the coding frame. Rather than do a third trial coding, you should reconsider your entire study and whether QCA really is the best method to use. If only minor revisions are necessary after the second trial coding, this is not considered a problem, and you can continue with the main coding after making these adjustments.

What happens to the material that was used for the trial coding?

This depends on the kind of material that you used for the trial coding and the scope of your revisions of the coding frame. If the material you selected for the trial coding is not part of your material for the main coding, it has served its purpose, and you can simply disregard it. If you used part of the material for your main study for the trial coding, you will have to recode this material to some extent, depending on the extent of your revisions of the coding frame. If you had to make only minor revisions, you can simply return to those units of coding that were assigned to the categories that were changed, and code them again. But if you substantially revised your coding frame, it would be best to recode all the material during the main coding phase.

End-of-chapter questions

- What does the pilot phase involve?
- How much of your material should you include in the trial coding?
- What would be good ways of subdividing the coding if your coding frame contains more than around 40 (sub)categories?
- What would be a good way of preparing for the discussion between the coders after the trial coding?
- Name two of the reasons why coders may have assigned a unit of coding to different categories.
- What do you do if two coders differ in their interpretation of a unit of coding?

9

WHAT TO KEEP IN MIND: EVALUATING YOUR CODING FRAME

Chapter guide

Now that you have tried out your coding frame, it is time to check how well it is doing, to assess its quality. The comparison of codes that was described in the previous chapter is an important part of this. But in addition, you as the researcher should carry out a more formal assessment. In this chapter the focus will be on the criteria that are commonly used in making this assessment: reliability and validity. In particular, we will look at:

- what reliability is, its role in QCA, and how to assess it;
- what validity is and how to assess the validity of data-driven and concept-driven coding frames.

Other criteria in evaluating coding frames are unidimensionality, exhaustiveness, saturation, and mutual exclusiveness. Because these should already guide you in constructing your coding frame, they are covered in Chapter 4.

Reliability

Reliability as a criterion in evaluating research in general and content analysis in particular is rooted in quantitative social science methodology. Because of this origin in quantitative research, it is easy to dismiss it as irrelevant for QCA. But this would be to throw out the baby with the bathwater. The decisive issue is not the origin of the concept, but whether it can serve a useful purpose in QCA. In this section, we will first look at what exactly reliability entails and what role it can play in QCA. We will then move on to the different ways of assessing reliability and interpreting reliability measures.

What is reliability?

Reliability is a criterion that is typically used in evaluating the quality of a specific instrument, such as a questionnaire, a test, or a coding frame. In general terms, an instrument is considered to be reliable to the extent that it yields data that is free of error. The idea behind this is actually quite similar to what we mean when we call another person reliable. Someone who is reliable will be true to her word and will be there for us in times of need. Someone who is unreliable, by contrast, will say that she will help us move house, but may then fail to show up. The actions of a reliable person will be predictable, and we will not be mistaken in 'relying' on her, whereas the actions of an unreliable person will fluctuate in unpredictable ways.

DEFINITION

An instrument is called reliable to the extent that it yields data that is free of error.

In quantitative research, a number of strategies have been devised for assessing the reliability of an instrument (Bryman, 2008, pp. 149ff.; Cresswell, 2009, pp. 190ff.). When assessing the reliability of a coding frame, only two of these are important:

- *Comparisons across persons.* Two (or more) coders use the same coding frame to analyse the same units of coding, and they do so independently of each other ('blind coding'). The underlying concept of reliability is called *intersubjectivity*. The coding frame is considered reliable to the extent that the results of the analysis are not only subjective, but *inter*subjective, i.e. apply across persons.
- *Comparisons across points in time.* One coder uses the same coding frame to analyse the same units of coding. The underlying concept of reliability is called *stability*. The coding frame is considered reliable to the extent that the results of the analysis remain stable over time.

This type of reliability is also called *internal reliability* (Bryman, 2008, pp. 154ff.; Seale, 1999, Chapter 10), and the common goal linking both procedures for assessing internal reliability is *consistency*. Whether the coding is compared by different persons or by one person at different points in time, the coding frame is considered reliable to the extent that the coding is consistent. When applied to QCA, reliability therefore translates into consistency.

KEY POINT

In assessing the reliability of your coding frame, you are looking at the consistency of the coding. You can do this by comparing coding across persons or across points in time.

Reliability is not an all-or-none, a yes-or-no type of criterion. The question is not whether your coding frame is reliable or unreliable, but to what *extent* it is reliable. Reliability is always a matter of degree.

Why reliability is useful in QCA

But what is the use of criteria such as reliability and consistency in qualitative research? As a matter of fact, reliability can be useful in two respects: it can tell you something about the quality of your coding frame, and it can provide you with information about the acceptability of your analysis (see also Boyatzis, 1998, Chapter 7).

In Chapter 5, we looked at how to define your categories in such a way that it becomes clear what each category stands for. The definition should enable you and others to recognise instances of the category in your data and to distinguish between one category and other, similar categories. Now imagine what will happen if the definitions you have come up with do not measure up to this standard: most likely, units of analysis will sometimes be coded as instances of one category, sometimes as instances of another category – in other words, the categories will be used inconsistently. In this way, low consistency will point you to flaws in your coding frame; it will show you that those categories that were used inconsistently need to be improved. This is the first way in which reliability can be put to use in QCA: as a pointer to flaws in your coding frame. Both reliability as intersubjectivity and as stability can be useful in this way.

To understand the second way in which reliability can be useful in QCA, remember why you would want to use the method in the first place. QCA is especially helpful when you are dealing with large amounts of qualitative data and want to describe what is in that data through classification. This act of classification invariably involves a claim: that the meaning you are describing in your categories is in fact present in your material.

––––––––––– **Example of the claims you are making in QCA** –––––––––––

Hsu et al. (2010) conducted interviews with 327 patients who had received complementary/alternative treatment for their back pain, such as acupuncture or yoga. They conducted a QCA of these interviews to determine what benefits patients experienced from these treatments. Their reasoning was that the existing standardised questionnaires for assessing treatment benefits were aimed at biomedical treatment and might therefore leave out other types of benefits that are not commonly associated with biomedicine. Their final coding frame contained the following themes that were only partially captured by standardised outcome measures: increased awareness of treatment options; increased ability to relax; positive changes in emotional state; increased body awareness; changes in thinking that increased the ability to cope with back pain; and other themes. By reporting their results the authors are making the claim that the patients who received complementary/alternative treatment for their back pain did indeed experience these benefits.

This type of claim would be meaningless if it were merely your own, subjective reading of the material. It strengthens your claim if you can show that others interpret the material in the same way: if two (or more) people independently agree on the meaning of your material, chances are that other members of your society and culture would most likely understand the material in a similar way, i.e. that the material 'has' this meaning for the members of this community. This is not to say this is the 'correct' meaning (assuming that such a thing as the 'correct' meaning exists…). But if two or more coders *cannot* agree (and provided that your category definitions are clear; see above), this shows that your material does not have a clear, unambiguous meaning and that you should be careful when presenting your results. That is to say, reliability and consistency also tell you something about the acceptability of your analysis for other members of the (scientific) community. This second use of reliability applies only to reliability in the sense of intersubjectivity.

KEY POINT

Reliability can be useful in QCA in two respects: first, low consistency can help to pinpoint flaws in the coding frame; second, low consistency between different coders shows where interpretations are likely to be contentious.

Assessing reliability – a contentious issue

While I am arguing here that assessing reliability in QCA is useful, the issue of reliability is a contentious one in qualitative research. Reliability (especially in the sense of intersubjectivity) will often be rejected on the grounds that meaning is highly context-dependent. According to this line of reasoning, to make the agreement between two coders a criterion in evaluating data analysis is to reduce the multiplicity of potential meanings to one meaning only. This is considered to decrease instead of increase the quality of the analysis (cf. Seale, 1999, Chapter 4; Steinke, 2004). Why is the criterion used in QCA nonetheless?

In the first place, not every data analysis aims to uncover multiple meanings. QCA, by reducing and summarising your data, does not. Of course different interpretations by different researchers can and should be taken into account when developing your coding frame. And of course any given unit of analysis can be coded and thereby assigned a meaning on several different dimensions. But coding for various simultaneous meanings on one and the same dimension is difficult using QCA (and is easier using other methods such as semiotics or discourse analysis; see Chapter 3 for a comparison between QCA and other qualitative methods for data analysis). QCA aims to determine one meaning for each unit of analysis on a given dimension; and, considering this aim, it makes sense to assess whether different coders agree on their reading (for a similar position see Boyatzis, 1998, Chapter 7; Seale, 1999, Chapter 10).

Second, qualitative researchers often make use of a criterion in evaluating their research which is actually not that different from reliability. This is the criterion of making your interpretation plausible and convincing to others (see Miles & Huberman, 1994, Chapter 10; Steinke, 2004). This refers both to your work in your research team and to the presentation of your analysis and results when writing up your research: you should show both your fellow analysts and your readers why you favour one interpretation over another. The focus here is on the process of making your interpretation plausible, but of course you do so with a specific goal in mind: you want to convince them of your interpretation – i.e. to make others *agree* with you. Making your interpretation plausible and achieving consistency are therefore two sides of the same coin, focusing on the process and the aim, respectively. You will see below that making your interpretation plausible to others is indeed one way of achieving reliability in QCA.

How to assess reliability

Conceptualising reliability as consistency implies a comparison: something can only be consistent with something else. As mentioned above, this can refer to the consistency between different persons or to the consistency between different points in time (Boyatzis, 1998, Chapter 7). If you work together with another coder, you can assess both types of consistency. If you code your material on your own, you can only determine consistency across time. In quantitative content analysis, reliability is assessed by calculating a *coefficient of agreement* (for an overview see Krippendorf, 2004, Chapter 11; Neuendorf, 2002, Chapter 7). In QCA, additional procedures for determining consistency have been developed. In the following, we will first look at coefficients of agreement and how to interpret them, and then move on to other methods for determining consistency.

Coefficients of agreement

The simplest way to arrive at a coefficient of agreement is to calculate the *percentage of agreement*:

$$\text{Percentage of agreement} = \frac{\text{Number of units of coding on which the codes agrees}}{\text{Total number of unites of coding}} \times 100$$

Obviously, the higher the reliability of the coding, the closer the resulting number is to 100%. But several concerns have been raised over the use of such a simple coefficient. What exactly does it mean, for instance, for two coders to 'agree'? Do they 'agree' only if they assign a unit of coding to the same category? Or does it also constitute a type of 'agreement' if they do *not* assign a unit of coding to certain categories? A second concern relates to the number of categories available. If two coders agree on a category for 75% of the units of coding, and only two categories are available to choose from, this is much less 'impressive' than if two coders agree on 75% of units when choosing from among 40 different categories. This is so because, depending on the number of categories to choose from, coders can be expected to agree on the same category a certain number of times purely by coincidence. With only two categories, such a chance agreement is much more likely than with 40 categories. These concerns point to some common problems in interpreting coefficients of agreement.

To address these concerns, a number of more complex coefficients have been developed, notably Scott's *pi*, Cohen's *kappa*, and Krippendorff's *alpha*. Because these have been described in detail elsewhere (Krippendorff, 2004, Chapter 11; Neuendorf, 2002, Chapter 7), they will not be covered here.

KEY POINT

The most common coefficients of agreement include the percentage of agreement, Scott's pi, Cohen's kappa and Krippendorff's alpha.

Looking for the extent of agreement is only meaningful where there may have been grounds for disagreement. Therefore, you calculate a coefficient of agreement only for those categories that constitute true alternatives during coding, i.e. for those categories that mutually exclude each other. You would typically *not* calculate a coefficient including all subcategories for all main categories in your coding frame all at once. Usually, one coefficient each is calculated for all subcategories in a given main category. Sometimes researchers calculate an additional coefficient for all main categories compared to each other (aggregating across the many subcategories).

— Example of using a coefficient of agreement to assess consistency —

In assessing the coding frame in our prioritising study, we used either Cohen's kappa or percentage of agreement. As a rule, we calculated one coefficient for all subcategories that were simultaneously applied to interviewees' replies to one related block of questions in our interview guide. We therefore calculated one coefficient comparing all the subcategories within the main categories: aspects of health care that have changed for the better; aspects of health care that have changed for the worse; aspects of health care that have remained unchanged. We likewise calculated one coefficient of agreement comparing all the subcategories within the main categories that we had created concerning the case of Terri Schiavo: opinions concerning the case; development of their line of reasoning;

criteria in favour of terminating her life support; criteria against terminating her life support; additional criteria; criteria that should not enter into the decision. Strictly speaking, we might have calculated separate coefficients for all subcategories in the first and for all subcategories in the second main categories, because only the subcategories within each main category were mutually exclusive. But considering the number of main categories and subcategories in the entire coding frame, this would have made things too complicated. We therefore opted for a more pragmatic solution.

Interpreting coefficients of agreement

The advantage of calculating a coefficient of agreement is that it provides you with a concise summary of consistency. But what exactly this summary means is not as clear and straightforward as it may appear at first sight.

Ultimately, the interpretation of any given coefficient depends on your material and on the kind of meaning you are looking at (Früh, 2007, Part II, Chapter 1). Some kinds of meaning are fairly standardised, whereas others require a greater amount of interpretation (on standardised meaning see below). The more standardised the meaning you are dealing with, the higher you can reasonably expect your coefficient of agreement to be. But if the meaning you are looking at is less standardised, you would expect your coders to have grounds for disagreement. In this case it would not be reasonable to expect the same high degree of consistency (Neuendorf, 2002; Scheufele, 2001).

Example of how the expected degree of consistency —————— depends on degree of standardisation ——————

If you are coding whether the persons shown in an advertisement are male or female, this constitutes a highly standardised type of meaning, and coding requires little interpretation. But if you analysed the same advertisement in terms of the role of the persons shown *vis-à-vis* the product (user, endorser, or symbolic; Skorek, 2008), much more interpretation would be required. Considering this difference, 75% agreement between coders concerning the role *vis-à-vis* the product might be acceptable. But if you obtained 75% agreement between coders concerning the sex of the persons shown in the advertisement, you would probably think that there must be an error in your calculation.

In qualitative research, you will typically be dealing with meaning that requires a certain amount of interpretation. Also, coding frames in QCA are often extensive, containing a large number of categories. In interpreting your coefficients of agreement, you should therefore never use guidelines from quantitative research as a cut-off criterion (on guidelines for kappa see Landis & Koch, 1977), as in: 'Oh, my kappa coefficient is below 0.40 – it looks like I will have to scrap these categories'. Instead, what looks like a low coefficient should make you take another closer look both at your material and your coding frame. Perhaps, considering your material and the number of your categories, a comparatively low coefficient of agreement is acceptable – this is simply the best you can do. But it may also be the case that your coding frame is not well written and that the criteria for applying the different categories are not clear. In this case you will have to revise your coding frame. Because you may find it difficult to look at the feasibility of your own coding frame 'from the outside', it may be a good idea at this stage to bring in someone else to give you advice about how to proceed.

KEY POINT

The interpretation of a coefficient of agreement depends on how much interpretation is needed in coding and on how the disagreement is distributed across your material and your categories.

Also, you should not interpret your coefficient in isolation, but in combination with a detailed examination of disagreements between coders, including a discussion of the reasons underlying their coding decisions (see Chapter 8). A coefficient may be relatively high (say, 92% percentage agreement). Yet in one study the 8% disagreements may be spread out over the various subcategories and may be due to a number of reasons: perhaps the coders differed in their interpretations of the material or were feeling increasingly exhausted. In this case, you would not need to revise your coding frame (although in research practice this is highly unlikely!). But the situation would be different if these 8% disagreements were the result of an overlap between two subcategories, and if coders sometimes used one subcategory, sometimes the other, being uncertain which one to choose. In this case you would definitely have to revise your coding frame, even though the overall consistency is quite high. It is therefore not the coefficient as such that tells you whether to change anything about your coding frame or leave it as it is. But based on your comparison of the coding and the coefficient you will have to discuss any cases of disagreement with the other coders and make your decision about whether and how to revise based on this discussion.

Can it nevertheless be useful to calculate a coefficient of agreement in QCA? If it is handled and interpreted with care, it certainly can be. This is especially so if you are dealing with complex coding frames where it is useful to have a summary of consistency across categories.

Other ways of establishing consistency in QCA

Even though coefficients of agreement provide you with a concise summary of consistency, some qualitative researchers may prefer not to use them – be it because the coefficients are in need of further interpretation anyway, or because the researchers argue that what matters most is not the consistency of the coding, but that the coders ultimately agree on a given interpretation. If the coders agree, this in itself ensures that the interpretation in question is shared, potentially by all members of a given community. Consistency in this sense of the term is quite a common criterion in evaluating qualitative research in general, not only in QCA (Miles & Huberman, 1994, Chapter 10C; Steinke, 2004). Here, the requirement is that other members of the research team can follow and share the interpretation of the material in question, and that you can make your interpretation sufficiently plausible to the other members of the research team. This is typically achieved by having all members of a research team meet and discuss their interpretations of the material in question. But because this is a very time-consuming procedure, it is usually not feasible for the large amounts of material to which QCA is applied. To make it feasible, the procedure first needs to be adapted.

Example of adapting the assessment of coding consistency to qualitative research

Hsu et al. (2010) used such an adapted procedure for establishing consistency in their study of benefits from complementary/alternative treatment of back pain. Two coders coded the material independently of each other. Then they met to discuss those units of coding which they had assigned to different categories and to resolve any disagreements. No coefficient was calculated.

One way of doing this would be to proceed as described in this and the preceding chapter, but without calculating a coefficient of agreement (for a similar suggestion, termed hermeneutic-classificatory content analysis, cf. Mathes, 1992). That is, you would code your material together with, but independently of a second coder, would compare the categories you used, and sit down together to discuss and resolve any disagreements. A second option would be that you and any other coders read the material first and then meet and do the coding together, again aiming for consensual interpretations. But if you decide to proceed like this, you should be aware that you are conceptualising consistency differently than is usually done in content analysis (for additional suggestions, see Schilling, 2006).

SUMMARY

A research instrument is considered reliable to the extent that it is free of error. In content analysis, reliability translates into consistency. Consistency is assessed by comparing coding across persons (intersubjectivity) or over time (stability). Even though the concept originates in quantitative research, it can be useful in QCA because it says something about the quality of the coding frame, pointing you to any flaws, and about the acceptability of your analysis. In this latter sense, consistency is closely related to the plausibility of your interpretation, and this is actually a common criterion in qualitative research. In quantitative content analysis reliability is usually assessed by calculating the percentage or a coefficient of agreement. This is useful for giving a summary impression of reliability, but has to be interpreted with the kind of material and the distribution of disagreements in mind. In QCA, discussion among coders can replace calculating a coefficient.

Validity

Although it is important to develop a coding frame that can be consistently applied, other considerations concerning the quality of the coding frame are at least as important. The most important among these is validity.

In the methodological literature, an instrument is considered valid to the extent that it in fact captures what it sets out to capture (Krippendorff, 2004, Chapter 13; Neuendorf, 2002, Chapter 6). Your coding frame can be regarded as valid to the extent that your categories adequately represent the concepts in your research question. While the role of reliability in QCA has been contentious, the importance of achieving a valid coding frame has never really been under dispute. Like reliability, validity is also not an all-or-nothing criterion. Therefore, your coding frame is not either valid or invalid, but it is valid to a certain degree.

DEFINITION

An instrument is considered valid to the extent that it captures what it sets out to capture. A coding frame is valid to the extent that the categories adequately represent the concepts under study.

While the definition of validity is simple enough, the discussion of the criterion in QCA has been quite complex, focusing on two contentious areas. The first of these concerns the validity of coding frames for assessing so-called manifest versus latent content. The second area relates to the scope of the conclusions drawn on the basis of content analysis (for an overview of these issues see Groeben & Rustemeyer, 1994). Even though this discussion is complex and takes us away from how to actually assess the validity of your own coding frame, it is important that you familiarise yourself with it, otherwise you will not understand what other authors say on this topic and why they hold such divergent views. In the following, we will therefore start out by looking at the discussions surrounding these two contentious issues. We will then move on to different kinds of validity and how to tell whether your own coding frame is sufficiently valid.

First contention: Manifest or latent content?

The origins of the debate

The discussion of validity in the context of assessing manifest as opposed to latent content dates back to the middle of the twentieth century. At this time a vigorous debate between the proponents of 'quantitative content analysis' and QCA was in full swing. Proponents of quantitative content analysis argued that the method should limit itself to the examination of so-called manifest content, because coding for latent content opened the door to subjectivity and highly individual interpretations.

But what exactly is manifest and what is latent content, and how is their assessment related to validity? Berelson (1952, p. 20), one of the major proponents of quantitative content analysis, gave the following definition:

If one imagines a continuum along which various communications are placed depending upon the degree to which different members of the intended audience get the same understandings from them, one might place a simple news story on a train wreck at one end (since it is likely that every reader will get the same meanings from the content) and an obscure modern poem at the other (since it is likely that no two readers will get identical meanings from the content).... The analysis of manifest content is applicable to materials at the end of the continuum where understanding is simple and direct, and not at the other. Presumably, there is a point on the continuum beyond which the 'latency' of the content (i.e., the diversity of its understanding in the relevant audience) is too great for reliable analysis.

Manifest meaning, according to Berelson, can therefore be characterised as simple, clear, direct, i.e. the kind of meaning on which different persons are likely to agree, whereas latent meaning is obscure and likely to be different for different readers.

Berelson's definitions have repeatedly been challenged, and not only by proponents of QCA (Kracauer, 1952; see also Früh, 2007, Part I, Chapter 2; Groeben & Rustemeyer, 1994; Holsti, 1969; Krippendorff, 2004, Chapter 1; Lisch & Kriz, 1978). It has been argued that to understand any kind of meaning, whether it concerns a 'simple news story on a train wreck' or an 'obscure modern poem', invariably requires some degree of interpretation. Communication content does indeed differ in a number of respects, but these are gradual differences, not fundamental differences that prevent consensual interpretation.

KEY POINT

Proponents of QCA argue that analysing meaning always requires interpretation, whether that meaning is manifest or latent.

Differences between manifest and latent content

Let us now take a closer look at these differences between manifest and latent content and whether they should prevent you from using QCA.

- A first difference, already mentioned earlier, concerns degree of standardisation. Manifest content is more standardised, and standardised content is easier to understand and will more readily be understood in similar ways by different persons. To say that '150 persons' had assembled will evoke more similar interpretations in readers than to say that 'quite a few persons' had assembled.
- Second, content differs in terms of what has, in linguistic terms, been called directness of speech. The idea underlying this concept is that communication follows certain rules. One such rule is to say no more and no less than is required in a given situation. Another rule is to be sincere (Grice, 1975). If someone communicates with us in a way that is not in accordance with these rules, we will assume that they mean something other than what they literally say. Let us assume that you promise to be home by 8.00 pm, but walk in the door at 11.00 pm. Your partner greets you by saying 'It's 11 o'clock'. In this situation, you immediately understand that s/he is not literally informing you about the time (this would be superfluous), but is implicitly reproaching for you being late. Again, direct speech is easier to understand than communication where the speaker is implying something other than what she literally says.
- Third, content differs in terms of the number of meanings it is intended to convey. Many instances of everyday communication are what is called monosemous (on monosemous and polysemous content see Groeben & Schreier, 1992): they have one meaning only, such as an instruction manual, the bus schedule, or (supposedly) Berelson's example of an article about a train wreck. Other instances of communication are polysemous: they are meant to convey several meanings simultaneously, as do poems or other works of art. Moreover, these meanings may be highly individualised, i.e. different people may read the poem very differently.

KEY POINT

Manifest and latent content differ in terms of standardisation, directness and number of meanings that are conveyed simultaneously.

Can QCA be applied to latent content?

Communication content differs in terms of degree of standardisation, directness, and number of meanings that are conveyed simultaneously. But is a valid

---

analysis of less standardised, indirect, and polysemous content really so difficult?

When it comes to degree of standardisation and directness, it is important to note that most of our everyday communication is anything but standardised and is often somewhat indirect. This, as a matter of fact, is precisely the reason why methods for interpreting meaning were developed in the first place. If our meaning was always perfectly obvious and clear, we would always know exactly what was being meant – and that would be it, no additional analysis would be needed. We would live in a world without misunderstandings – a very clear and standardised, but also a very boring world in many ways! But in fact what we mean is often different from what we say, and the less standardised and the more indirect our way of expressing ourselves is, the more interpretation is required to get to the meaning 'beneath' the words. And with the degree of interpretation, the room for misunderstandings and for error also increases. But nevertheless communication works, we do manage to make ourselves understood a lot of the time, and we have the impression of understanding what others mean.

The situation when applying QCA to less standardised and indirect content is no different from understanding indirect meaning in everyday situations. You will have to engage in more interpretation, and you may have to look at the context in more detail. But usually it is perfectly possible to arrive at a given meaning, and coders will be able to give their reasons why they favour one interpretation over another. Latent content in the sense of indirect and non-standardised meaning is therefore perfectly accessible to QCA (cf. Früh, 2007, Chapter 4; Groeben & Rustemeyer, 1994).

When it comes to polysemous content, QCA is not the best method for capturing the meaning of this type of communication. But the reason is not, as Berelson claims, that these meanings are not manifest. Instead, the reason has to do with the number and simultaneity of the different meanings (Früh, 1992; Rustemeyer, 1992). QCA, by summarising and reducing your material, aims to limit, not to expand upon meaning. Although a unit of coding can be coded on several main categories simultaneously and can in this way be assigned different meanings, there are limits to this. Overall, other interpretive methods (such as semiotics) are better suited to capturing a multiplicity of simultaneous meanings (see Chapter 3).

How to increase validity when analysing latent meaning

Berelson was right in wanting to exclude polysemous material from content analysis, but he was mistaken with respect to less than fully standardised and indirect meanings. QCA can be used to analyse these, and can yield valid results, even though this may be more difficult than an analysis of direct meaning. When you are saying something explicitly and in so many words, there are very few ways of doing so, and others will easily understand what you mean.

But if you are saying something in an indirect way, there are numerous ways of doing so, and it is less easy to tell what you mean. In particular, indicators will be of little help in recognising the meaning, because the meaning is not expressed on the surface in so many words (on the role of indicators in QCA, see Chapter 5).

To help you and other coders with inferring latent meaning and assigning the segments to the right categories, you should phrase your categories in conceptual terms more than in terms of concrete indicators and examples. The following is an example taken from a coding frame used to assess whether one of Kipling's narratives from his collection *The Second Junglebook* about the character Mowgli constitutes an escapist, 'trivial' text or is to be considered an example of 'high literature' (Marlange & Vorderer, 1987). This QCA is itself part of a larger study that also included a survey with readers of the narrative (see below).

─────── **Example of a QCA concerned with latent meaning** ───────

Marlange and Vorderer (1987) started out by identifying major narrative strategies that had been associated with a trivial, escapist type of literature. These included a lack of complex (socio-economic, cultural, political, or psychological) structures at the expense of simple, omnipotent hero characters, affirmation of existing norms, and others. On this basis they constructed a coding frame that contained two types of categories: the one type exemplified the escapist and affirmative strategy, the other type a more realistic and critical strategy. The following categories are meant to capture the presentation of Mowgli as a heroic as opposed to a realistic character (Marlange & Vorderer, 1987, p. 200):

- *Mowgli as a heroic character:*
    o The hero is omnipotent, he succeeds at anything he undertakes, he can do anything, he is invincible, strong, and 'clever'. He may occasionally resort to brute force, but he is always morally justified in doing so.
    o The main character does not experience any inner conflicts; he is noble, brave, and discreet. He is endowed with authority and autonomy. He is successful, active, and 'good'.
    o The character has great, supernatural charisma, is beautiful and mysterious. Unrealistic expectations are raised.

- *Mowgli as a realistic character:*
    o The character is shown to make mistakes and to possess certain weaknesses. He does not invariably succeed at everything. He meets with resistance from the outside, and he cannot always overcome these obstacles. Sometimes he is 'weak'.
    o Psychological conflicts are addressed. The character meets with strong inner resistance, he is not invariably autonomous and successful, and he sometimes lacks authority.
    o The character is described in realistic terms. He is not invariably beautiful and the like. No unrealistic expectations are raised.

Second contention: Scope of inferences

The debate

Another contentious issue is whether the results of content analysis apply only to the material that was analysed or whether they go beyond. This question dates back to the origins of content analysis in communication studies. Here, the method has often been situated within a model of communication going back to the so-called Lasswell formula: 'Who says what in which channel to whom with what effect?' (Lasswell, 1948, p. 37). Results that apply to the content only would be results that are limited to describing the material. In many instances, however, content has not been of intrinsic interest, but because of the information it may convey about the situation in which it was produced, about the communicator, or about the effects on the recipient.

— **Examples of research questions in QCA involving wider inferences** —

In propaganda analysis during the Second World War, for instance, where the Lasswell formula originates, the primary concern was with the intentions of the communicators – the enemy who had released the propaganda material (see Chapter 1). Likewise, in much of communication analysis, the analysis of the content serves as a vehicle for drawing conclusions about the effects on the recipients. The analysis of violent media content, for instance, has not primarily been concerned with the prevalence and presence of different types of violence *per se*, but with the possibility that the reception of violent content may cause aggression in the recipients and may provide them with models for violent action. A similar concern underlies the analysis of trivial literary texts (see the example above): researchers feared that readers would adopt what they read in a one-to-one fashion, i.e. if the world and characters were presented in simplified terms, readers would assume and in fact expect the world to be like this, becoming increasingly unwilling to deal with complexity. Within a social science context, communication content has also been studied as an indicator of the situation in which it was produced. When studying the presentation of men and women in contemporary advertising, for instance, a change in the portrayal of men and women over time has typically been taken to indicate a corresponding value change in society.

Some proponents of content analysis have argued that content analysis proper should always aim to make inferences that go beyond the actual content. Klaus Merten, a German methodologist, has suggested calling an analysis that focuses on the content only 'textual analysis', to distinguish textual description from content analysis proper whose goal he defines as making inferences from communication content to social reality (Merten, 1995, Chapter 1; a similar position is held by Früh, 2007; Krippendorff, 2004; Mayring, 2010).

Other methodologists, however, have argued that, interesting as such inferences undoubtedly are, they also run the danger of lacking validity. Compared to an analysis that results in conclusions about the text only, such inferences require an additional 'leap'; and this leap in turn needs additional substantiation (Groeben & Rustemeyer, 1994; Lisch & Kriz, 1978; Ritsert, 1972). Krippendorff (2004, Chapter 3) combines both positions.

KEY POINT

If you use QCA to make inferences about the communication situation, the communicator, or the recipients, this involves a 'leap' beyond the analysis. Additional substantiation of these conclusions is needed.

I will assume here that it is perfectly justified to conduct a QCA that focuses on simply describing your material. In fact, such a QCA is much easier to validate because it does not require any inferences beyond the text (Rustemeyer, 1992). Before describing how this is done, I would like to show you some of the pitfalls of inferences that go beyond your material.

Inferential 'leaps'

In the following, we will take a closer look at what is involved when making inferences from QCA of textual or visual material to the social situation, the communicator, or the recipients.

If you use texts to draw conclusions about the social situation in which they were produced (if you analyse advertising in order to say something about the position of men and women in society, for instance), this will often be justified and involves the smallest inferential 'leap'.

Nevertheless your material does not automatically reflect the social situation. In repressive societies, censorship may prevent the public expression of values and opinions of large parts of the population. Or a value change may have taken place in society, but there may be a delay until it 'translates' into public documents. If you analysed newspaper content or advertisements while the value change was taking place, chances are that your material would not yet reflect this change. You would conclude that there is no value change, but you would be mistaken: your inference from your analysis of the material to the social situation would not be valid. Texts and visual material often do reflect the social situation in which they were produced, but they do not do so automatically. If you want to make inferences from the material to the social situation, you have to say why you believe that this is justified.

─ Example of a QCA concerned with inferences to the social situation ─

In her QCA of advertising for various types of alcoholic beverages in Italy, Beccaria (2001) was especially interested in the relationship between the representations in the advertisements and the consumption patterns in Italian society. Beccaria stressed the dual role of advertising in both reflecting and shaping social values. To explore this relationship, she compared the results of her analysis with statistics about consumption patterns. This comparison showed that advertising indeed mirrored some of these patterns, such as the increasing consumption of alcoholic beverages by women, but did not reflect others, such as the integration of alcohol consumption into everyday life. In this way, Beccaria cross-checked the validity of her results, using statistics about consumption patterns as an indicator, and did not jump to conclusions about Italian society based on her analysis of commercials.

Matters become even more difficult if you want to say something about the communicator, her intentions, motives, state of mind, or personality, based on what she has said or written. For any number of reasons, people may choose to make their intentions less than clear. Moreover, in order to infer a speaker's intentions, you need much background and contextual knowledge about what counts as the 'normal' and 'standard' way of communicating in that situation; otherwise you are likely to commit all kinds of errors, mistaking direct meaning for indirect, and vice versa. Also, people differ widely in their ways of expressing themselves. Speaking in a loud voice and making wild gestures may be a sign of inner turmoil in one person; with another person, this may just be her normal way of speaking. Therefore, if you want to make inferences about the communicator, QCA is not enough. You will have to provide additional evidence showing that the content that you have identified is indeed a valid indicator of the state of mind that you are inferring. This is called external validation.

─────── KEY POINT ───────

Drawing conclusions from the material you have analysed to the communicator requires additional external validation.

Example of an external validation of QCA-based
─ inferences about communicator motives ─

The Thematic Apperception Test is a psychological test that aims to find out about the motives that drive a person: motive to be in the company of others (affiliation), to be successful, to have power over others, etc. (see Chapter 1). In the test, persons are presented with a series of images and are asked to tell the story behind each image. David McClelland, John Atkinson, David Winter and other collaborators have developed several coding frames, one for each motive (overview in Smith, 2008). The stories participants tell are content-analysed using these coding frames. On this basis the researchers draw conclusions about the strength of each motive in that person. In this case, the conclusions are justified: Each of the coding frames has been validated through additional research. Winter (2008a; 2008b) was able to show, for instance, that persons with a high frequency of power-related imagery (identified through the coding frame) frequently held positions of power in society and showed other signs that were typically connected with wanting to have power over others. The researchers carried out this external validation for all the coding frames they had developed.

If you want to draw conclusions about the effects of the material you have analysed on recipients, this requires the biggest leap and entails the greatest dangers concerning validity. It means that you want to say something about how others have understood the material you are analysing. But to understand texts or images is invariably a constructive process (see Chapter 1): recipients construe meaning by bringing together the information they have extracted from the text with what they already know about the topic. An expert on respiratory disease will extract very different information from the latest article on advances in the treatment of asthma published in a medical journal, for instance, than someone without a medical background who has just been diagnosed with asthma and is now trying to put together some information about treatment options. It is simply not possible to say how someone else will understand a given text by analysing that text. The only way to find out how others understand textual or visual material is to ask them about it, i.e. to conduct a reception study.

KEY POINT

It is not possible to say how others understand a text by doing a QCA of this text. Such conclusions require an additional reception study.

Example of a reception study to test QCA-based conclusions about recipients

Marlange and Vorderer (1987), in their study of the narrative about Mowgli, first conducted a QCA of the text, in order to identify escapist versus realist content. They showed that the narrative can indeed be described as escapist in certain respects. On the basis of these results they then constructed a questionnaire, turning the categories they had used into questionnaire items, and used these to assess readers' expectations and gratifications concerning the text. They were able to show that readers did not simply take the text at face value, but that their reading entailed a complex process of taking up some of the potential for escape that was present in the text, while rejecting and critically reflecting upon other aspects.

In this way, the scope of the inferences that you might want to make in QCA increases from a QCA focusing on the communication content itself, where little inference is required, to an analysis where you aim to draw conclusions about the situation in which the content was produced, to an analysis that is designed to uncover the intentions of the communicator, to an analysis about the effects on the recipient (Rustemeyer, 1992, Section 7.1). In focusing on a description of the material, achieving validity is quite straightforward, and it is this type of validity that we will look at in the following sections. External validation that goes beyond QCA (see the examples above) will not be covered here.

The exception to the rule

The distinction between these different kinds of inferences was largely developed in the context of quantitative research. But if you use QCA on the data collected in a qualitative study, it becomes increasingly difficult to uphold these distinctions. Here, the description of your material may coincide with a description of the inner state of the communicators or even of the ways in which the recipients have understood a given text. This is because in qualitative research, you will collect data from the communicators or from the recipients, and this data is your material.

Example of a conflation of material, communicators, and recipients in qualitative research

In her reception study, Odağ (2007) collected written protocols by readers about their reading experience in order to compare the effects of four texts which varied in terms of fictionality (fiction/non-fiction) and focus (inner world of the characters/external world). In conducting a QCA of the protocols, she was concerned with describing her material. This analysis of the material coincided with an analysis of the experience of the communicators. Moreover, the communicators in this case were identical to the recipients of the four texts. In this way, her QCA of the reading protocols simultaneously yielded a description of the material (i.e.

> the interviews – not the narrative texts), of the opinions of the communicators (i.e. the interviewees – not the authors of the narrative texts), and the effects of the texts on the readers.

If your material itself contains a description of the social situation, the inner state of the communicators, or the experience of the recipients, you simply have to make sure that your categories adequately capture what is in your material. In this case, no additional steps of validation are required.

Assessing the validity of coding frames

In the following, we will look at different types of validity. We will then focus on two of these which are especially important in QCA and will discuss how to assess the validity of inductive and of deductive coding frames.

Types of validity

Four types of validity are commonly distinguished in the literature: face, content, criterion, and construct validity (see Neuendorf, 2002, pp. 114ff.). *Face validity* refers to the extent to which your instrument gives the impression of measuring what it is supposed to measure; Neuendorf (2002, p. 115) aptly describes it as 'WYSIWYG (what you see is what you get)' validity. *Content validity* is assumed to be present to the extent that an instrument covers all dimensions of a concept.

Whereas face and content validity concern only the relationship between a concept and an instrument, criterion and construct validity involve additional measures and, in the case of construct validity, additional concepts. You establish *criterion validity* by determining the relationship between your instrument and another indicator of the concept in question whose validity has already been established.

─────────── **Example of assessing criterion validity** ───────────

Marlange and Vorderer (1987) showed that their QCA of *Mowgli* had only low criterion validity as an indicator of reader expectations and gratifications. They did this by comparing the results of their analysis of the literary text with readers' descriptions of their expectations and gratifications in a survey.

Construct validity is even more complex. Here you take into consideration the relationship between the concept under study and other concepts. You derive hypotheses about the relationships between the indicators of these constructs from a theory and test them.

Criterion and construct validity are only important if you want to validate inferences that go beyond the description of your material. If you want to validate a coding frame that simply describes your material, you will primarily be concerned with face validity (in dealing with inductive coding frames) and with content validity (in dealing with deductive coding frames). Because of this, criterion and construct validity will not be discussed any further.

KEY POINT

Four types of validity are distinguished: face, content, criterion, and construct validity. If you use QCA to describe your material, you need only be concerned with face and content validity.

Assessing the validity of data-driven coding frames

Face validity may seem almost too simplistic at first sight, but it is actually a very helpful concept, especially if you are developing your categories from the data. When you do this, you want to provide an exact description of your material – and this is exactly what face validity is all about.

KEY POINT

To assess the validity of data-driven coding frames, face validity is most useful.

To assess the face validity of your data-driven coding frame, you can use the results of your pilot coding. You should start by looking at your residual category or categories. If you have assigned many segments to your residual categories, this is typically a bad sign. If you are unable to describe a considerable part of your material in terms of your substantive categories, but have to assign them to the residual category, this shows that your substantive categories are not able to capture the meaning of these segments. And, by definition, if the categories of your coding frame do not cover the meaning of your material, your frame has low face validity. Frequent use of the residual category or categories therefore indicates low face validity. If this happens, you should take a closer look at the segments that you assigned to the residual category. List them, try to determine what they have in common, and create some additional substantive categories.

To assess the face validity of your data-driven coding frame, you should also look at each main category and how the segments are distributed across the subcategories. If you have assigned the majority of segments to one subcategory over and above the other subcategories, this is often a sign that your coding frame is not sufficiently differentiated. Often, that one subcategory that you have used much more often than the others summarises several considerations at a fairly abstract level. Because of this, this subcategory would not describe the material in sufficient detail. High coding frequencies for one subcategory compared to the other available subcategories can therefore act as yet another indicator of low face validity. If this happens, it is worth examining your material for additional differentiations within that one subcategory. If you are able to divide that subcategory into further subcategories, this will add to the validity of your coding frame.

— Example of a QCA with high coding frequency for one subcategory —

In Skorek's (2008) QCA of the working and non-working roles in which men and women are portrayed in contemporary advertising, it turned out that both men and women were far more frequently shown in a decorative than in any other role (although this applied to women even more than to men). The subcategory *decorative role* was underdifferentiated by comparison to the other subcategories (*working*, *family*, and *recreational roles*). A closer look at the advertisements coded under this subcategory showed that the advertisements differed in terms of the symbolism used. This would have been an interesting differentiation to make. But she did not pursue this idea any further because the coding frame was in fact not purely data-driven, and one of her goals was to compare her results with those of other, previous studies (see below).

A final consideration in assessing the validity of your data-driven coding frame concerns its level of abstraction. QCA summarises and reduces your material, and by categorising your material, you will invariably lose some individual information – but if your categories are too abstract and you lose too much information, your coding frame will not have sufficient face validity. This consideration is closely related to the question of how many main and subcategories you should create in the first place (see Chapter 4). There are no clear criteria for assessing face validity in this respect. But as a rule of thumb you should ask yourself whether your coding frame justifies the effort you have made in conducting your research. If your coding frame gives you results that you would also have obtained using a much less time-consuming quantitative procedure, your coding frame is probably underdifferentiated and low on face validity. If this is the case, you should have another look at your material, search for those aspects that are not yet covered by your coding frame, and generate additional main and subcategories. If you find it difficult to see such additional aspects, it would be a good idea to go through your material together with someone else and brainstorm for ideas.

—————— **Example of an underdifferentiated coding frame** ——————

If, in assessing interviewees' opinions concerning the case of Terri Schiavo, we had classified only their opinion and stopped there, our coding frame would have had low face validity. By reducing participants' complex considerations of the case to a simple classification into *morally justified, long overdue, morally wrong, refusal to take any decision, unclear*, we would have carried abstraction too far. And we would have obtained the same results with much less effort by simply asking participants to indicate their opinion on a five-point Likert scale.

In other words, these three signs can help you identify low face validity in data-driven coding frames: high coding frequency for residual categories, high coding frequency for one subcategory compared to the other subcategories on that dimension, and high level of abstraction. But these three signs are not equally 'foolproof'. The one sign that is clear and unambiguous (when dealing with data-driven coding frames!) is a high coding frequency for your residual categories. If this emerges from your pilot coding, the face validity of your coding frame is almost invariably too low.

===================== **KEY POINT** =====================

The following are telltale signs of low face validity for data-driven coding frames: high coding frequencies for residual categories; high coding frequencies for one subcategory compared to the other subcategories on a given dimension; and underdifferentiated abstract categories.

But this is not necessarily the case if one subcategory is used more frequently than the other subcategories on this dimension. High coding frequencies for one subcategory may simply reflect a corresponding distribution of themes in your material. This would be an empirical finding, not a reason to change your instrument.

Example of high coding frequency for one subcategory
—————— **that does not reflect low validity** ——————

In our prioritising study, more than 60% of the participants were classified as believing that turning off the life support for Terri Schiavo was morally justified. That is to say, the coding frequency for this subcategory was much higher than for any of the other subcategories on the dimension *Opinion concerning the case of Terri Schiavo.* Nevertheless, this category is not underdifferentiated: the high coding frequency for the subcategory simply reflects that the majority of our participants believed that turning off the life support was the right thing to do. Moreover, we did not just look at the participants' opinion in isolation. Instead, we examined their opinions together with the reasons they gave, the way they arrived at their decision, and their opinions on the other cases and scenarios we presented them with.

When you are assessing the face validity of your coding frame, you should therefore look at all your categories and how they fit together, not just at individual categories in isolation. This also applies to the problem of abstract categories. As the previous example shows, a high level of abstraction in one category need not be a problem if the category is combined with other, more concrete categories.

Assessing the validity of concept-driven coding frames

Typically, you will make use of concept-driven categories when you already have certain concepts in mind and want to find out whether there is any evidence of these concepts in your material. With this kind of research question, your coding frame is valid to the extent that your categories adequately capture these concepts. The type of validity that relates to the adequate representation of a concept in a research instrument is content validity. In evaluating the validity of concept-driven coding frames, you should therefore make use of content validity.

KEY POINT

To assess the validity of concept-driven coding frames, content validity is most useful.

In QCA, a good way to assess content validity is by expert evaluation. That is to say, you should have someone look at your coding frame who is familiar with the concepts on which the frame is based. If such an expert is of the opinion that your categories adequately represent these concepts, you can consider your coding frame to be sufficiently valid.

Some authors have suggested that the validity of your coding frame is also related to the consistency of your coding, i.e. to reliability (Früh, 2007, Part II, Chapter 1; Lissmann, 2008, Chapter 7). They assume that the researcher herself is the best expert. To assess content validity, they suggest calculating the agreement between the researcher and another coder. In this way, content validity is assumed to coincide with reliability if you yourself act as one of the coders – which will usually be the case in qualitative research.

If you are constructing a data-driven coding frame, high coding frequency for one subcategory compared to other subcategories on the same dimension may indicate low validity (see the previous section). In dealing with concept-driven coding frames and content validity, the situation is different. Because your subcategories are created on a conceptual basis, and because you are concerned with the presence of these concepts in your material, you should not change your categories from a conceptual point of view, regardless of the distribution of the coding frequencies.

Example of acceptable high coding frequencies for selected subcategories

In her analysis of gender role portrayals in magazine advertisements, Skorek (2008; Skorek & Schreier, 2009) used one set of categories that goes back to Goffman's (1979) analysis of dominance in the presentation of couples in advertising. Goffman had at the time distinguished between men being shown as dominating over women and women being shown as dominating over men; other researchers had in the meantime added a third category that captures the genders being depicted as equals (Klassen, Jasper & Schwartz, 1993). Skorek wanted to conduct a comparison over time, comparing her findings to those of earlier studies. The results showed that presentation of the genders as equal was by far the most frequent type of dominance role found in the material. Because these three types of dominance portrayals were exactly the ones she wanted to distinguish from a conceptual point of view, she evaluated these findings with a view to content validity, not face validity. From this perspective, she did not consider the results a sign of low validity, and she did not differentiate the equality subcategory any further.

SUMMARY

In addition to being reliable, coding frames should be valid, i.e. the categories should adequately represent the concepts in your study. This is easier to achieve for manifest than for latent meaning which is less standardised and less direct, but a valid QCA of latent meaning is perfectly possible. It is also easier to achieve if your QCA is limited to describing your material. Conclusions from the material to the situation in which it was produced, the communicator, or the effects on the recipients require bigger and bigger 'leaps' and therefore additional steps of external validation that go beyond QCA. In assessing the validity of data-driven coding frames, face validity should be used. High coding frequencies for the residual categories, disproportionally high coding frequencies for one subcategory compared to other subcategories on one dimension, and disproportionally abstract, reductive categories are signs of low face validity. In assessing the validity of concept-driven coding frames, content validity should be used. This can involve the assessment of the coding frame by an expert or a comparison of your coding with that of another coder.

Frequently asked questions

Why does QCA still make use of positivist constructs like reliability and validity?

Reliability and validity are rooted in a quantitative, positivist conception of research. While introducing QCA as a qualitative research method, I continue to use these terms for two reasons. In the first place, there is no clear dividing line between QCA and quantitative content analysis (see Chapter 2). They are closely related, they are often discussed together in the literature, and in this context the terms 'reliability' and 'validity' continue to be used. To switch to a different terminology would be to cut QCA off from this tradition and these discussions. Second, there is no obvious alternative. Within the qualitative research community, different positions can be found concerning quality criteria. Although suggestions have been made for alternative, qualitative quality criteria, such as credibility, trustworthiness, auditability, or authenticity, qualitative researchers do not agree on a single set of criteria and sometimes use the names of these alternative criteria to refer to different concepts (see the overview in Seale, 1999, Chapter 4; Steinke, 2004). Because of this, adopting any of these at the expense of others seems arbitrary and might be confusing, especially to someone just starting to use QCA.

Which should I use in assessing reliability: inter- or intra-coder reliability?

The idea underlying reliability is to show that you have applied your coding frame to the material in a consistent manner and that your interpretation of the material is systematic and reasoned and does not just occur on the spur of the moment. Keeping this in mind, inter-coder reliability is the stronger measure, because two persons differ more with respect to the background that they bring to the understanding of the material than does one person at two different points in time. If possible, inter-coder reliability should therefore be used.

Are there no situations where intra-coder reliability would be preferable over inter-coder reliability?

Yes and no. Conceptually speaking, inter-coder reliability is always 'stronger' and therefore preferable, as long as a second suitable coder is available. But if no suitable second coder can be found, intra-coder reliability based on one expert coder is preferable to inter-coder reliability based on the coding of the researcher and a second unsuitable coder (on what is required of a good coder see Krippendorff, 2004, Chapter 7). The suitability of a coder depends on whether s/he is sufficiently familiar with the research topic: this familiarity provides the relevant context that you need to adequately understand and interpret the material. It may be familiarity with a specific life world (what it is like to work for a particular company, according to what internal rules does the company operate, etc.), theoretical knowledge (e.g. about argumentation theory in carrying out a content analysis of functional roles in argumentation), or familiarity with the context of your research.

Which coefficient of agreement should I use?

The simple percentage of agreement is the easiest to calculate. But because it does not take into account chance agreement between coders, it will often *over*estimate actual agreement. From this point of view a chance-corrected coefficient such as kappa is often used and has been implemented in common statistical software, such as SPSS/PASW. But with extensive coding frames (as are typically used in QCA), kappa can yield incorrect results, massively *under*estimating actual reliability (see Neuendorf, 2004, p. 151). Therefore, a simple percentage of agreement will often be sufficient, as long as you guard against overinterpreting high percentages.

How do I know that my coding frame is not reliable or not valid?

Reliability and validity are not absolutes, but a matter of degree. Therefore, coding frames cannot be described as 'reliable' or 'unreliable' (or as 'valid' or 'invalid'), but as (not sufficiently) reliable or valid in this or that respect. Moreover, clear criteria do not exist, and reliability and validity always need to be assessed in the context of your research question, the kind and number of your categories. If you are uncertain whether your coding frame meets the requirements, go and ask for the opinion of another researcher on the frame and the results of the pilot phase.

————————————— **End-of-chapter questions** —————————————

- What is meant by reliability?
- How do you assess the reliability of a coding frame?
- What are the two considerations you should keep in mind when interpreting a coefficient of agreement?
- What is meant by validity?
- Which type of validity should be used in evaluating data-based coding frames, and what are the telltale signs of low validity?
- Which type of validity is most suitable for assessing the validity of concept-based coding frames?

10
THE MAIN ANALYSIS PHASE

Chapter guide

If you have come this far, you have completed all your preparations. You have built your coding frame, tried it out, looked at the reliability and validity of your trial coding, and you have probably modified your coding frame. Now you are all set for the main analysis phase. During this phase, you will have to prepare for the main coding, do the main coding, i.e. apply your coding frame to all your material, compare codes and decide upon the final meaning of your units of coding, and transform your results from the level of the unit of coding to the level of the unit of analysis. In the following, we will look at:

- how to prepare for the main coding;
- the main coding and the steps you have to go through;
- what to do with the codes from the main coding;
- how to prepare your results for presentation or further analysis.

How to prepare for the main coding

Before you get started on the main coding, a little preparation is necessary: you should give the coders the opportunity to get to know the coding frame, and you must divide your material into units of coding.

Getting to know the coding frame

Before you get started on the main coding, you should have done a pilot coding, trying out your coding frame. If you are working together with other coders, the coders who participated in your pilot phase should be the same as the persons doing the main coding. If so, they will already be familiar with the coding frame. Nevertheless it would be a good idea to have one more phase of getting to know the coding frame. Based on the results of the pilot coding, you probably modified your coding frame: you collapsed separate categories into one, you introduced new categories, perhaps you even changed the structure of your frame. If this is what you did, it is important that you tell other coders about these changes and why you made them.

If you do not do so, the other coders will have the old version of the coding frame in mind when they get started on the main coding. Because of this, they will not be aware of new categories and new coding options. They will not adjust their understanding of categories whose definition you changed. And they will probably code the material the same way as they did before. But this was not the best way of coding – otherwise there would have been no need to modify your coding frame in the first place. In other words, to make sure that all coders really make the best possible use of your modified coding frame, you have to tell them about the changes you made.

If you are working on your own, you obviously do not need to describe the changes you made to anyone else. But it would still be a good idea to take a moment to sit down and go through your revised coding frame.

Dividing the material into units of coding

To make sure that you and any other coders really are working with the same material (and to make sure that you really take all your relevant material into account), you must segment your material before you get started on the actual coding. That is to say, you must divide it into units in such a way that each segment/unit fits into one category of the coding frame. In Chapter 7, we looked in detail at the steps this involves, namely: marking relevant parts of your material; deciding upon your criterion of segmentation; and marking your units of coding.

Once you have reached your main analysis phase, you have already chosen your criterion of segmentation (formal or thematic), i.e. you know how to decide where one unit ends and another one begins. This leaves only the other two steps: you still have to indicate which parts of your material are relevant, and you still have to mark your units of coding within these relevant parts.

KEY POINT

Segmenting your material for the main coding involves only two steps: indicating the relevant parts of your material; and marking the units of coding within these relevant parts.

Indicating which parts of your material are relevant

The main coding usually involves much more material than the pilot phase. Because of this, it is even more important now than it was during the pilot phase that you indicate which parts of your material are relevant to your research question. Otherwise it is all too easy to get lost. Coders can typically keep track of approximately 40 categories (including subcategories) at a time (see Chapter 8). If this is about the size of your coding frame, you now go through one unit of analysis after another, marking those parts that are relevant to your research question.

If your coding frame is larger, it is best to apply only a part of that frame at a time. You can divide this task into the following steps:

- First, go through your units of analysis one after another, marking those parts to which the first part of your coding frame applies.
- Second, go through your units of analysis again, marking those parts to which the second part of your coding frame applies.
- Repeat as many times as there are parts of your coding frame.

If you have conducted interviews or focus groups, your topic guide can help you divide your coding frame into smaller parts.

Example of dividing the coding frame into smaller parts

In our prioritising study, we used our interview guide to divide our very large total coding frame into smaller parts. Each set of interview questions focusing on one topic corresponded to one part of the coding frame. The interview questions that we asked about Terri Schiavo, for instance, corresponded to one such section of the coding frame. In this way, we arrived at 13 sections of the coding frame. Because some topics yielded far more material than others, they also required more categories than others. As a result, the sections of the coding frame differed considerably in size. Some contained only 30 categories or less, while two contained approximately 70 categories. We went through the interviews 13 times, marking the relevant parts for one section of the coding frame at a time.

Marking your units of coding

Once you have identified the relevant parts of your material, you then mark and number your units of coding within each of these. That is to say, you note where each unit ends and the next one begins. In Chapter 7, we distinguished between formal and thematic criteria in identifying units of coding.

If you use a formal criterion, you make use of the inherent structure in your material (such as words, sentences, paragraphs). Because it is clear where each unit ends and the next one begins, you can mark and number the units and do the coding at the same time. Because of this, there is no need to mark and number each unit before doing the coding.

KEY POINT

If you use a formal criterion to identify your units of coding, marking the units and doing the coding can be done in one step. A separate step of marking your units of coding is only necessary if you are using a thematic criterion for identifying these units.

If you are using a thematic criterion in identifying and marking your units of coding, you have two strategies to choose from (see Chapter 7). The first strategy implies that you, as the researcher, mark and number the units. The second strategy is only applicable if you work together with another coder. Here, the material is divided up between you and the other coders; each coder marks and numbers the units in her part of the material. To make sure that you and any other coders conceptualise the themes in a similar way, it is usually a good idea that you all sit down together at the beginning and jointly mark some units of coding (see Chapter 7 for more detail). If you have a lot of material, it is best to repeat this a few times, at regular intervals. This helps you and the other coders keep track of what is meant by a theme in the context of your coding frame. It also prevents you from going off in different directions when marking units of coding. Because the main coding usually involves far more material than the pilot coding, it is even more important during the main coding that you and the other coders agree on what a theme is and cross-check for this at regular intervals.

SUMMARY

Before you get started on the main coding, a little preparation is necessary: you should inform other coders about any changes to the coding frame after the pilot phase and you must divide your material into units of coding. In a first step, this involves indicating which parts of your material are relevant to your research question. If your coding frame contains more than 40 categories, it is best to do this separately for each part of your coding frame. In a second step, you have to identify and mark your units of coding. If you are using a formal criterion to distinguish between units of coding, there is no need to mark the units now; you can do this as you do the main coding. If you are using a thematic criterion, you have to identify and number all units of coding. If you are working together with another coder, it is best that you mark some units together at regular intervals.

Doing the main coding

You are now ready to do the main coding. Because you have reached the phase of your research where you code *all* of your material, it is essential that you use the final version of your coding frame. At this stage, you can no longer make any changes to your frame. If you did, you and the other coders would have to code all your material yet again. This is why it is so important to make your coding frame as good as you can while developing it.

KEY POINT

During the main coding, you can no longer make any changes to your coding frame.

In this section, we will look at how to proceed during the main coding and what to do if you notice any shortcomings in your coding frame at this late stage.

How to proceed

In coding your material, you proceed exactly as described in Chapter 8 for the trial coding. If you are working on your own, you first code and then recode your material after an interval of about 10–14 days. If you are working with another coder, the coders independently of each other assign each unit of coding to one of the categories of your coding frame and enter their choice on a coding sheet (for how to do this using software, see Chapter 12). In this, the coders should not be aware of the codes the others have chosen ('blind' coding).

If you have a lot of material, it may simply not be possible to read and code every single unit of coding twice (if you are working on your own) or to have two persons read and code all the material twice. There are several strategies for how to proceed at this stage:

- *You are working on your own, but have found someone who is willing to help.* If this is mostly your project and you bring in someone else to help you, you will and should do most of the coding yourself. The second person will only code a part of your material. In this, it is less important how much the other person codes; it is more important that she codes all the different kinds of material that you are dealing with (e.g. material from different sources; see Chapters 5 and 8 on the importance of variability). There are no strict rules for how much the second person should code. The more, the better. But even if she codes only two out of a total of 20 interviews, this is much better than nothing and helps you check your own coding against someone else's.
- *You are working in a team.* If there are several of you working on the project, the best strategy is to divide your material into three parts. You will code the first part, the other coder will code the second part, and both of you will code the third part – and then compare your codes. Obviously, no comparison is needed for those parts that were coded by only one of you. If you want to be extra certain that your interpretations are shared by the other person, you might want to skim-read over each other's parts of the material and codes. You can then alert each other to any interpretations where you would strongly disagree.
- *You are working on your own.* If you are working completely on your own, you obviously cannot divide the material between two coders. In this case, you should recode part of it after a time interval of 10–14 days (or longer). Again, there are

no strict rules on how much of your material to recode. But as when you are working with one other coder, recoding some part of your material (however small) is better than not recoding any at all. Likewise, including all the different kinds of your material in your recoding is more important than the amount of recoding as such.

─────── **Example of dividing the material between different coders** ───────

In the prioritising study, we were working in a team. We therefore followed the second strategy, dividing the material into three parts. One part was coded by the first coder, the second part was coded by the second coder, and the third part was coded by both of them independently of each other. In addition, both coders skim-read the parts coded only by the other person and pointed out any passages where their own reading disagreed from the reading of the other coder.

Because the pilot phase usually leads to some changes in the coding frame, the coding frame that you used for your trial coding is typically not identical to the coding frame that you are now using for the main coding. Because it is important that all your material is coded with the final version of the coding frame, you may now have to recode the material from your pilot phase. If you made extensive changes to your frame following the pilot phase, it is best to simply recode all the material from the pilot phase. If you changed only a few selected categories, it may be enough to recode those units of coding on which you used the categories that you changed. If you used additional material for trying out the coding frame, i.e. material that is not part of your main study, you do not need to do any recoding.

What if you do notice shortcomings during the main coding?

Because you should not make any further changes to your coding frame at this stage, it is important that you make your coding frame as good as possible while you are developing it. This is the best way to safeguard against any shortcomings during your main coding. We discussed two ways to improve your coding frame and make it a good fit with your material. The first way is to watch out for any differences, any variation in your material, and to use all the variability there is when developing your coding frame (see Chapter 5). The second way is to make good use of the pilot phase. If the pilot phase showed that you had to change the first version of your coding frame in many ways, it is best to have a second pilot phase before beginning to do the main coding. If you had to make many changes to the first version, chances are that the second version will need some fine tuning. If this is the case, it is better to find out during a second pilot phase – even though this can seem quite time-consuming – than during the main coding when it is too late.

If you are not certain that your coding frame 'works', it is best to run a second pilot phase.

Even if you take all the care you possibly can in building your coding frame, it can nevertheless happen that you notice some shortcomings during the main coding.

If these shortcomings are minor, it is best to remind yourself that there is no such thing as the perfect study or the perfect coding frame. It is important to be aware of such problems and to mention them in the discussion section when evaluating your study, but it is not worth making changes and repeating the entire main coding. If you find, for instance, that the consistency between coders for a few subcategories is actually a little lower for the main coding than for the trial coding, this would be an example of a minor shortcoming.

You may also realise during the main coding that an aspect that was rare in your material when you were building the coding frame now keeps recurring. Because it was rare when you were building the coding frame, you did not create a subcategory to cover it. Because it now keeps recurring, you wish you had created a subcategory. If this concerns only two or three subcategories, it also qualifies as a minor shortcoming. It is a pity that you are now not able to analyse this more systematically, but you can always include it in a follow-up study.

Example of a minor shortcoming of the coding frame

In our prioritising study, we presented the participants with a scenario involving two patients who were both in need of heart surgery. The first patient was responsible for a large number of employees, whereas the second patient nursed his wife who was also very ill. The participants were asked to decide which of the two patients should have surgery performed. Those who argued that the second patient should be preferred frequently did so by referring to his responsibility towards his wife. We included this as one subcategory in our coding frame. During the main coding it became apparent that participants mentioned his responsibility towards his wife in different contexts. Some argued that he should be enabled to continue nursing his wife, because otherwise the state would have to pay for in-home care. Others argued that his wife was dependent on him. These different contexts were not represented in our coding frame. Nevertheless we decided that this was a comparatively minor point that did not justify redoing the main coding. We simply took note of it and will, in a future study, look more closely at the values that underlie the choices participants make and the reasons they give for these choices.

It can also happen that you become aware of major shortcomings during or following the main coding. If this happens, you may indeed have to make more changes to your coding frame and to redo the main coding. What you intended to be the main coding would then turn into a second trial coding. This would be the case if the consistency between the coders was too low to be acceptable or if a number of relevant aspects in the material were not covered by your coding frame.

KEY POINT

If you change your coding frame during the main coding, the main coding becomes your second trial coding. When you have made all the changes that are needed to your coding frame, you have to start again on the main coding.

But even in this case other solutions exist. If the consistency between coders is too low, one option is to simply continue with your study – but without reporting any results for the categories with low consistency. If the inconsistencies occur because decision rules between two subcategories are still not sufficiently specific, you can decide together with the other coders what to do about such cases when you are comparing codes (see below).

If you find new aspects in your material that are not covered by your coding frame, you can assign these units of coding to the residual subcategories. Following the main coding, you can return to these units, determine what they have in common, and report this with your other results. While this is not a proper QCA, at least it allows you to make use of this information and to present it to your readers.

SUMMARY

For the main coding, you have to use the final version of your coding frame. It is not necessary to code every unit in your material twice, but part of your material should be double-coded by two different persons or at two points in time. If you are working in a team, you should double-code one third of your material. In all other situations, you should make sure that different parts of your material are coded twice. You also have to recode material from the pilot phase at this stage. If you notice minor shortcomings of your coding frame during the main coding, there is no need to change your coding frame. If you notice major shortcomings, you may have to make additional changes to your frame. In this case, the main coding becomes a second trial coding and you have to repeat your main coding based on the revised final version of your frame.

Comparing codes and follow-up discussion

As a result of the main coding, you want to be able to describe the meaning of your material in all those respects that interest you, i.e. on all those dimensions that you have identified and around which you have built your coding frame. To do so, you have to determine the meaning of each unit of coding *vis-à-vis* your coding frame. The first important step in this is the main coding; this you have already done, and this provides you with the meaning of those units that were coded only once. The meaning of these units is identical to the (sub)category to which they were assigned. But a certain part of your material should have been double-coded (by yourself or by another coder). To determine the meaning of these units, you have to compare the two codes, and if they differ, you have to make a decision between them. This is an important point in which the main analysis differs from the pilot phase.

KEY POINT

Following the main coding, you have to compare the codes for those units that were double-coded. If the codes differ, you have to decide between them.

In the following, we will look at the comparison process and at the situations that may come up when determining the meaning of a unit of coding.

Comparing codes

Why it is important to compare codes during the main analysis phase

You are already familiar with the process of comparing codes from the pilot phase. In the pilot phase, this comparison serves one main purpose: to help you identify shortcomings of your coding frame and misunderstandings on the part of any other coders. Because you are now working with the final version of your coding frame that should not be changed any further, you are no longer concerned with identifying such sources of error (at least this is no longer your primary concern). Comparing codes is still an important step, but it serves different purposes:

- If you are using summary measures of coding consistency (such as percentage of agreement or kappa), it would be a good idea to calculate these again following the main coding. They provide information about the quality of your coding frame.

- You must first compare codes in order to identify those units that were coded differently by different coders or by yourself at different times. This is an important step in preparing the following discussion between you and any other coders (if any other coders are involved) and for deciding on the meaning of these units.

KEY POINT

During the main analysis phase, comparing codes serves a double purpose: first, summary measures help you with reporting the quality of your coding frame; second, you have to compare in order to identify units that were coded differently.

Obviously, you can only compare codes for those parts of your material that were coded by two persons or by yourself at different points in time. For those parts of the material that were coded only by yourself and only once, you can skip this step and continue with preparing your results for presentation (see below).

Preparing for the comparison

To prepare for the comparison of codes, you start out as you did following the trial coding. You again create a comparison coding sheet for each dimension of your coding frame, where each line corresponds to one unit of coding (see Chapter 8 for details). But there is one important difference between the comparison coding sheet for the trial and for the main coding. The sheet for the trial coding contains only two columns, one for each coder or point in time. The sheet for the main coding should contain *three* columns: one for each coder or point in time, and one for the final code assigned to any unit of coding. In other words, following the main coding, it is not enough to simply note which codes were used by the different coders or at different points in time. The main coding always ends with deciding on one code, even if (especially if) a given unit has been coded differently, and you have to leave some space for this on the comparison coding sheet (see Table 10.1). To prepare for this, it would be a good idea to mark all those units of coding that were coded differently (see unit 2.1 in Table 10.1).

Reporting the quality of your coding frame

As during the pilot phase, there are different options for what to do with the information you have now recorded. One option is to calculate a measure of coding consistency, such as percentage of agreement or kappa (see Chapter 8 on the advantages and disadvantages). If you do so, you should again calculate such a measure for each dimension in your coding frame and one measure across all dimensions. These measures can be especially useful for comparing

Table 10.1 Comparative coding sheet for dimension 1

Unit no.	First code	Second code	Final code
1.1	1.3	1.3	
1.2	1.5	1.5	
...	...	...	
2.1	1.3	1.7	
...	...	...	
3.1	1.5	1.5	
...	...		
n.n	...	...	

the trial with the main coding. Because the pilot phase helped you identify shortcomings and you changed your coding frame accordingly, coding consistency should be higher for the main than for the trial coding. By reporting this, you demonstrate that the quality of your coding frame has improved. In addition, the information on the comparative coding sheet serves as a starting point for determining the final meaning of your units of coding (see below).

Example of comparing coding consistency for the trial and the main coding

In the prioritising study, we calculated the percentage of agreement as a measure of coding consistency within each dimension and across all subcategories and dimensions, both following the trial and the main coding. The percentage of agreement across all subcategories was 73.9% following the trial coding and 83.7% following the main coding. The percentage of agreement across the dimensions was 87.1% following the trial and 96.6% following the main coding. This shows that we had indeed managed to improve our coding frame following the pilot phase.

Alternatively, if you did not calculate any measures of agreement during the pilot phase, you need not calculate any such measures following the main coding either. In this case, the information on the comparative coding sheet only serves as your starting point for determining the final meaning of your units of coding.

Deciding on the final meaning of your units of coding

The purpose of the main coding is to decide on the meaning of each of your units of coding with respect to the dimensions in your coding frame. This is easy

Table 10.2 Comparative coding sheet for dimension 1, including final codes

Unit no.	First code	Second code	Final code
1.1	1.3	1.3	1.3
1.2	1.5	1.5	1.5
...	...	...	
2.1	1.3	1.7	
...	...	...	
3.1	1.5	1.5	1.5
...	...		
n.n	...	...	

whenever the codes assigned to a unit of coding coincide across coders or points in time. In this case you simply enter that code into the third column of your comparative coding sheet (see Table 10.2). The same applies to all units that were coded only once (by one out of two coders or by you at one point of time): this is the final meaning, and you simply enter it into the third column.

If a unit was coded twice and the codes do not coincide, matters are more complicated, and there are different ways of proceeding. Whichever way you choose, you should again (as you did following the trial coding) sit down with any other coders and talk about the reasons why you assigned that particular code to that particular unit of coding. This may result in the following situations:

- As after the trial coding, it may turn out that one of the coders has made a mistake. If this is the case, you will easily be able to agree on one 'correct' meaning, and this should be entered into the third column.
- It may also be the case that both coders had good reasons for interpreting the unit in a particular way. But perhaps one coder is able to convince the other of her reasons. Again you can agree on one meaning, and this should be entered into the sheet.
- It may turn out that the decision rule between two subcategories was not clear. In this case, you can introduce a decision rule during the discussion phase. That is to say, you and the other coder can agree to always assign doubtful cases to one of the two subcategories. In this way you can resolve all disagreements relating to these two subcategories in a consistent way.
- Finally – and this is the most difficult situation – both coders may have had good reasons for interpreting the unit in a particular way, and both reasons may be equally valid. In this case, the coders cannot agree on a final meaning.

━━━━━━━━━━━━━━━━━━━━━━━ **KEY POINT** ━━━━━━━━━━━━━━━━━━━━━━━

If the decision rule between two subcategories was not clear during the coding, you can introduce a clearer decision rule after the coding to resolve any disagreements between the coders.

No standard solution exists if the coders cannot agree on a final meaning. There are different ways of handling this situation:

- You simply disregard this unit of coding. You do not enter anything into the coding sheet, and you do not include it when reporting your results. This is OK if you do it occasionally. But if you do it more often, you lose a lot of information.
- You take turns between the interpretations of the two coders. The first time this happens, you enter the first coder's interpretation as the final meaning; the second time it happens, you enter the second coder's interpretation; the third time, you again take the first coder's interpretation, and so on. This is a little arbitrary, but at least you preserve some of the coding information.
- You bring in a third person, ideally someone with some expertise on your research topic. You decide on the interpretation that is favoured by the third person. In quantitative content analysis, researchers sometimes work with three coders from the start. Typically, two of them will agree on an interpretation. In this case, the code that was chosen by the majority of coders is also chosen as the final meaning. But bringing in three coders is difficult to realise in QCA. Bringing in a third person where two coders disagree is usually more feasible and is a good way of dealing with disagreement between two coders.
- You make a distinction between the coders, valuing one opinion over another. This makes sense if you have good reasons for doing so. You might argue, for instance, that you as the person who conducted the research and developed the coding frame are a better judge than someone who only helps with the coding. Or else you might argue that a person who conducted interviews has more background information and therefore an advantage over someone who only reads the material, but was not present during data collection. This is a good solution if you really have grounds for valuing one opinion over another.

KEY POINT

If two coders cannot agree on the meaning of a passage, you can resolve the disagreement by bringing in a third person with some knowledge about the research topic.

Example of resolving disagreement between two coders

In the prioritising study, we were working in a large team. In this situation, it was easy to bring in a third person if the two coders could not agree on the meaning of a unit of coding. Usually, this was another research associate who had also been involved in conducting the interviews.

In this way, you should try to achieve consensus among the coders if their codes differ. If this is not possible, you should adopt one of the above suggestions in order to arrive at a final meaning for each unit of coding. If you are working on your own and coded a unit differently at two points in time, you should try to reconstruct your reasons for each code and decide on one of them. If both codes seem equally valid, perhaps you can bring in another person at this stage, asking her to cross-check those units about which you are uncertain.

You are done with this step once you have filled in the third column for all units of coding and all dimensions.

SUMMARY

Following the main coding, you must compare the codes for those units of coding that were double-coded. This is a necessary step in order to identify units that were coded differently. If you are using a measure of consistency to summarise your comparison, this also provides information about the quality of your coding frame. To prepare for the comparison, you create a comparative coding sheet containing three columns. Into the third column you enter the final meaning of that unit of coding. This is obvious where the two codes coincide. If they do not, the unit must be discussed by the coders. They should each give their reasons for interpreting the unit in a particular way and should try to achieve consensus. If this is not possible, a number of strategies exist for handling the situation, such as bringing in a third person with some expertise on the research topic.

Preparing your results

At this point, you are done with your QCA in the narrow sense. But you may not yet be able to answer your research question. The reason is that your comparative coding sheet gives you the final meaning of each unit of *coding* – but research questions usually relate to units of *analysis*. Units of coding and units of analysis typically differ in size (see Chapter 7), and each unit of analysis usually contains several units of coding. If your units of analysis are identical to your units of coding, no further preparation of your results is needed. But if your units of analysis are larger than your units of coding, you have to transform your results on to the level of your units of analysis before you can present them or write them up.

KEY POINT

If your units of analysis are larger than your units of coding, you have to transform your results to the level of the units of analysis in order to answer your research question.

—Example of a study where units of analysis and of coding coincide—

In her analysis of Italian alcohol advertising, Beccaria (2001) examined 41 television advertisements. These served as her units of analysis and her units of coding, i.e. the units of analysis and of coding were identical in this study. Beccaria recorded for each advertisement what kind of alcohol was consumed, in what kind of environment, by whom, and what the underlying values were. Because the units of analysis and coding were identical, she merely had to record the final code for each unit of coding on each dimension. This provided her with the information about the type of alcohol, the persons consuming it, and so on, for each of the advertisements. She could answer her research question based on the coding alone, and there was no need to transform the results.

Example of a study where units of coding have to be
———————— transformed to the level of units of analysis ————————

In our prioritising study, we were interested in the decisions and underlying criteria of our interviewees. Each interview constituted one unit of analysis, and each of these contained hundreds of units of coding. To answer our research question, we therefore had to transform our results from the level of the units of coding to the level of the units of analysis.

Transforming your results from one level to another involves two steps:

- creating a matrix across the dimensions of your coding frame;
- integrating information about the repeated use of codes into the matrix.

Creating a matrix

You have already created your comparative coding sheets as matrices. In the comparative coding sheets, each line corresponds to a unit of coding, and each column corresponds to one coding (by one coder, at one point in time, or the final meaning). Depending on how many dimensions there are in your coding frame, you have probably created several such comparative coding sheets (see Table 10.2).

In the data matrix that you will now create, you will bring together all these coding sheets. Here, each line of the matrix corresponds to one unit of analysis, and the columns correspond to the categories of your coding frame. Your data matrix will have as many lines as there are units of analysis in your study, and it will have (at least) as many columns as there are dimensions in your coding frame. How exactly you set up the columns of this matrix depends on the structure of your coding frame. More specifically, it depends on whether you can code only one subcategory on a given dimension for each unit of analysis or more than one subcategory.

KEY POINT

The set-up of your data matrix will be different for dimensions where you can only code one subcategory per unit of analysis and dimensions where it is possible to code more than one subcategory.

If you can code only one subcategory for a given dimension, you typically create one column to represent this dimension. Into the cells of this column you enter, for each unit of analysis, the name or number of the subcategory that you coded for this dimension. At this stage, you enter only the final code. If you want to use an analogy taken from quantitative research, you may want to think of your dimensions as variables and of your subcategories as the possible values of these variables (see Chapter 4). The column in your data matrix that represents a given dimension contains the values of this variable for each of your units of analysis.

Example of a dimension where only one subcategory can be coded per unit of analysis

The coding frame for the case of Terri Schiavo contained, among others, the dimension whether the participants considered terminating Terri Schiavo's life support to have been morally right or wrong. For each interviewee (unit of analysis), only one subcategory could be coded (*morally justified, long overdue, morally wrong, refusal to take any decision, unclear*). For instance, a participant could not refuse to take any decision and at the same time consider it morally justified that her life support had been terminated. Because of this, the dimension was represented in our data matrix by a single column. Here we entered for each participant (unit of analysis) the final code representing her opinion on this issue.

If more than one subcategory on a given dimension can be coded for one unit of analysis (but for different units of coding within this one unit of analysis), it is best to set up your data matrix in such a way that each column represents a *sub*category within this dimension. In your data matrix you record whether the subcategory was coded for a given unit of analysis or not.

Example of a dimension where several subcategories ———————— can be coded for each unit of analysis ————————

Another dimension in our coding frame for the case of Terri Schiavo concerned the reasons why participants considered it justified that Terri Schiavo's life support had been terminated. Altogether 11 reasons were distinguished as subcategories. We had chosen our units of coding in such a way that exactly one subcategory could be coded per unit. But throughout the interview, an interviewee could of course mention several reasons why she considered it justified that Terri Schiavo's life support had been terminated. A participant might say, for instance, that Terri Schiavo might not have wanted to be kept alive like this (*right to die*), that it was terrible for her relatives to see her like this (*burden on her relatives*), and that she was unlikely to ever regain consciousness, considering how long she had already been in a coma (*duration of her comatose state*). We therefore represented each subcategory, i.e. each reason, by a separate column in our data matrix. Altogether, the dimension was represented by 11 columns. For each reason we entered whether a participant had or had not mentioned this reason.

When creating your data matrix, you simply add columns as needed. Most coding frames will contain some categories where only one subcategory can be coded per unit of analysis and other categories where several subcategories can be coded. Because of this, your matrix will most likely contain some columns that represent an entire dimension and other columns that represent subcategories. It is all the more important that you label the columns in your matrix accordingly and clearly (see Table 10.3 for an example).

The information in the column labels and the cells of the data matrix can be entered using names (as in Table 10.3). But if you are dealing with a lot of material and a large coding frame, this can quickly become cumbersome. Alternatively, you can use numbers to identify the categories and subcategories. The information whether a certain subcategory was coded or not can be represented as '0' (was not coded) and '1' (was coded). Table 10.4 shows how the information in Table 10.3 can be represented in this format.

Integrating information about the repeated use of codes

As you are creating your data matrix, you will again be confronted with the fact that you may have coded some subcategories more than once for the same unit of analysis. If you followed my earlier suggestion (see Chapter 8), you assigned each unit of coding to a subcategory, regardless whether this was a second, or third (and so on) coding of that subcategory for that case. If this is important information in the context of your research – because you take

Table 10.3 Partial data matrix for the case of Terri Schiavo

Interviewee no.	Opinion	Relatives	Duration	Costs	Burden	Machines	Quality of life	Right to die	No change	Suffering	Organ donation	Miscellaneous reasons pro
1	justified	yes	yes	no	yes	no	no	no	no	no	no	yes
2	overdue	no	yes	no	no	yes	yes	yes	yes	yes	no	no
3	wrong	no	no	no	no	no	no	no	no	no	no	no
4												
⋯												
N												

Table 10.4 Partial data matrix for the case of Terri Schiavo, numerical form

Interviewee no.	C1	C2.1	C2.2	C2.3	C2.4	C2.5	C2.6	C2.7	C2.8	C2.9	C2.10	C2.11
1	1	1	1	0	1	0	0	0	0	0	0	1
2	2	0	1	0	0	1	1	1	1	1	0	0
3	3	0	0	0	0	0	0	0	0	0	0	0
4												
...												
N												

repetition to indicate a stronger opinion, for instance – you have to include this information in the data matrix you are creating. In this case, your data matrix will contain coding frequencies, i.e. information on how many times a category or subcategory was used for each unit of analysis.

KEY POINT

If information about coding frequencies is necessary to answer your research question, you have to include this information in your data matrix.

This is easy when you are dealing with dimensions where more than one subcategory can be coded. In this case, each column in your data matrix represents one such subcategory. As you create your data matrix, you go through one case after another, and you increase the count for each subcategory by 1 whenever this subcategory occurs as the final code for any unit of coding. Once you have entered the information on all units of coding for a given case into your data matrix, the matrix will contain the coding frequency for all your subcategories.

Example of integrating frequency information into your data matrix

The – fictitious – comparative coding sheet in Table 10.5 contains information about the units of coding where participant no. 2 (corresponding to one unit of analysis) talked about the reasons why she considered it morally justified that the life support of Terri Schiavo was terminated. Remember that in creating your data matrix, you enter only the final code.

Table 10.5 Comparative coding sheet on reasons concerning the case of Terri Schiavo

Unit no.	First code	Second code	Final code
1.1	2.2	2.2	2.2
1.2	2.10	2.5	2.5
1.3	2.2	2.2	2.2
1.4	2.6	2.6	2.6
1.5	2.7	2.7	2.7
1.6	2.5	2.5	2.5
1.7	2.9	2.9	2.9
1.8	2.2	2.10	2.2
1.9	2.8	2.8	2.8

The resulting data matrix is displayed in Table 10.6. It shows that the participant mentioned three times that she considered it morally justified that the life support had been terminated, considering that Terri Schiavo's coma had already lasted for more than 15 years (reason 2.2: the long duration of her comatose state); compared to the other reasons, this clearly carries the greatest weight for participant no. 2. She also mentions twice that Terri Schiavo is only kept alive by the support of the machines (reason no. 2.5). The remaining reasons are mentioned only once by the participant (low assumed quality of life, 2.6; her right to die, 2.7; that her condition is unlikely to change, 2.8; that the life support was only prolonging her suffering, 2.9).

Table 10.6 Data matrix for participant no. 2 showing coding frequencies for Terri Schiavo

Interviewee no.	C2.1	C2.2	C2.3	C2.4	C2.5	C2.6	C2.7	C2.8	C2.9	C2.10	C2.11
2	0	3	0	0	2	1	1	1	1	0	0

If you want to include frequency information on subcategories for dimensions where only one subcategory per dimension can be coded, this is more difficult (e.g. participants' opinion about terminating the life support for Terri Schiavo). Here, the dimension is represented by one column where you are supposed to enter the number of the subcategory that was coded to represent this participants' opinion (e.g. '1' to represent the first subcategory, namely that the participant considers this to have been morally justified). In this case, you cannot simply increase this number by 1 whenever the participant repeats this opinion in a later unit of coding. In the context of this dimension, '2' does not stand for 'mentioned the first subcategory twice', but for the second subcategory, namely 'considers this to have been long overdue'. If you were to increase the number, you would be mixing two different kinds of information: the numbers representing the subcategories (these are simply names) and the frequency information.

The best way to include this kind of information into your data matrix is by creating a scale that integrates the opinion and the number of times a participant repeats this opinion. This is called scaled QCA (Mayring, 2010, Chapter 5).

Example of integrating scaled information into your data matrix

For participants' opinions concerning the case of Terri Schiavo we created the following subcategories: *morally justified, long overdue, morally wrong, refusal to take any decision, unclear*. The first three subcategories are easily ordered in a sequence: long overdue, morally justified, morally wrong. But this scale is not symmetrical: it contains two values for considering the decision morally justified, but only one value for considering it morally wrong. On this basis, we might have constructed the following scale for representing the degree to which participants considered the decision morally justified or morally wrong:

```
4————————3————————2————————1
Highly justified   Justified        Wrong      Highly wrong
```

If a participant considered the decision justified, this would be represented by entering a '3' into the data matrix. If the participant repeated this opinion in a later unit of coding, this can be taken to indicate a stronger opinion on the issue which would be represented by entering a '4' for that person (replacing the original '3'). A '4' would also have been entered if the participant had expressed the opinion that the decision was long overdue. Because this is already the end point of the scale, the scale does not allow you to represent a repetition of this already strong opinion. Also, more than one repetition of any opinion would not be represented on the scale. If one wanted to represent additional repetitions, the scale would have to be more strongly differentiated, such as:

```
6————————5————————4————————3————————2————————1
Highly      Justified   Somewhat   Somewhat   Wrong     Highly
justified              justified   wrong                wrong
```

On this scale, up to three repetitions of an opinion can be represented.

So far, the scale does not include the subcategories *refusal to take any decision* and *unclear*. These could be summarised into 'no decision taken' and be represented by a '0' (note that this would not allow you to code a repetition of the refusal to take a decision).

In your data matrix, the respective dimension continues to be represented by a single column. Into that column, you enter each participant's value on the scale that you have created. Table 10.7 shows an example of a data matrix integrating frequency information both for participants' opinion (column headed '1') and the various reasons they give to support their opinion (the remaining columns). Here, the participant is of the opinion that terminating Terri Schiavo's life support was morally justified, and she only says so once, coded as a '3' according to the four-point scale suggested above.

If you do not want to take repetitions into account, you simply enter into your data matrix which subcategory was coded or whether a given subcategory was coded (compare Table 10.4 above). If you find, as you are entering the information from your comparative coding sheet, that the subcategory for a unit of coding has already been entered into your data matrix, you ignore this unit and move on to the next unit of coding, without entering

Table 10.7 Data matrix for participant no. 2 showing coding frequencies and repetitions

Interviewee no.	C1	C2.1	C2.2	C2.3	C2.4	C2.5	C2.6	C2.7	C2.8	C2.9	C2.10	C2.11
2	3	0	3	0	0	2	1	1	1	1	0	0

anything into your data matrix. Along these lines, you would ignore units 1.3 and 1.10, because they repeat the information in unit 1.1; you would likewise ignore the information in unit 1.6 which repeats the subcategory for unit 1.2.

SUMMARY

If your units of analysis are larger than your units of coding, you have to transform your results to the level of the units of analysis in order to answer your research question. To do so, you have to create a matrix that covers all your units of analysis (represented in the lines of the matrix) and all your dimensions (represented in the columns of the matrix). Dimensions where only one subcategory can be coded per unit of analysis are represented by one column. Dimensions where several subcategories can be coded per unit of analysis are represented by one column per subcategory. If the repetition of a subcategory carries important information, this must also be integrated into your matrix. For dimensions where each subcategory is represented by a column, this information is represented by the coding frequency for this subcategory for any one unit of analysis. For dimensions that are represented by a single column, it is best to integrate information on the subcategory and the coding frequency by creating a scale and entering the value on that scale into the matrix.

Frequently asked questions

What do I do if new categories emerge during the main coding?

Once you start doing the main coding, you should use the final version of your coding frame. If you cannot avoid creating new categories, what was intended as the main coding turns into a second trial coding. You have to start again on the main coding once you have truly finalised your coding frame. If this concerns only certain parts of your coding frame, you may simply want to report that it would be useful to explore these categories in more detail in a future study (instead of creating new categories now). This means that these parts of your coding frame are not as valid as they should be, and you should discuss this in the context of the validity of your coding frame.

What if the reliability for some categories is too low after the main coding?

This means that you did not manage to improve your frame sufficiently after the trial coding. If this concerns only a few categories, it is only a minor problem. You should disregard the results concerning these categories. You should also report this in your discussion section. If reliability is a problem with more than about a quarter of your categories, either you should try to improve your coding frame some more and do another main coding (turning what was intended to be your main coding into a second trial coding), or, if you have already tried this, you should reconsider your study and whether QCA really is a good method for answering your research question.

What if reliability is lower for the main coding than for the trial coding?

Usually this will only be the case for a very few categories. You should definitely report this in your discussion section. Also try to find the reason why consistency is so low and try to introduce a rule for consistently resolving these cases when deciding upon the final meaning of the units of coding that are affected by this.

Isn't the matrix covering all units of analysis and all dimensions a very quantitative way of presenting my results?

The matrix is not necessarily the way in which you present your results. It is only a means to give you an overview of all your results. What you then do with these results and how you present them is a different question that will be discussed in the next chapter.

End-of-chapter questions

- Imagine that you are working on your own, but a friend of yours is willing to help you with the coding. What part of your material would you ask your friend to code, to be able to compare your codes with hers? What would your decision depend on?
- Imagine that you realise during the main coding that your coding frame does not allow you to describe important parts of what your participants are saying. Because of this, you add new categories to your coding frame. What do you do now? Can you continue with the main coding? Why (not)?
- What strategies are there for handling cases where two coders cannot agree on the meaning of a unit of coding?

- Under what conditions is it necessary that you transform your results on to the level of your units of analysis?
- Imagine that you have been working with a coding frame that consists of three dimensions. The first dimension contains 5, the second dimension 8, the third dimension 4 subcategories. For each dimension, more than one subcategory can be coded for each unit of analysis. How many columns are needed in your transformed matrix to represent the codes for these dimensions?
- Imagine that you also want to integrate repetitions of subcategories into the above matrix for the three dimensions. How do you represent information about code repetitions in this kind of matrix?

11

HOW TO PRESENT YOUR RESULTS

Chapter guide

Now that you are done with your QCA, you want to write up your study and present your results. There are different ways of doing this, and some of these involve some additional data analysis. What would be the best option for you depends on your study and your research question. In this chapter, we will look at two basic ways of presenting the results of QCA:

- presenting your results in qualitative style;
- presenting your results in quantitative style.

Presenting your results in qualitative style

In qualitative research, the different research phases (data collection, data analysis, presenting your findings) are often not distinct, but merge with each other (see Chapter 2). Keeping this in mind, your coding frame itself may be your most important finding. This is the case whenever you want to explore or describe your material in certain respects and are using data-driven categories to do so.

─── **Example of a study where the coding frame is the main finding** ───

> Rachel Tambling and Lee Johnson (2010) conducted a study in which they wanted to explore and examine expectations concerning couple therapy – a topic about which little is known. To do so, they first conducted interviews (before the first therapy session and following the second, third and fourth therapy sessions) and examined these for expectations using data-driven categories. The categories that they created to describe these expectations are their main finding, and they describe their coding frame in qualitative style.

If your coding frame is your most important result, you will probably present your results so as to describe one category after another. If you organise your results section in this way, your cases (units of analysis) feature in your results only to the extent that they illustrate certain categories (as in the above example). If your research question is more focused on describing your cases, it is better to first give a brief overview of your coding frame. Then, in the main part of your results section, you describe each of your cases in terms of your coding frame. Which way is best for you depends on your research question.

KEY POINT

There are two ways to organise your results section when presenting your results in qualitative style: by categories or by cases.

There are three main strategies for presenting your results in qualitative style:

- describing and illustrating your findings using continuous text;
- describing and illustrating your findings using text matrices;
- doing additional data exploration and analysis and presenting these results.

Using continuous text

In using continuous text, you simply describe your categories or your cases one after the other. If you are organising your findings by categories, you start out by saying what each category is about. In this, you do not repeat the category definition (the full coding frame, including all category definitions, should be provided in the appendix), but summarise the core of the category and the concept underlying it. You then illustrate the category by providing a few examples from your material. This is especially important in QCA because it allows you to show your readers how the category was expressed in your material.

—— Example of using quotations to illustrate the results/categories ——

In their study on the characteristics of peak experiences in wilderness settings, McDonald et al. (2009) identified seven themes that characterised the experiences of the participants. In addition to giving an overview of their findings in a table, their results section consists mostly of a description of the various themes using continuous text. The following excerpt illustrates the first theme (McDonald et al., 2009, pp. 376ff.):

'Theme 1: Aesthetic Quality: One's Focus of Attention was Absorbed in the Aesthetic Qualities of the Wilderness Setting'

The most common theme to emerge from the participants' descriptions of their peak experiences was the aesthetic qualities of the wilderness setting. Wilderness settings dwarf human beings by their sheer size, age, ecological complexity, and uniqueness. The most commonly cited objects of attention at the time of the participants' peak experiences were sunlight (particularly late afternoon sunsets), forests, mountains, wild animals, and valleys.

'Watching the sun set, I was alone watching the most beautiful shades of mauve and pink on the clouds near the acropolis; I felt a sense of awe.' (Participant 5)

'As we skied up to the head of the glacier, I remember peering over the very edge and saw this other magnificent glacier spill down into the adjoining valley. It was such an incredible sight, especially for someone who had never seen mountains on this scale before. My first reaction upon seeing this sight was to start laughing; it just seemed so unreal, like I was on another planet. There was no other way to respond, it was such an amazing feeling.' (Participant 2)

The example shows how to integrate additional information into your description of the categories. The authors start out by saying that aesthetic experiences were the ones most frequently described by their participants. In this way, they integrate a comparison between their categories into their description, and they also integrate what is really frequency information, but without giving you the numbers as part of their text (they do provide frequencies in a separate table). They also provide information on the most distinctive aspect of this aesthetic experience, namely feeling dwarfed by one's surroundings. They say what aspects of the wilderness were mentioned by the participants as giving rise to this particular kind of experience, such as late afternoon sunsets, forests, or wild animals. In this way, they summarise some important aspects of their findings, adding detail over and above the category description. Finally, each category is illustrated by several quotes from their material. As you can see, each quote relates to a different aspect of the wilderness which gave rise to the experience (a sunset and a glacier). In this way, the quotes also illustrate some of the wilderness aspects that are enumerated in their text.

When describing your findings in this way, you can also use the continuous text to comment upon the relations of the themes to each other if this is in any way noteworthy.

Example of using continuous text to comment on the relations between categories

In their study of expectations concerning couple therapy, Tambling and Johnson (2010, p. 326) use continuous text to point to the way in which some of their clients' expectations are not entirely consistent:

All clients were informed on intake that their therapist was a graduate student. This information helped them identify an approximate age range:

'...Oh well I'm assuming he is in graduate school here in some capacity but so I'm thinking he probably gonna be in his I'll say mid to late twenties maybe.' (052.1)

> '... But I would have thought, being that it's with the university it would be somebody young.' (742.1)
>
> Despite believing that their therapist would be both young and a student, many participants also expected that their therapist be experienced and professional.
>
> > 'I would hope that they have a certain amount of experience even if they were still relatively new at their job.' (852.1)
>
> > 'Um, hopefully informed, hopefully know what they are talking about. I'm sure they will, I mean that's why we're here.' (741.1)
>
> > '... you know I was expecting a level of professionalism...' (051.1)

When using continuous text to present your findings, you can organise your results section either by categories (as in the above examples) or by cases. Continuous text is suitable for presenting your results either way. If you are organising your findings by cases, you provide quotes for each case on those categories that best describe the case.

Using matrices to describe your coding frame

If your coding frame is large, it may be cumbersome to describe and illustrate every single category using only continuous text – as well as making dull reading. Likewise, if you have studied many cases, you cannot present every single one of them in this way. In this situation, you may want to focus on summarising some key findings in your continuous text and supplement the text with tables where you provide more detail. Tables that contain mostly text instead of numbers are commonly called text matrices. Text matrices allow you to summarise and at the same time illustrate various aspects of your findings. They can be organised in many different ways, depending on what you want to show; Huberman and Miles (1995) provide numerous examples of how to do this (not with a view to QCA in particular, but their suggestions are perfectly suitable). Text matrices are always used together with continuous text, and text and matrices should relate to and illustrate each other.

-- KEY POINT --

If your coding frame or your number of cases is large, text matrices allow you to summarise and at the same time illustrate selected parts of your findings. They are used together with continuous text.

In the following, we will look at three ways in which text matrices are particularly useful for reporting the findings of QCA:

- illustrating categories;
- describing cases;
- comparing (groups of) cases.

Using text matrices to illustrate categories

Using text matrices to illustrate categories is the easiest way to employ matrices in presenting your findings. In the simplest case, these matrices contain only two columns: one column for the category name and a second one for quotes illustrating the category. This type of text matrix is especially useful for summarising information about your coding frame.

Example of using a matrix with two columns

In her marketing study, Birklbauer (2009) examines the reasons why women drink beer and the barriers that keep them from consuming beer. The coding frame is Birklbauer's main finding, and she uses a text matrix for presenting and illustrating the entire frame. Table 11.1 shows a small excerpt.

Table 11.1 Paraphrases from the interviews and categories (Birklbauer, 2009, pp. 817ff.)

Motives for drinking beer	
You can have it with your meal, without getting drunk right away	Low on alcohol
It isn't as strong as wine	
I like the slightly bitter taste, it goes with the food	Taste
Has a pleasant cooling effect	
Got into the habit when I was about 18 or 19	Relaxation, habit, company
It is kind of sociable	
I acquired the taste; beer is something you have to get used to	
The price is OK compared to other drinks	Low price
Barriers to drinking beer	
I don't like the aftertaste	Taste
I find it too bitter	
I've never liked the taste of it	
Beer is associated with men sitting drunk in front of the TV	Negative (male) image
Fat man, beer belly, a bit unappetising, sitting on the sofa and drinking beer from the bottle	
Boozy proles, that's what beer makes me think of	
Beer has a cheap image, it's not really elegant; wine is more festive	
It's embarrassing, if you're sitting with men and don't know which beer to order	Insufficient knowledge

---

You can easily enlarge this kind of matrix by adding a third column where you give a brief description of what each category is about.

Using text matrices to describe cases

You can also use matrices to provide an in-depth description of your cases. Here, each line in your text matrix corresponds to a (sub)category of your coding frame. For each of these, you provide a quote for the case that you want to illustrate. This is especially useful in a study where you want to explore a few cases in depth. With this kind of research question it would be useful to create one such matrix for each of your cases: the text matrix summarises each case and illustrates it at the same time. Again, matrices and continuous text are used alongside each other and should illustrate each other.

KEY POINT

Creating case-related matrices to describe the results of your QCA is especially useful for describing a small number of cases in depth and for illustrating a particular kind of case.

Another way to use case-related matrices is to create a text matrix for selected cases only. How you select these cases depends on your research question and your findings. If you have a group of cases that resemble each other, you might want to create a matrix for each of these to illustrate a case that is typical of this group. Alternatively, you might want to illustrate an extreme case or a case that is very different from all the others.

Example of using matrices to illustrate cases

As part of our prioritising study, we had conducted interviews with one representative each of the large health insurance funds. Because each fund has distinctive interests in the field of health care, we are planning (in addition to the analyses we have already done) to look at each of them in depth. To present these findings, case-wise matrices would be suitable. Table 11.2 shows such a matrix illustrating the opinions of the representative of the AOK (the largest public health insurance fund in Germany) concerning the case of Terri Schiavo.

Using text matrices to compare cases

A third way in which text matrices are helpful for presenting results is when you want to compare cases on selected categories. The matrix shows you what

Table 11.2 Case-related matrix: The representative of the AOK on the case of Terri Schiavo

Opinion: Morally justified	Personally, I can agree with this kind of decision, but I would say, sort of, that this is an extremely difficult decision to make and that it is a tragic decision and that there always remains some uncertainty in the end.
Reasons in favour: Duration of the coma	Well, this strongly depends on the time factor. The longer someone has been in a coma, the fewer the chances.
The relatives agree	And I would say that it depends on the relatives...
Diagnosis	That would be the personal opinion of the doctor who is treating her. ... And I would say that it depends on the relatives and the doctor who is treating her.
Miscellaneous	If this was me, I would agree. And it would not take 15 years. For myself, I would say after two or three years maybe, when the chances are really–
Reasons against: She might regain consciousness	... and you never find out whether you have done the right thing. Because, if you turn the machines off now, I suppose that the chances are 99.99% that you didn't rob this woman of a single day of being conscious and alive. But you never know, you can never be 100% certain.

each case says on your topic of interest. Usually, the text matrix is arranged so that each case corresponds to a column. Because of space restrictions – a page is only so wide – you will have to limit the number of cases to around four. Table 11.3 shows an example of such a matrix, presenting the views of three representatives of the large German public health funds on the case of Terri Schiavo. While none of them opposes the decision to terminate her life support, the matrix clearly shows that their opinions are for the most part based on very different reasons.

Doing additional data exploration and analysis

There are numerous ways in which you can further examine and analyse the results of your QCA. In this section, I will focus on two such strategies which are especially prevalent in qualitative research: exploring your results for patterns and co-occurrences and constructing a typology.

Exploring your results for patterns and co-occurrences

So far, in doing your QCA, you have determined what each of your units of coding means. In examining the results of your QCA for patterns and co-occurrences, you move beyond the individual unit of coding and beyond your results for individual categories; and now you focus on the *relations* between your categories. Gibbs (2007, Chapter 6) has called this 'comparative analysis'; Dey (1993, Chapters 11 and 12) writes of linking data and looking

Table 11.3 Matrix comparing representatives of health insurance funds on the case of Terri Schiavo

Category/Representative of	AOK	BKK	KdAK
Decision	Justified: Personally, I can agree with this kind of decision, but I would say, sort of, that this is an extremely difficult decision to make and that it is a tragic decision and that there always remains some uncertainty in the end.	Not clear: This is an extremely difficult question....	Justified: ... if the relatives agree, this is ethically justified
Reasons in favour:			
The relatives agree	And I would say that it depends on the relatives....		
Duration of the coma	Well, this strongly depends on the time factor. The longer someone has been in a coma, the fewer the chances.		
Only machines keeping her alive		On the other hand, prolonging her life by these measures, this is also a way of interfering with nature	
Prolongation of her suffering		I was wondering whether it was really necessary to prolong her suffering by 15 years	
Miscellaneous	If this was me, I would agree. And it would not take 15 years. For myself, I would say after two or three years maybe, when the chances are really-		
Reasons against:			
Criminal/unethical procedure		And everyone should be aware that they are acting the part of God, a bit, they are interfering with life.	

Table 11.3 (Continued)

Category/Representative of	AOK	BKK	KdAK
She might regain consciousness	… and you never find out whether you have done the right thing. Because, if you turn the machines off now, I suppose that the chances are 99.99% that you didn't rob this woman of a single day of being conscious and alive. But you never know, you can never be 100% certain.		
Additional criteria: Diagnosis	That would be the personal opinion of the doctor who is treating her. … And I would say that it depends on the relatives and the doctor who is treating her.		If this was a medical decision, it cannot be contested. The physician has to make the decision
Social consensus		I would say that you have to try and reach a consensus in the society, concerning these ethical kinds of cases: How do you deal with such cases? These kinds of questions – it is really important to have a discussion on them, to be able to refer to a consensus in these situations. This helps the relatives, and it helps the doctors who are treating the patient. And of course it is easier to make this kind of decision if there is a broad consensus that this is the way to proceed in such cases.	
Decision makers			It depends on who makes the decision. If this is the decision of the relatives and the doctors treating the patient, it cannot really be contested.

for connections; Miles and Huberman (1994, Chapter 4) refer to looking for patterns; and in the literature on using software to support you in your analysis of qualitative data, the term 'looking for co-occurrences' has become common (Lewins & Silver, 2007, Chapter 12).

KEY POINT

In looking for patterns and co-occurrences, you focus on how your categories are related.

The process of exploring your results for relationships between your categories is similar to what you do in grounded theory methodology when you move to the stage of selective coding (see Strauss & Corbin, 1998; see also Chapter 3 above). Here the focus is also on the interrelation between your codes, although grounded theory methodology takes this much further than looking for simple interrelations. In examining your QCA results for patterns, you ask questions such as:

- Do some of my categories occur together?
- Do some of my categories occur near each other?
- Are some of my categories related in specific ways (e.g. the one being named as an antecedent, a consequence, or an indicator of the other)?

To examine your material along these lines, software can support you in many ways; it can even help you spot interrelations that you had not previously considered (see Chapter 12). Looking for patterns can be helpful both within and across your cases.

Example of examining the results of QCA for co-occurrences

In our prioritising study, we presented the participants with a vignette that contrasted two patients in terms of own responsibility for their heart disease and their role in society. One patient was described as engaging in an unhealthy lifestyle, but being responsible for 2000 employees (Stephan); the other patient was presented as suffering from hereditary heart disease, but leading a very healthy life (Martin). The participants were asked to decide whose heart surgery should be financed by public health care. When looking at the results of our QCA, the physicians stood out compared to the other stakeholder groups: they were the only ones who mentioned Stephan's social status as a consideration in their decision. When examining our results for patterns, it turned out that this was not because the physicians were of the opinion that Stephan was more deserving of surgery because of his higher social status. Instead, it turned out that the subcategories *own responsibility, higher social status*, and decision in favour of *surgery on Martin* co-occurred among the physicians. They argued that Stephan, because of his unhealthy lifestyle, was at least in part responsible for his own bad state of health. Moreover, they argued, he should have known better: as someone in charge of 2000 employees he was sufficiently intelligent to have known that his lifestyle would be harmful to his health. In the eyes of the physicians, Stephan's high social status actually increased his responsibility for the bad state of his health: they held him even more accountable and in consequence argued for surgery on Martin.

When looking at co-occurrences and patterns, frequency information can also be important and can be integrated into your analysis.

Constructing a typology

Especially if you are doing a large-scale study, you may want to reduce and summarise your results further before presenting them. Constructing a typology is a method that is particularly useful for doing this.

--- KEY POINT ---

Creating a typology is a useful way of summarising and condensing the results of QCA.

By creating a typology, you sort your cases into groups in such a way that the cases making up one group are similar to each other in some way, and the cases that go into different groups are different from each other. The groups help you to summarise your results: Instead of describing your results case by case, you can now present your results group by group – and the whole idea behind creating groups is that there are fewer groups than individual cases. At the same time, you can make your description rich by presenting one or two cases for each of your groups in more detail. This helps to make the groups come alive.

The crucial point about creating groups is to identify those characteristics of your cases that are most helpful for sorting them into groups. Having done a QCA, your dimensions/categories are your characteristics. A good starting point is to look at those dimensions where your cases/units of analysis differ a lot. Those units that you assigned to similar subcategories on these dimensions should go into one group. Creating typologies is a method in its own right, and it is impossible to describe it here in much detail. It is only possible to give you the bare bones; to actually construct types, you will have to read up on the method (see Kluge, 2000, for a concise introduction).

——————— **Example of a study making use of types based on QCA** ———————

Gorski (2009) examined 45 syllabi from multicultural teacher education courses in the US using a mixture of grounded theory-type coding and QCA. Categories included the awareness of and respect for diversity (or lack thereof), the type of language used, degree of cultural sensitivity and self-reflection, and several others. Based on his coding, Gorski then created a typology consisting of five groups:

- Teaching the other, characterised by: use of *othering* language; presenting non-dominant groups as homogeneous; defining multicultural education through a market-centric lens;

- Teaching with cultural sensitivity and tolerance, characterised by: framing multicultural education as respecting diversity; cultural sensitivity and self-reflection; but also a lack of attention to educational inequity;

- Teaching with multicultural competence, characterised by: a focus on multicultural competence; a focus also on pragmatic skills; but likewise a lack of attention to inequities in education;

- Teaching in socio-political context, characterised by: a focus on the critical analysis of educational policy and practice; situating this analysis in a larger socio-political context; and the use of critical theory;

- Teaching as resistance and counter-hegemonic practice, characterised by: a focus on the critical analysis of educational policy and practice; situating this analysis in a larger socio-political context; and the use of critical theory; plus determination to resist oppression.

Gorski summarised his findings even further by sorting these five approaches into three smaller groups: conservative (corresponding to the first group), liberal (corresponding to the second and third groups), and critical (containing the fourth and fifth groups).

████████████████████████ SUMMARY ████████████████████████

There are three main strategies for presenting your findings in qualitative style: using continuous text, using text matrices, doing an additional qualitative data exploration and analysis. You can use continuous text to describe your findings by either focusing on categories or focusing on cases. Text matrices are tables that contain text instead of numbers. They can be arranged to illustrate the categories in your coding frame, or to illustrate a few cases in depth, or to compare cases on a few selected categories. The two most important strategies for doing additional data exploration and analysis are looking for patterns and constructing a typology. In looking for patterns, you move beyond the results for your individual categories and examine how your categories relate to each other. Constructing a typology is especially useful if you are dealing with a large number of cases. This means sorting your cases into groups depending on how similar to or how different from each other they are on selected categories.

Presenting your results in quantitative style

In conducting a QCA, you are sorting your material into distinct categories. This procedure easily lends itself to counting. In fact, constructing a data matrix where you enter the codes for each of your cases/units of analysis and each of your categories almost takes you there (see Chapter 10). Because counting is so easy with the results of QCA, it is actually rare – although perfectly possible – to find a presentation of the results of a QCA that does not include some frequencies somewhere. Because you usually count across your units of analysis, presenting your results in quantitative style typically means that you focus on your categories, not your cases. If you want to focus on describing your cases, a qualitative strategy of presenting your findings would be better.

KEY POINT

Presenting your results in quantitative style usually means that you are placing your focus on your categories, not on your cases.

In the following sections, we will look at three strategies for presenting your findings in quantitative style:

- providing absolute frequencies;
- doing descriptive group comparisons;
- using inferential statistics.

Absolute frequencies

Absolute frequencies tell you how often each of your categories and subcategories was coded for your material. They are most useful if you want to compare the subcategories for one category/dimension. You calculate absolute frequencies by going back to the data matrix that you created after you had completed your QCA (see Chapter 10). Each line in your matrix corresponds to one case, and each column represents a category or a subcategory. Adding up the numbers in the cells for a given column tells you how often that category or subcategory was used across all units of analysis. If you have only a few categories and cases, it is easiest to do this using a calculator; if you are doing your QCA using software, the software will usually provide you with such frequency counts (see Chapter 12). If your data matrix is large (and if you are not making use of software in the first place), you might want to enter it into Excel or into a data analysis program such as SPSS/PASW. Excel is a good choice if you want to provide only absolute frequencies. If you want to do group comparisons or use inferential statistics, a data analysis program would be the better choice.

KEY POINT

Absolute frequencies tell you how often a (sub)category was coded across all units of analysis. They are often used together with continuous text.

Presenting absolute frequencies as part of the continuous text

Absolute frequencies are often presented together with continuous text. Some authors provide them as part of their text, giving the frequencies, sometimes in parentheses, as they describe their categories.

--- **Example of including coding frequency in continuous text** ---

The following excerpt is taken from the text where we present the results of our prioritising study for the stakeholder group of representatives of health insurance funds (Otten, Schreier & Diederich, 2010, p. 20):

Two representatives of public health insurance funds were of the opinion that turning off the life support system for Terri Schiavo was morally justified; an additional representative in fact considered this to have been overdue. One participant did not want to make a decision, and the two remaining representatives did not state a clear opinion.

Concerning the reasons why turning off her life support was morally justified, three participants said that keeping her on the machine had been paramount to unduly prolonging her suffering:

'... and you have to ask yourself: ... Is this kind of life really worth living? I personally would not want to live like this.'

Two interviewees each mentioned that Terri Schiavo would already have died a natural death if it had not been for the machines, and that her state was unlikely to change:

'... This is to overdo what medicine can do – if you know that there is no way the patient will make any further progress...'.

If your number of cases is small, you might wonder whether there is any point in reporting frequencies at all (as in the above example where the findings are reported for the six representatives of one stakeholder group). But as long as you use frequency-related terminology when reporting your results, you should also report the actual frequencies, however small your sample. Frequency-related terminology includes phrases such as: the *majority* of participants; the category with the *highest* coding frequency; only *few* participants mentioned, and the like. If your sample is so small that this feels odd, another option is to use frequency-related terminology in your continuous text and to provide a frequency table in the appendix or with your text.

KEY POINT

If you are using frequency-related terminology when reporting your results, you should also provide the frequencies.

Integrating absolute frequencies into text matrices

Another way of reporting absolute frequencies is to integrate them into any text matrices that you have created for presenting the categories in your coding frame (see above). To integrate the frequency information, you simply add another column and enter the frequency there.

—— Example of integrating frequency information into text matrices ——

In presenting their findings on the features of wilderness settings that contribute to peak experiences, McDonald et al. (2009) integrated a matrix into the presentation of their findings in continuous text. In this matrix they provided the name of each category ('theme' in their terminology), the number of participants who mentioned this aspect (i.e. the coding frequency), a brief description of the theme, and what they call the 'spiritual expression' of the theme (this is related to their theoretical framework). Table 11.4 shows an excerpt from this matrix.

Table 11.4 Excerpt from the matrix presenting themes in experiences of wilderness settings (McDonald et al., 2009, p. 376)

Theme	No. of participants	Description of theme	Spiritual expression
1 Aesthetic qualities	15	Focus of attention was absorbed in the aesthetic qualities of the wilderness setting	Sacrednesss of life
2 Being away	15	Escape from the pressures, people, distractions, and concerns of the human-made world	Sacredness of life
3 Meaningful experience	13	The experience was significant to the individual's life	Meaning and purpose in life

Reporting absolute frequencies in charts

Absolute frequencies are useful, but reporting them in numbers only is also a little abstract and dry. A more vivid and descriptive way of presenting frequencies is to create charts. Charts transform the abstract frequency information into graphics, and the graphics show you at one glance what the coding frequency for one category is in comparison to another. Many different types of chart are available – bar charts, histograms, pie charts, and others. Play around with Excel or SPSS/PASW if you have not made much use of charts in the past – it can be fun!

Example of using charts to present frequency information

Odağ (2007) uses charts to present the results of her analysis of reading protocols. Figure 11.1 shows the coding frequencies for those aspects of the texts which readers mention in their protocols as reference points of their reading experience (Odağ, 2007, p. 328). You can see at a glance that readers refer to the characters and the plot much more than they do to the language of the text or its author.

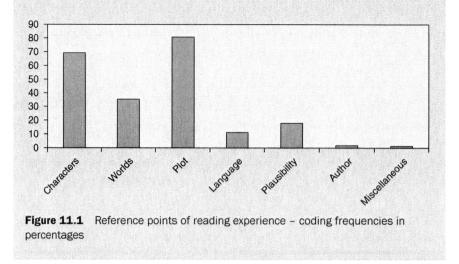

Figure 11.1 Reference points of reading experience – coding frequencies in percentages

Transforming absolute frequencies into percentages

Sometimes percentages are reported instead of absolute frequencies. In principle, this is a perfectly legitimate alternative way of presenting your findings. But other than absolute frequencies, reporting percentages carries a number of pitfalls.

One such pitfall is reporting percentages when your absolute frequencies are small. If you write that one aspect was mentioned only by 20% of your participants, whereas the other aspect was mentioned by 80%, this sounds like a huge difference. Instead, if you say that one aspect was mentioned by one person and the other aspect was mentioned by four persons (out of a total of five participants), this sounds very different. If your frequencies are small, absolute frequencies present a more accurate picture than percentages.

KEY POINT

Presenting percentages instead of absolute frequencies can be misleading, especially if total frequencies are small.

Another pitfall results if you switch back and forth between different points of reference and if your percentages sometimes refer to one total and sometimes to a different total. In this case, it is very difficult to keep track of what exactly your results are.

—— **Example of changing reference points in reporting percentages** ——

We did this ourselves when reporting and comparing the results of our prioritising study across different subgroups. In the following passage, percentages alternately refer to our complete sample across all stakeholder groups, to physicians, nursing staff, and healthy participants. At the beginning of the results section, we describe how it is organised and what the different percentages refer to, and we also provide absolute frequencies, but nevertheless this style of presenting the results is somewhat confusing:

'The main reason why our interviewees would be willing to pay more for medical services is that they consider the present medical services to be insufficient (14 interviewees = 31.1%). Especially members of the medical professions (4 physicians = 57.1%; 3 nurses = 50%) and healthy persons (4 = 44.4%) argued along these lines.' (Heil et al., 2010, p. 61)

Group comparisons

If you have collected your data from different sources, you may want to compare coding frequencies between groups of sources (e.g. men and women; novices and experts; documents from one time period and documents from another time period). To do so, you can again make use of all the different options mentioned in the previous section. You can integrate frequencies or percentages into continuous text, you can create tables, or you can create charts.

If your groups differ in size, absolute frequencies can be misleading; in this case it is actually better to report percentages. If you say, for instance, that 20 women mentioned a certain point, but only five men did, this gives the impression that women made this point much more often than men. This impression would be correct if you had 20 female and 20 male participants. But the picture would be very different and the absolute frequencies would be misleading, if altogether 40 women and five men had participated. Transforming absolute frequencies into percentages makes this obvious – only 50% of the female, but 100% of the male participants mentioned the point.

KEY POINT

If you want to do a group comparison and the number of cases in the different groups is unequal, absolute frequencies can be misleading. In this case you should report percentages.

Example of using percentages to report the results of QCA

The findings of our prioritising study concerning opinions about the case of Terri Schiavo would lend themselves to being summarised in a table, comparing percentages across the different stakeholder groups. In Table 11.5 the subcategories (i.e. the different opinions) are represented in the columns, and the stakeholder groups are shown in the rows. Each row shows what percentage of participants from the respective stakeholder group endorses each of the opinions that we distinguish in our coding frame, i.e. the percentages add up to 100% per row across the columns of the table. The final row represents the percentage of all participants, across the stakeholder groups, endorsing the various opinions. By inspecting the table, it is immediately obvious, for example, that the majority of healthy participants are in favour of terminating Terri Schiavo's life support and that the members of the nursing personnel are strongly divided in their opinions.

Table 11.5 Opinions of different stakeholder groups concerning the case of Terri Schiavo

Opinion / Stakeholder group	Morally justified	Long overdue	Morally wrong	Refusal	Unclear
Healthy persons	66.7%	22.2%	0%	0%	11.1%
Patients	50%	33.3%	8.3%	0%	8.3%
Physicians	0%	42.9%	28.6%	14.3%	14.3%
Nursing Personnel	33.3%%	33.3%	33.3%	0%	0%
Politicians	20%	0%	40%%	0%	40%
Health Insurance Representatives	33.3%	16.7%	0%	16.7%	33.3%
Total	37.8%	26.7%	15.6%	4.4%	15.6%

If you compare groups by presenting coding frequencies (or percentages) for each group, you have to be careful not to overinterpret your findings. It would be very tempting, for instance, to conclude from Table 11.5 that physicians are more likely than members of the other stakeholder groups to consider the termination of Terri Schiavo's life support to have been long overdue. But you would only be able to draw this conclusion if the sample included in our study was in fact representative of the population; considering the low number of participants, however, this is quite unlikely.

KEY POINT

If you compare groups by presenting coding frequencies (or percentages) for each group, you have to be careful not to overinterpret your findings.

Likewise, we do not know whether the difference between the coding frequencies for the stakeholder groups (in this case, for the subcategory *Opinions: long overdue*) are indeed significant differences; i.e., we do not know whether these differences are so large that they are probably not due to coincidence, but reflect a true difference between the physicians and the other stakeholder groups. To know for sure, you have to do some calculations using inferential statistics over and above presenting the purely descriptive tables displaying frequencies or percentages.

Using inferential statistics

As described in the previous section, inferential statistics are useful if you want to go beyond descriptive group comparisons. Inferential statistics allow you to say whether any differences between groups are so large that they are unlikely to have occurred by chance. Any group differences that meet this criterion are termed *significant*.

KEY POINT

Inferential statistics allow you to say whether any differences between groups are so large that they are unlikely to have occurred by chance.

To make use of inferential statistics, it is best to enter your data into a statistics program such as SPSS/PASW. The data matrix you have to create to do so looks just like the matrix you set up at the end of your QCA: each line corresponds to a case, and each column corresponds to a (sub)category. To these, you have to add one column for each variable on which you want to compare your groups (e.g. gender, time period of publication); for details see a textbook on statistics software such as Pallant (2010).

From among the many procedures that have been developed in inferential statistics, the following are especially useful if you want to test for significant differences between groups:

- *Independent t-test.* The t-test is used for comparing coding frequencies between two groups. The t-test works best, however, if your frequencies follow the normal distribution. With the type of results that you get with QCA, this is not always the case. Statistics programs such as SPSS/PASW allow you to automatically check for this when running a t-test.
- *Analysis of variance.* This is like the t-test, but it allows you to compare three or more groups at a time. As with the t-test, however, your data must meet certain requirements. Again, statistics software allows you to check whether these are met as you are running the test.
- *Chi-square test.* The chi-square test allows you to compare as many groups as you like at the same time. It requires your data to meet only a few conditions, but this comes at a price: it is slower to recognise significant differences between groups than are the t-test and analysis of variance. If you do not know much about statistics and want to be on the safe side, you should do a chi-square test when using inferential statistics to do group comparisons.

━━━━━━━━━━━━━━━━━━━━ KEY POINT ━━━━━━━━━━━━━━━━━━━━

If you want to compare coding frequencies between groups and do not know much about statistics, a chi-square test would be the best test to use.

─── **Example of using the chi-square statistic in group comparisons** ───

In reporting her results about differences in reading experience depending on the kind of text and the gender of the readers, Odağ (2007) made use of inferential statistics. Figure 11.1 showed the coding frequencies for the aspects of the texts the readers mention in their protocols (characters; worlds; plot; language; plausibility; author; miscellaneous). Chi-square analysis with the two factors *text type* (focus on the inner or the outer world) and *aspects of the texts* that readers mention as the reference point for their reading experience (i.e. the above categories) showed significant differences between the two text types for the two categories *characters* and *worlds* ($X^2 = 164.34$; $df = 3$; $p < 0.001$). The two texts that focus on the inner world more often give rise to comments about the characters (*standardised residual* $_{text\ 1} = 2.6$, *standardised residual* $_{text\ 2} = 3.5$), whereas the two texts that focus on the external world do so significantly less often (*standardised residual* $_{text\ 3} = -4.9$, *standardised residual* $_{text\ 4} = -2.8$). Conversely, the two texts with a focus on the inner world evoke significantly fewer comments about the textual world than would have been expected (*standardised residual* $_{text\ 1} = -3.9$, *standardised residual* $_{text\ 2} = -3.2$), whereas the two texts with a focus on the outer world evoke significantly more such comments (*standardised residual* $_{text\ 3} = 2.9$, *standardised residual* $_{text\ 4} = 5.4$; overall $X^2 = 97.002$; $df = 3$; $p < 0.001$; Odağ, 2007, p. 329).

Apart from these statistical measures for group comparisons, many other statistical procedures and tests exist that can be used on the results of QCA.

─────── **Example of using cluster analysis following upon QCA** ───────

Odağ's (2007) total coding frame was large, containing dozens of categories. At a later stage of her analysis she wanted to integrate the results of her QCA with the results of a questionnaire about reading experience that she had given out to her participants. To keep the number of calculations that would be necessary to a minimum, she summarised the results of her QCA before conducting further analyses. To do so, she carried out a cluster analysis on each dimension of her coding frame. Cluster analysis is a (descriptive) statistical procedure for sorting data into groups, similar to creating a typology. In the case of the reference points participants mentioned for their reading experience, cluster analysis showed that these could be divided into two groups: one group, termed *characters*, which combined the coding frequencies for characters and actions; and a second group, termed *world*, which combined the remaining categories (Odağ, 2007, pp. 327ff.).

═══════════ SUMMARY ═══════════

When presenting your results in quantitative style, the focus is usually on your categories (not your cases). There are three strategies for presenting your results in quantitative terms: providing absolute frequencies; doing descriptive group comparisons; and using inferential statistics. To present absolute frequencies, you calculate how often each (sub)category was coded across all units of analysis. Absolute frequencies can be integrated into continuous text; they can be integrated into text matrices; or they can be presented in charts. Alternatively, absolute frequencies can be transformed into and reported as percentages, but this can be misleading especially if total frequencies are small. (Descriptive) group comparisons are useful if you have collected data from different sources and want to compare coding frequencies for categories across these sources. But as long as you show only frequencies or percentages, you have to be careful not to overinterpret your findings. In order to tell whether any differences between groups that you observe are indeed significant differences (i.e. unlikely to have occurred purely by chance), you have to make use of inferential statistics. For group comparisons, the chi-square test is particularly useful, but there are many other measures and tests that can be used on the results of QCA.

Frequently asked questions

Is presenting coding frequencies really compatible with QCA?

If you are interested in describing your material and in finding out which of these aspects (categories) occur most frequently, conducting a QCA and then presenting coding frequencies is exactly the right way to proceed. Calculating frequencies is something that you do when you have completed your QCA. It does not make the method any less qualitative, and it is perfectly compatible with conducting qualitative data analysis. But one might argue that it turns the design of your study into a so-called mixed methods design, i.e. a design that combines qualitative and quantitative features (on mixed methods, see Cresswell & Plano Clark, 2007, Chapter 1).

I have data from different sources. Do I have to use statistics in reporting my results?

If you want to compare and contrast different sources after having done a QCA, this will usually involve reporting both frequencies and providing quotes that highlight the differences between the groups (if coding revealed any such differences). Strictly speaking, even absolute frequencies qualify as 'statistics', but they are called descriptive statistics.

If your question refers to inferential statistics, the answer depends on your research question. If you want to know whether your sources are 'really' different in some way, then yes, you should use inferential statistical tests. But if your number of cases is very small (three or four cases for each group), statistics cannot really tell you very much. In this case there is little point in using inferential statistics, and it is better just to report your results descriptively. In fact this allows you to explore any differences in greater depth and more detail than if you were using statistics.

Can I use frequencies if I present my results on a case-by-case basis?

Frequencies are typically used for presenting results with a focus on categories, not cases; and presenting results in qualitative style is more often done with a focus on cases rather than categories. But as long as you counted repeated coding of the same categories, there is nothing to prevent you from using frequencies when reporting your results for each of your cases. In fact this may be a very good idea – if you are doing comparisons within cases across time, for instance.

--- **End-of-chapter questions** ---

- What are the main strategies for presenting your findings in qualitative style?
- What is a text matrix, and how can you make use of text matrices in presenting your findings?
- What does looking for patterns and co-occurrences involve?
- What are the main strategies for presenting your findings in quantitative style?
- Name three ways of presenting absolute frequencies in your results section.
- In what respect do you have to be careful not to overinterpret your findings when comparing descriptive coding frequencies across groups?

12

USING SOFTWARE IN DOING QUALITATIVE CONTENT ANALYSIS

Chapter guide

QCA was developed at a time when computers did not yet exist, so you can do QCA without making use of software. But especially if you are working on a large-scale project, software can support you in many of the steps that I have described in the previous chapters. In this chapter, we will look at:

- the kinds of software for text analysis and which of these is suitable for doing QCA;
- how software can support you in each of the steps involved in doing QCA.

Types of software for analysing text

Nowadays, there is a lot of software out there that promises to support you in analysing qualitative material, especially in analysing text. Unfortunately, the situation is also confusing for the researcher engaging in QCA. On the one hand, you will find software packages such as NVivo, MAXQDA and ATLAS.ti which are expressly designed to support the qualitative research process. Yet authors writing about these packages will also tell you that these do not support content analysis or do so only to a limited extent or only by adding another module (Lewins & Silver, 2007, p. 7). On the other hand, you will find software such as Textpack or the General Inquirer that has been designed for computer-aided content analysis. But when you look at descriptions of this software, you will not find it very useful for doing the type of QCA that has been presented in this book (Skalski, 2002). In the following, we will take a brief look at the main features of these two types of software.

Software for qualitative data analysis

Software that supports qualitative data analysis is usually referred to under the umbrella term of *computer-assisted qualitative data analysis* (CAQDAS). The packages that were created in the early 1990s started out with distinct features, each supporting a different task. Depending on what a package focused on, Weitzman and Miles (1995) distinguished between five types of software: text retrievers, textbase managers, code and retrieve packages, code-based theory builders, and conceptual network builders.

─────────────── **Examples of CAQDAS software** ───────────────

Commercial software packages include AQUAD, ATLAS.ti, C-I-Said, HyperRESEARCH, Kwalitan, MAXQDA, NVivo (formerly NUD*IST), QDA Miner, Qualrus. You will find brief descriptions in Lewins and Silver (2007, Appendix E) and at http://caqdas.soc.surrey.ac.uk/Support/Choosingsoftware/software-options.html and http://www.textanalysis.info/.

In addition to the commercial packages, freeware has also been developed. These programs have fewer functions and have less to offer for theory building and visualising your results, but they handle all other core functions well. These include: AnnoTape, Answr, CAT, RCDQA, and Weft. For descriptions, see http://www.textanalysis.info/; Answr is described at http://www.cdc.gov/hiv/topics/surveillance/resources/software/answr/index.htm.

Today, software for qualitative data analysis generally supports all of these tasks (for an overview see Lewins & Silver, 2007; Evers et al., 2011). All the leading packages help you manage your data, for example by creating groups of files where you bring together and link all the data forming part of the same research project. They let you do text searches for any words that you specify and bring up the text containing these words. Coding and retrieval in particular are at the core of CAQDAS software: you can create codes and assign multiple codes to passages or segments in your material. And once you have assigned your codes, you can retrieve the results in many different ways: you can ask the program to list all the passages that were assigned the same code; you can look for passages that were assigned the same multiple codes; you can search for codes (and related passages) that follow upon each other in close sequence, and much more. All software packages also support you in writing comments ('memos') about both your data and your codes and in searching these. Finally, the more commercial packages allow you to format and visualise your results in many different ways.

By integrating all these functions, CAQDAS software offers you very powerful tools for your qualitative data analysis. But at the same time it is also important to realise that it operates differently from quantitative software for data analysis such as SPSS/PASW. With quantitative software, you enter the data, you choose the analysis you want to perform, and the software does it for you and provides you with an output of the results. CAQDAS software does not work like this. With CAQDAS software, you enter the data – and then you still have to do the analysis: you have to create the codes and to assign them. The software merely supports you in this, and it also supports you at the later stages of bringing it all together, in seeing relationships emerge between categories, and in recognising similarities or differences between your cases.

CAQDAS software does not automate qualitative data analysis.

CAQDAS software has been designed to support all kinds of qualitative data analysis, especially various kinds of descriptive and interpretive coding. It has not been designed for doing QCA in particular. But even so (and even though authors like Lewins and Silver explicitly exclude – quantitative – content analysis from the scope of CAQDAS software), the programs can support you in the process of carrying out your QCA in many different ways.

Software for quantitative content analysis

The second type of software is usually described as supporting content analysis (Lewins & Silver, 2007; Neuendorf, 2002). In this, however, content analysis is typically equated with *quantitative* content analysis.

KEY POINT

So-called content analysis software usually supports only quantitative content analysis.

This kind of software dates much further back than CAQDAS software (for overviews and program descriptions, see: http://www.textanalysis.info/; Skalski, 2002).The first program of its kind, the General Inquirer, was in fact developed as early as the 1960s, and since then many more programs have followed. The idea underlying these programs is automatic coding based on so-called dictionaries. The researcher creates a coding frame where each category is defined through a list of key terms. The software then automatically codes the category whenever a word from the dictionary for this category is found in a text under analysis. At the same time, the frequency count for this category is increased by 1.

Example of using a dictionary to support quantitative content analysis

The Harvard IV-4 categories constitute a huge coding frame for the quantitative content analysis of texts under many different perspectives; this coding frame is used by the General Inquirer. One dimension of this coding frame refers to the language used by different institutions. The following institutions are included: academics, organised systems of knowledge, commerce, self-expression, legal, military, politics, and religion. The legal category consists of 192 key terms: accuse, acquit, acquittal, allegation, amendment, amnesty, etc. Whenever the software encounters one of these words in the text that is being analysed, it increases the frequency count for the legal category by 1 (http://www.wjh.harvard.edu/~inquirer/).

Some software for content analysis comes with one or more inbuilt dictionaries (such as the General Inquirer, LWIC, or PCAD); others let you build your own dictionary (Textpack, TextQuest). In either case and despite of the name by which the software goes, these programs do *not* support you in doing QCA. Because of this, they will not be discussed any further.

Recent developments

During the last decade, some bridges have been built between these two software traditions. Developers of CAQDAS software have begun to integrate features supporting quantitative content analysis, such as keyword searches, tools for automatic coding, and additional modules for building dictionaries into their packages. Developers of quantitative software have for many years been aware of the potential pitfalls of relying only on automatic coding. Because of this, software that lets the researcher build her own dictionaries typically also allows for semi-automatic or interactive coding. This means that the decision whether to code the category that is suggested by the software lies with the researcher, not with the software.

Moreover, software has now been developed that integrates features of qualitative and quantitative data analysis. These programs are especially suitable for QCA: over and above what CAQDAS programs can do, they support you in creating and using mutually exclusive categories, and some programs also allow you to compare the codes assigned by different coders and let you calculate inter- or intra-coder agreement.

Examples of integrative software

Software that integrates qualitative and quantitative features and is especially helpful with QCA includes: Answr (http://www.cdc.gov/hiv/topics/surveillance/resources/software/answr/index.htm); C-I-SAid (http://www.code-a-text.co.uk/index.htm); and Qualrus (http://www.ideaworks.com/qualrus/index.html).

━━━━━━━━━━━━━━━━━━━━━━━━━ SUMMARY ━━━━━━━━━━

Software for analysing text largely falls into two groups: CAQDAS software and software for content analysis. CAQDAS software has been
designed to support descriptive and interpretive coding. It can support
many of the steps in QCA, even though it was not designed for QCA
and even though (quantitative) content analysis is explicitly excluded
from the scope of these programs. Software for content analysis typically
supports only quantitative content analysis and is not suitable for QCA.
In addition to these two types of software, a few programs explicitly
integrate features of qualitative and quantitative data analysis. This
makes them especially helpful for doing QCA. These include Answr, C-I-
Said, and Qualrus.

How software can support you along the way

During the previous chapters of this book, I have taken you through the steps
of a QCA: building your coding frame, defining your categories, dividing your
material into units of coding, trying out the coding frame, evaluating and revising the coding frame, doing your main analysis, and pulling together and interpreting your results. In the following, we will look at whether and how
software can support you in carrying out these steps.

Building your coding frame and defining your categories

Building your coding frame

Because coding is at the heart of CAQDAS software, it can considerably support you during this stage of your work. All software that allows you to do
qualitative data analysis also allows you to create a coding frame. This can be
a concept-driven, data-driven or mixed frame.

Software packages differ, however, when it comes to the organisation of your
frame. Most packages let you create hierarchical frames that can go down a
certain number of levels (such as Answr, C-I-Said, Qualrus, QDA Miner,
MAXQDA, NVivo, and Weft). But some programs can only accommodate 'free'
codes that are not hierarchically organised (ATLAS.ti and HyperRESEARCH
would be cases in point). These packages are so powerful that you can usually
find a way of working around these limitations. Nevertheless, packages that
allow you to create hierarchical frames are better suited to support QCA.

Software packages also differ in the extent to which they support you in
creating categories which are mutually exclusive. Of course it is up to you to
make mutual exclusiveness part of the definition of any of your categories, and
all CAQDAS packages support this (see below). But, as mentioned above,
some programs allow you to set up mutually exclusive categories in such a way
that later, when it comes to coding, a segment can be assigned to one of these

categories only. Most of these packages let you set up both kinds of categories, i.e. categories which are mutually exclusive as well as categories which are not (CAT, C-I-Said, Qualrus). Answr is the only package that allows only mutually exclusive categories.

Where software really comes in useful at this stage of your analysis is when you are not yet sure how to structure your coding frame, when you are still playing around with different versions.

KEY POINT

As you are building your coding frame, software is particularly helpful with trying out different ways of structuring the frame.

Software helps you by providing the following functions:

- If you are working on a large-scale project, you can make use of software features to identify relevant passages. If you are building your coding frame around inter-view questions, for example, you can do a first round of very basic coding where you assign codes that identify passages as relating to question no. 1, 2, and so on. If answers to a specific interview question always contain a certain keyword or phrase, you can also do a keyword search to identify the relevant passages. In a next step, the software can show you all passages for one case (or across all cases) where the keyword has been found or where the selected code has been assigned. This provides you with a good overview of your material on this particular issue and helps you focus on a selected dimension of your coding frame.
- It is easy to change the order of the categories and subcategories.
- You can change the names of categories at any time.
- If your categories are data-driven and you want to make use of the terminology in your material to label your categories, most CAQDAS packages offer an *in vivo coding* feature: they let you turn a phrase in your material into a category name or label.
- If you change your mind about where to put a subcategory, you can simply drag and drop it elsewhere, making it a subcategory of a different dimension – or turning it into a new dimension altogether.
- Alternatively, you can copy categories into different places in the hierarchy. This way, you have different versions of your coding frame available at the same time (MAXQDA, NVivo).
- If you are still playing around with the structure, Qualrus offers a nice feature: the program lets you sort categories into different stacks and move categories around between stacks, until the structure looks right to you. This is really no different from the usual way of moving categories around in a tree-like structure. But it offers a different kind of visualisation that might be more appealing to some users.
- Qualrus is also the only software to offer so-called intelligent coding strategies. That is to say, the software is able to extract information from your material, to suggest

categories to you, and to learn from the choices you make. While this may be tempting, it is important to keep in mind that the task of interpreting your material and building a coding frame is ultimately a conceptual task that is up to you and cannot be taken over by software.

Defining your categories

In a next step, you have to define your categories. This step is essentially the same, regardless of whether you are using software or working with pen and paper.

In traditional CAQDAS software, you will have to make use of the memo function to enter category definitions. The software lets you attach a memo to your codes where you can enter the definition. By clicking on the memo, the definition is displayed whenever you want to see it.

Two integrative programs also include category definitions in the narrow sense. In CAT, you have to enter category definitions before you can get started on the coding (whereas most other software also lets you work with category labels, with no definitions attached). And Answr includes different fields for accommodating the different parts of category definitions: the code name, a brief definition, a more extensive definition, explanations for when to use the code, explanations for when not to use the code, and examples.

Where you have to watch out

Traditional CAQDAS software has been created to support interpretive data-driven coding. In this, you will usually create and assign your codes in one step. That is to say, interpretive data-driven coding does not distinguish between the steps of creating a coding frame and coding, but collapses the two steps into one. The coding frame is constantly being modified as new codes are created and assigned. This is very different from QCA, where you have to finalise your coding frame before the pilot or the main coding. In this respect, using CAQDAS software can be dangerous when you are doing QCA. Particularly if you are building a data-driven coding frame, it is very tempting to create categories and do the coding at the same time. Do not give in to temptation. Or if you do, always make sure that you have saved an uncoded version of your project. You can then import your final coding frame into this uncoded version once you and any other coders start on the pilot or the main analysis phase.

Traditional CAQDAS software also offers many additional features and options at the stage of building your coding frame. These are very helpful when you are using other qualitative methods, but they do not really help you with QCA. These include, for instance, the option to create hyperlinks between text passages (ATLAS.ti, HyperRESEARCH); this is especially useful in narrative analysis. Another such option is to establish semantic links between codes – 'is a', 'is similar to', 'is the opposite of' (ATLAS.ti, Qualrus); this is especially helpful in constructing grounded theory.

Segmenting your material

Because CAQDAS software does not conceptually distinguish between building your coding frame and doing the actual coding, the step in-between, namely the segmentation process, is also not explicitly supported in most software packages. To divide your material into units of coding, you have to make use of other software features such as the coding facility.

To do so, you should open an uncoded version of your files. In this, you mark one unit after another and assign it an appropriate code, such as *unit dimension 1, unit dimension 2*, and so on. Every unit of coding that is to be coded on a given dimension should be assigned the same code. In using software, you do not need to number these units, as you should do when working manually (see Chapter 7). If you want to code a passage on more than one dimension, this is not a problem. Because CAQDAS software lets you assign as many codes as you like to any one passage, you can easily assign one code for each dimension to any one passage. At the end of this process, you should have a file in which all relevant passages have been assigned unit codes.

KEY POINT

To divide your material into units of coding, you have to adapt the coding facility of software packages. You use this to assign unit codes which indicate on which dimensions a given segment is to be coded.

Those software packages that have been designed to integrate features of qualitative and quantitative data analysis (such as Answr, CAT, and C-I-Said) are more likely to include segmentation features. These packages require you to prepare your data files in such a way that segments are clearly indicated and can be recognised by the software. Usually, the program will assume that segments can be distinguished according to a formal criterion, such as the beginning of a new paragraph or another speaker taking over. The software also assumes that your segments are the same across your entire coding frame. In this way, software that provides segmentation features actually limits you in these respects.

If you are using a formal criterion for segmentation and if this criterion remains the same throughout your coding frame, software that provides segmentation features can automate the segmentation process. Otherwise, the work involved in segmentation remains the same, whether you are using software or working manually.

Trying out your coding frame

To try out your coding frame, you make use of the coding features offered by all software for qualitative data analysis. Each of these packages lets you assign categories to units of coding in your data files. The process is the same whether you are using software or working manually.

One feature of most CAQDAS software, however, that is very useful when coding is interactivity: when clicking on a passage that you have coded, the context in which the passage occurs is shown on the screen. Remember that in the days before software, coding was referred to as 'cut and paste'. By cutting, a passage was removed from its context and placed alongside other passages which had been coded in the same way. CAQDAS software lets you perform both actions simultaneously, so to speak: you can code a passage and display it together with other passages that were coded the same; but at the same time the passage remains in its original context and you can look at it within its context any time you like.

Another software feature that supports trial coding is the memoing function, i.e. the option to write memos and link them to codes or segments of your material. In this way, coders can jot down any problems they experience when applying a code to a segment at the very time when the problem comes up (see Chapter 8). Moreover, the note will be linked to the code or passage where the problem occurs; none of you will lose sight of it, and you will be sure to take it up when discussing the results of the trial coding.

KEY POINT

CAQDAS software supports the trial coding through interactivity and through the memoing function.

Software can also make your life easier when selecting cases for the trial coding. Remember that it is important to include a heterogeneous set of cases; otherwise you will not be able to try out the full range of your coding frame. Software helps you with this because many packages let you create variables and assign a value for a given variable to each case. In this way you can see where each case 'stands' with respect to these variables, and you can select cases for the pilot phase to be as different from each other as possible. This software feature is also useful at the stage of building your coding frame, if you want to base it only on a part of your cases.

Example of using the variables feature of software in case selection

In our prioritising study, we had included participants from six different stakeholder groups. Moreover, within each stakeholder group we had also selected cases on a number of other variables: age, other socio-demographic characteristics, extent of professional experience, and others. We used software and created a variable for each of these, and entered the appropriate values for each case. On the basis of this information it was easy to put together a very heterogeneous group of cases on which to try out our coding frame.

This not only works with features such as socio-demographic factors, i.e. information that you already have when starting on your analysis. If you notice aspects on which your cases differ as you are looking through your material, you can create memos that tell you what is characteristic of each case. If you are very systematic in putting this information together, you can again turn it into a variable on which you then classify each of your cases.

At the stage of pilot coding, you may want to work together with other coders, assigning segments to categories independently of each other ('blind coding'). Many CAQDAS programs support teamwork. This, however, can mean something very different depending on the specific package. In particular, it does not necessarily mean that two coders can independently code the same file and then compare their work. This feature has only been implemented in a few packages, among them Answr, CAT, C-I-Said, and QDA Miner. Other software requires that coders work on different versions of the project and that these are merged into a master project at a later stage.

Evaluating and revising your coding frame

Evaluating your coding frame

In Chapter 9 we looked at the two main criteria that are important for evaluating your coding frame: reliability and validity. Other criteria that should guide you when constructing your frame are: unidimensionality, exhaustiveness, saturation, and mutual exclusiveness (see Chapter 4). Software can strongly support you in evaluating your coding frame in many of these respects.

Reliability

The criterion of reliability requires you to check whether the coding has been done consistently, either by different coders or by you at different points in time. The first step in this is to create a spreadsheet showing the codes that were assigned to each unit of coding (i.e. to create a comparative coding sheet; see Chapter 8). Traditional CAQDAS software can support you in this if it supports teamwork. If it does (like ATLAS.ti or NVivo), you can usually display each unit of coding together with the codes assigned to it. But the software does not provide you with a spreadsheet. Instead, it lets you see the text in one window of the screen and the codes assigned to the text in another window. If all you want is to go through the text and discuss any inconsistencies, this is perfectly sufficient. If you want to have an overview of categories that were handled inconsistently and how they were handled by the different coders, you will have to create a comparative coding sheet by hand, despite using software. If you want to determine coding consistency, you will also have to do this by hand based on the coding sheet, or you will have to import your comparative coding sheet into Excel or SPSS/PASW.

KEY POINT

Recent developments in software support creating a comparative coding sheet, whereas traditional CAQDAS software usually does not.

Recent developments in software, however, have increasingly started to take into account the requirements of QCA. Packages such as Answr, CAT, C-I-Said and the latest version of MAXQDA let you create a spreadsheet that compares different coders; these packages also let you calculate measures of coding consistency. In this way, these programs automate coding comparisons and assessment of reliability. In addition, CAT lets you determine which coder (if you are working with several coders) differs the most from the others and might require additional coder training.

Validity

In Chapter 9 we looked at different kinds of validity and how to increase the validity of your coding frame. If you are building your coding frame in a data-driven way, telltale signs of low validity include high coding frequencies for residual categories and high coding frequencies for one subcategory compared to the other subcategories on a given dimension. All CAQDAS software can support you in this by providing you with coding frequencies for all your codes at a mouse click. All you have to do is generate coding frequencies for all residual categories and coding frequencies for all the subcategories in one dimension (for each of the dimensions in your coding frame).

KEY POINT

All CAQDAS software can support you in assessing the validity of your coding frame by calculating coding frequencies for selected categories. Recent software often offers additional tools.

If your coding frame is partly concept-driven, it can be useful to bring in an expert to assess your coding frame and to code part of your material (and you may be this expert). In this case, you can determine validity by calculating the consistency between the coding by the expert and any other coders. If you assess validity in this way, determining validity coincides with determining reliability. CAT and Qualrus offer additional program features to support this kind of validity assessment: they let you calculate the consistency between any coder and an expert opinion, i.e. you can define a 'valid' way of coding within the program and use this as the standard to which other coders are compared.

Validity refers to the extent to which your coding frame captures the concepts that you set out to capture. As you are using your coding frame, it can happen that you come across passages in your material that sort of fit a category, but do not quite capture the core. As you continue coding, perhaps you assign more and more passages to that category and, by so doing, gradually change its meaning. This can be a threat to the validity of your study. Software helps you check whether this is happening. For each of your categories, the software can provide you with a list of all the units of coding that were assigned to this category. In this way, you can easily check whether the meaning of your category has remained constant or has begun to change in the course of coding.

Recent CAQDAS software frequently offers additional tools that help with evaluating a coding frame in terms of validity. ATLAS.ti, for instance, lets you check for redundant coding, i.e. helps you identify categories which are very similar and had better be combined into one. Qualrus contains a so-called concept refinement and a concept generalisation tool. Both of these are designed to help you identify categories that may either be too broad or too narrow.

Other evaluation criteria

Other criteria for evaluating your coding frame are unidimensionality, mutual exclusiveness, exhaustiveness, and saturation.

Unidimensionality refers to the requirement that each dimension of your coding frame capture only one aspect of your material (see Chapter 4). This is only relevant as you are building your coding frame. It is an issue of how you conceptualise your frame, and only you yourself and the input from other researchers can help you with this. Software is irrelevant here.

Mutual exclusiveness means that each unit of coding should be assigned to only one subcategory per dimension. Virtually all CAQDAS software helps you check for this. Typically, you can display your material in one window and the codes assigned to it in the margin next to it or in another window. Some programs (MAXQDA, QDA Miner, etc.) allow you to use different colours for different codes. This is very useful when checking for mutual exclusiveness. If you use different colours for the dimensions in your coding frame, it is easy to see whether the same colour comes up twice for one unit of coding. If it does, your subcategories for this dimension are not mutually exclusive, and you should revise your definitions and your coding.

Your coding frame is exhaustive if every unit of coding has been assigned to a category. If you have used a separate code to mark all units of coding that are to be coded on a given dimension (see above on how software can support you during the segmentation process), software can again be helpful. To check for exhaustiveness, you make use of the same display feature that you use when checking for mutual exclusiveness. By looking at the code marks shown next to each unit of coding, any units that have not been coded are easy to spot.

A final criterion in evaluating your coding frame is saturation. It is met if you have assigned at least one unit of coding to each of the subcategories in your coding frame. As mentioned in Chapter 4, the criterion is somewhat controversial. But if it does play a role in your research, all CAQDAS software can help you check for it. To do so, you again request coding frequencies for each of your subcategories. If the coding frequency for any one subcategory is 0, your coding frame is not saturated.

KEY POINT

All CAQDAS software can support you in evaluating your coding frame for mutual exclusiveness, exhaustiveness, and saturation.

Revising your coding frame

After doing the trial coding and evaluating your coding frame, you will want to change your frame in some respects. You may need to revise code definitions and add decision rules. You may even want to change the structure of your frame in some respects: move subcategories to a different dimension, combine several subcategories into one, or create new subcategories. CAQDAS software can support you with all of these tasks, especially when it comes to changing the structure of your frame:

- *Revising code definitions.* To revise code definitions, you simply go to the memo containing the definition and change it, as you would change any text using text processing software.
- *Moving categories.* Most CAQDAS software facilitates regrouping your categories/ codes. Typically, you can access a separate window where you can see and manage all your codes. You simply use the mouse to move the selected categories to a different part of your coding frame (copy and insert).
- *Merging categories.* Most traditional CAQDAS software (such as ATLAS.ti, MAXQDA, NVivo) lets you combine selected codes into one – and at the same time automatically recodes all segments which were coded using these codes.
- *Creating new (sub)categories.* To create new categories, you proceed the same way as you do when creating your coding scheme.

To help you keep track of the changes you are making, it is usually a good idea to save the earlier versions of your project. In addition, you may want to write memos documenting these changes. This helps you create an audit trail and lets you follow your project as it evolves. Creating an audit trail was first suggested by Lincoln and Guba (1985, pp. 382ff.) to document the validity of a qualitative study.

KEY POINT

CAQDAS software supports you at every step of revising your coding frame. To keep track of the changes you make, it is a good idea to save earlier versions of your project and to document all changes.

Once you have fully revised your coding frame, you are set for your main analysis. In this, you again make use of the coding functions provided by all CAQDAS software, as you do during the trial coding.

Putting together your results

It is at the final stage of putting together your results that CAQDAS software is particularly helpful.

Using software to present your results in qualitative style

If you would like to simply present your coding frame in qualitative style, illustrating your categories with quotes, it takes only one click of your mouse to generate a list of all segments that were assigned to a particular category. You can then use this output to construct tables, as described in Chapter 11.

If you would like to illustrate not your categories, but your cases or groups of cases, most packages offer a filter function that lets you select cases according to specific criteria. This may be membership in a particular stakeholder group, a socio-demographic characteristic, or anything else that fits your data and the questions you have concerning your data. Of course, in order to use information about your cases as a criterion for selecting results, you first have to enter this information into the software (usually as a variable; see above).

If you want to explore your cases further for relationships between your categories, software also offers you many options. This is called interrogating your dataset. In the first place, software allows you to look for co-occurrences between codes, i.e. to determine how often one code is used together with another code. You can also check how often one code is followed or preceded by another code, how often one code is embedded in another, and whether a certain code is not used at all in analysing a specific part of your material.

You can use software to help you look for co-occurrences between codes; look for codes which follow upon each other; look for codes embedding other codes; and determine whether a code has not been used in analysing a part of your data.

In QCA, looking for co-occurrences can be especially helpful. But because in QCA subcategories are meant to be mutually exclusive, the term 'co-occurrence' takes on a more general meaning than in interpretive coding. In interpretive coding, it refers only to the application of two codes to the same unit of *coding*. In the context of QCA, it refers to the application of two or more codes to the same unit of *analysis*. Interrogating your dataset for co-occurrences helps you identify patterns both within and across your cases.

Example of identifying patterns in the data

In our prioritising study, we presented our participants with a number of case vignettes. Participants were asked to decide which of two patients should receive treatment and why. Examining our dataset for co-occurrences revealed a pattern across these different vignettes in terms of taking patients' individual circumstances into account. Participants who did consider patients' individual circumstances more often based their decisions on personal and emotional grounds. Another group of participants tended to base their decisions on costs and benefits, abstracting from the individual patients.

In addition to these basic query options, the more commercial packages (such as ATLAS.ti, HyperRESEARCH, MAXQDA, NVivo, Qualrus) offer more complex search options such as looking for code sequences or combining several queries into a more complex one. In addition, virtually all packages offer additional, software-specific options for searching your project. ATLAS.ti, for example, lets you combine queries into so-called supercodes; moreover, you can calculate a coefficient indicating the strength of association between two co-occurring codes. C-I-Said lets you follow how sequences of codes develop over time. MAXQDA offers you powerful filtering options. In this way, you can, for instance, compare how often two subcategories occur together in one subgroup of your material compared to another subgroup. This is merely a selection of package-specific functions. Other packages offer yet other options. How useful these are to you depends on your data and on your research question.

Software also supports you in creating data displays, i.e. in visualising the results of your searches. This is especially true for commercial packages (such as ATLAS.ti, MAXQDA, NVivo, Qualrus); freeware usually does not include many display options. When presenting your findings in qualitative style, maps are a very powerful visualisation tool. There are two ways in which you can create maps. One way is to draw a map, using the codes in your coding frame (or text passages, or memos) as the nodes in the map. How these nodes are linked depends on your interpretation of your findings, and you have to create these links. Another way to create a map is to visualise the co-occurrences that you have discovered between categories. In this case, you focus the map on selected codes, and the software will place overlapping codes on the map and relate them to the code that you started with.

Text matrices are another way of displaying your results. In software language these are called summaries. While most software offers you the option to create tables, these are typically code frequency tables, not text matrices. But the software can support you in creating text matrices by allowing you to generate lists of the kind of information that you would like to display in a matrix and export the list to a text processing program where you can then create the actual matrix. This saves you much time compared to creating the matrix from scratch.

Using software to present your results in quantitative style

Because we are looking here at software that was developed to support qualitative data analysis, software features to support presenting your results in quantitative style are of necessity limited. Nevertheless, the software packages offer some basic features that can support you in putting together a quantitative report of your results:

- *Simple coding frequencies.* In the first place, all packages let you generate lists of coding frequencies. Using this feature, you can determine for each of your categories how often it was coded. Many packages also let you generate frequency outputs for selected groups of cases (e.g. how often a certain category was applied to the cases in one of your stakeholder groups).
- *Cross-tabulations.* All commercial packages also let you generate cross-tabulations for two types of codes, showing you the frequencies of co-occurrences. Cross-tabulations are especially useful in QCA if you want to know how often the subcategories for one dimension were coded together with the subcategories for a second dimension.
- *More advanced quantitative output.* Apart from these basic features, the various packages differ considerably in their support of presenting your results in quantitative format. MAXQDA provides an especially extensive interface between qualitative and quantitative features of your analysis, letting you generate different kinds of frequency tables.

But if you are planning to run some inference statistical tests on your QCA results, you will have to leave behind software that supports you in your qualitative data analysis and turn to statistical software such as SPSS/PASW. Some commercial packages, especially MAXQDA, let you export your coding frequencies to SPSS/PASW.

Table 12.1 provides a summary of software features that are relevant to QCA.

Table 12.1 Special software features relevant to QCA

Software/Features	Answr	Atlas/.ti	CAT	C-I-Said	MAXQDA	QUALRUS
Segmentation required	Yes	No	Yes	Yes	No	No
Comparison between coders	Yes	No	Yes	Yes	Yes	No
Features that support creating the coding frame	Categories must be mutually exclusive		Requires category definitions before coding; includes different fields for the different parts of the category definition			Sorting categories into stacks
Features that support evaluating the coding frame		Identification of redundant categories	Calculating consistency between any coder and an expert; identification of a coder who differs most from the others			Calculating consistency between any coder and an expert; supports identification of overly broad and narrow categories
Features that support data analysis and presentation		Combination of queries into 'supercodes'	Powerful filtering options; powerful interface to quantitative data analysis	Analysis of code sequences		

━━━━━━━━━━━━━━━━━━━━━━ SUMMARY ━━━━━━━━━━━━━━━━━━━━━━

Software can support you along the entire way of conducting QCA. It is especially useful for: trying out different ways of structuring your coding frame; selecting cases for and doing the pilot coding; assessing the validity of your coding frame; checking your coding frame for the mutual exclusiveness of your categories, exhaustiveness, and saturation; revising your coding frame; analysing your results for patterns by looking for co-occurrences; and presenting your results in either qualitative or quantitative style. One aspect of QCA that is typically not explicitly supported concerns the segmentation of your material into units of coding.

Frequently asked questions

Do I have to use software to do QCA?

No, certainly not. Methods for qualitative data analysis, including QCA, have been around for much longer than computers, and you can apply all of these methods without using software. In fact, Nigel Fielding and Raymond Lee (1998) conducted an interview study about the use of qualitative software and found that their participants mentioned not only advantages, but also a number of disadvantages of such programs. For example, some participants suspected that software might encourage certain types of qualitative data analysis at the expense of others, and that interrogating your dataset might deteriorate into a purely mechanical, aconceptual activity (Fielding & Lee, 1998, Chapter 3). Admittedly this was an early study, and today users might respond differently (see 'The experiment: user's perspectives,' in Evers et al., 2011, for a present-day view). But these results serve to underline the point I want to make here: that using software is not a must. Software can be extremely useful and support you in many ways, especially if you are dealing with a large-scale project. It is much easier to change your coding frame around, to look at coded passages in context, and to keep track of your results. But people have different preferences, and some find using software easier than others. If you are among those people who prefer to do things by hand, this is fine.

Which software package is best for doing QCA?

There is no straightforward answer, I'm afraid. There is no best package as such – what is best always depends on the nature of your project, your research question, and on the kind of person you are. If you are working on your PhD, have to watch how much money you spend, and your research question does not require any sophisticated searches of your material, freeware will work really well for you. If your research question requires you to do some inference statistical testing based upon your QCA, you will need a package that offers the option to export your coding frequencies to SPSS/PASW. Also, each package has a distinct 'feel' to it. ATLAS.ti, for example, was developed with grounded theory methodology in mind. NVivo works with the notion of nodes, and texts, variables and codes can all function as nodes. Some people find this confusing, whereas others find it liberating. To choose a package, you should go to one of the websites that provide reviews (such as http://caqdas. soc.surrey.ac.uk/Support/Choosingsoftware/softwareoptions.html; or http:// www.textanalysis.info/) and read through these reviews. You should then download trial versions of the packages that you find most appealing; such free trial versions are available for all commercial packages. You should play around a bit with each of these programs to see which one works best for you.

End-of-chapter questions

- What types of software are there for doing textual analysis?
- Which of these can support you in doing QCA?
- Which steps of QCA are especially well supported by software?
- How do you go about segmenting your material into units of coding using software?
- Which strategy for interrogating your dataset is especially helpful in doing QCA?

REFERENCES

Allport, Gordon (1942). *The use of personal documents in psychological science*. New York: Social Science Research Council.

Allport, Gordon (Ed.) (1965). *Letters from Jenny*. New York: Hartcourt, Brace & World.

Altheide, David (1996). *Qualitative media analysis*. Thousand Oaks, CA: Sage.

Baldwin, Alfred L. (1942). Personal structure analysis. *Journal of Abnormal and Social Psychology, 37*, 163–183.

Bales, Robert F. (1950). *Interaction process analysis. A method for the study of small groups*. Cambridge, MA: Addison-Wesley.

Bartlett, Frederic (1932). *Remembering. A study in experimental and social psychology*. Cambridge: Cambridge University Press.

Beccaria, Franca (2001). Italian alcohol advertising: a qualitative content analysis. *Contemporary Drug Problems, 28*, 391–414.

Berelson, Bernard (1952). *Content analysis in communication research*. Glencoe, IL: Free Press.

Berelson, Bernard (1954). Content analysis. In Gardner Lindzey (ed.), *Handbook of social psychology* (Vol. 1: Theory and method, pp. 488–522). Cambridge, MA: Addison Wesley.

Berelson, Bernard & Lazarsfeld, Paul (1948). *The analysis of communication content*. Chicago: University of Chicago and Columbia University.

Berg, Charles & Milmeister, Marianne (2008). Im Dialog mit den Daten das eigene Erzählen der Geschichte finden. Über die Kodierverfahren der Grounded-Theory-Methodologie [From dialoguing with data to finding one's own way of telling the story. On grounded theory methodology coding procedures]. *Forum Qualitative Sozialforschung/Forum: Qualitative Social Research, 9*(2), Art. 13, http://nbn-resolving.de/urn:nbn:de:0114-fqs0802138.

Berger, Arthur A. (2000). Content analysis. In Arthur Berger (ed.), *Media and communications research methods* (pp. 173–185). Thousand Oaks, CA: Sage.

Bernard, Russell H. & Ryan, Gery W. (2010). Content analysis. In Russell Bernard & Gery Ryan (eds.), *Analyzing qualitative data: Systematic approaches* (pp. 287–310). Los Angeles: Sage.

Bilandzic, Helena, Koschel, Friederike & Scheufele, Bertram (2001). Theoretisch-heuristische Segmentierung im Prozess der empiriegeleiteten Kategorienbildung [Theoretical-heuristic segmentation with data-driven coding frames]. In Werner Wirth & Edmund Lauf (eds.), *Inhaltsanalyse: Perspektiven, Probleme, Potentiale* (pp. 98–118). Cologne: Herbert von Halem Verlag.

Birklbauer, Valerie (2009). Frauen und Biertrinken. Auf der Suche nach Motiven und Gewohnheiten [Women and beer consumption. Looking for motives and habits]. In Renate Buber & Hartmut Holzmüller (eds.), *Qualitative Marktforschung* (pp. 805–822). Wiesbaden: Gabler.

Bowen, Glenn A. (2009). Document analysis as a qualitative research method. *Qualitative Research Journal, 9*(2), 27–40.

Boyatzis, Richard E. (1998). *Transforming qualitative information. Thematic analysis and code development.* Thousand Oaks, CA: Sage.

Breuer, Franz (2009). *Reflexive grounded theory.* Wiesbaden: VS Verlag.

Bryman, Alan (2008). *Social science research methods* (3rd ed.). Oxford: Oxford University Press.

Bux, Shahid M. & Coyne, Sarah M. (2009). The effects of terrorism: The aftermath of the London terror attacks. *Journal of Applied Social Psychology, 39*(12), 2936–2966.

Chandler, Daniel (2007). *Semiotics. The basics* (2nd ed.). New York: Routledge.

Chilton, Paul & Schäffner, Christina (1997): Discourse pragmatics. In Teun van Dijk (ed.), *Discourse as social interaction* (pp. 206–230). London: Sage.

Coffey, Amanda & Atkinson, Paul (1996). *Making sense of qualitative data.* Thousand Oaks, CA: Sage.

Cresswell, John W. (2007). *Qualitative inquiry and research design. Choosing among five approaches* (2nd ed.). Thousand Oaks, CA: Sage.

Cresswell, John W. (2009). *Qualitative, quantitative, and mixed methods approaches* (3rd ed.). Thousand Oaks, CA: Sage.

Cresswell, John W. & Plano Clark, Vicky L. (2007). *Designing and conducting mixed methods research.* Thousand Oaks, CA: Sage.

Czarniawska, Barbara (2004). *Narratives in social science research.* London: Sage.

Dey, Ian (1993). *Qualitative data analysis. A user friendly guide for social scientists.* London and New York: Routledge.

Diederich, Adele & Schreier, Margrit (2009). Kriterien der Priorisierung aus gesellschaftlicher Sicht [Criteria for priority setting: A societal perspective]. *Zeitschrift für Ärztliche Fortbildung und Qualitätssicherung, 103,* 111–116.

Dieris, Barbara (2006). 'Och Mutter, was ist aus dir geworden?!' Eine Grounded-Theory-Studie über die Neupositionierung in der Beziehung zwischen alternden Eltern und ihren erwachsenen, sich kümmernden Kindern ['Ah Mom, what's happened to you?!' A grounded theory-study about repositioning in the relationship between elderly parents and their adult, care-giving children]. *Forum Qualitative Sozialforschung/Forum: Qualitative Social Research, 7*(3), Art. 25, http://nbn-resolving.de/urn:nbn:de:0114-fqs0603253.

Döring, Nicola & Pöschl, Sandra (2006). Images of men and women in mobile phone advertisements. A content analysis of advertisements for mobile communication systems in selected popular magazines. *Sex Roles, 5–6,* 173–185.

Dovring, Karin (1954). Quantitative semantics in 18th century Sweden. *Public Opinion Quarterly, 18,* 389–394.

Eco, Umberto (1978). *A theory of semiotics.* Bloomington: Indiana University Press.

Elo, Satu & Kyngäs, Helvi (2008) The qualitative content analysis process. *Journal of Advanced Nursing, 62*(1), 107–115.

Evers, Jeanine C., Mruck, Katja, Silver, Christina & Peeters, Bart (eds.) (2011). The KWALON experiment: Discussions on qualitative data analysis software by developers and users. *Forum Qualitative Sozialforschung/Forum: Qualitative Social Research, 12*(1). http://www.qualitative-research.net/index.php/fqs/issue/view/36.

Fairclough, Norman (2003). *Analysing discourse: Textual analysis for social research.* London: Routledge.

Fielding, Nigel & Lee, Raymond (1998). *Computer analysis and qualitative research.* London: Sage.

Flesch, Rudolf (1948). A new readability yardstick. *Journal of Applied Psychology, 32,* 221–233.

Flick, Uwe (2009). *An introduction to qualitative research* (4th ed.). London: Sage.

Franzosi, Roberto (ed.) (2008). *Content analysis.* London: Sage.

French, Steven (2008). The structure of theories. In Statis Psillos & Martin Curd (eds.), *The Routledge companion to the philosophy of science* (pp. 269–280). London: Routledge.

Früh, Werner (1992). Analyse sprachlicher Daten. Zur konvergenten Entwicklung 'quantitativer' und 'qualitativer' Methoden [The analysis of verbal data: The converging development of 'quantitative' and 'qualitative' methods]. In Jürgen Hoffmeyer-Zlotnik (ed.), *Analyse verbaler Daten. Über den Umgang mit qualitativen Daten* [The analysis of verbal data. How to deal with qualitative data] (pp. 59–89). Opladen: Westdeutscher Verlag.

Früh, Werner (2001). Kategorienexplikation bei der Inhaltsanalyse. Basiswissengeleitete offene Kategorienfindung [Explicating categories in content analysis: knowledge-guided open creation of categories]. In Werner Wirth & Edmund Lauf (eds.), *Inhaltsanalyse: Perspektiven, Probleme, Potentiale* (pp. 117–139). Köln: Herbert von Halem Verlag.

Früh, Werner (2007). *Inhaltsanalyse* [Content analysis] (6th ed.). Konstanz: UVK.

George, Alexander L. (1959). Quantitative and qualitative approaches to content analysis. In Ithiel de Sola Pool (Ed.), *Trends in content analysis* (pp. 1–32). Urbana: University of Illinois Press.

Gerbner, George, Holsti, Ole, Krippendorff, Klaus, Paisley, William J. & Stone, Philip J. (eds.) (1969). *The analysis of communication content. Development in scientific theories and computer techniques.* New York: Wiley.

Gibbs, Graham (2007). *Analyzing qualitative data.* London: Sage.

Gläser, Jochen & Laudel, Grit (2009). *Experteninterviews und qualitative Inhaltsanalyse* [Expert interviews and qualitative content analysis] (3rd rev. ed.). Wiesbaden: VS Verlag für Sozialwissenschaften.

Goffman, Irving (1979). *Gender advertisements.* New York: HarperCollins.

Goldman, Susan R., Graesser, Arthur C. & van den Broek, Paul (eds.) (1999). *Narrative comprehension, causality, and coherence. Essays in honor of Tom Trabasso.* Mahwah, NJ: Erlbaum.

Görnitz, Anja (2007). *The Airbus crisis in the French and German quality press* (unpublished course paper). Bremen: Jacobs University Bremen.

Gorski, Paul C. (2009). What we're teaching teachers: An analysis of multicultural teacher education coursework syllabi. *Teaching and Teacher Education, 25,* 309–318.

Gottschalk, Louis A. & Gleser, Goldine C. (1967). Theory and application of a verbal behavior method of measuring transient psychological states. In Kurt Salzinger & Susanne Salzinger (eds.), *Research in verbal behavior and some neurological implications* (pp. 299–335). New York: Academic Press.

Gottschalk, Louis A., Gleser, Goldine C. & Hambidge, G. Jr. (1957). Verbal analysis. Some content and form variables in speech relevant to personality adjustment. *Archives of Neurology and Psychiatry, 77,* 300–311.

Grice, H. Paul (1975). Logic and conversation. In Peter Cole & Jerry Morgan (eds.), *Syntax and semantics* (Vol. 3, pp. 41–58). New York: Academic Press.

Groeben, Norbert (1987). Möglichkeiten und Grenzen der Kognitionskritik durch Inhaltsanalyse von Texten [Potential and limitations of criticism of discourse through content analysis]. In Peter Vorderer & Norbert Groeben (eds.), *Textanalyse als Kognitionskritik?* [Textual analysis as cognitive critique?] (pp. 1–21). Tübingen: Narr.

Groeben, Norbert & Rustemeyer, Ruth (1994). On the integration of quantitative and qualitative methodological paradigms (based on the example of content analysis). In Inger Borg & Peter Mohler (eds.), *Trends and perspectives in empirical social research* (pp. 308–326). Berlin: De Gruyter.

Groeben, Nobert & Schreier, Margrit (1992). The hypothesis of the polyvalence convention: A systematic survey from a historical perspective. *Poetics, 21,* 5–32.

Guiller, Jane & Durndell, Alan (2007). Students' linguistic behaviour in online discussion groups: Does gender matter? *Computers in Human Behaviour, 23*, 2240–2255.

Heil, Simone (2010). *Youth exchange and the 'special relations' between Germany and the state of Israel: Interdependence of structure and agency* (unpublished dissertation). Bremen: Jacobs University Bremen.

Heil, Simone, Schreier, Margrit, Winkelhage, Jeannette & Diederich, Adele (2010). *Explorationsstudien zur Priorisierung medizinischer Leistungen: Kriterien und Präferenzen verschiedener Stakeholdergruppen* [Exploratory studies about prioritising in health care: Criteria and preferences of different stakeholder groups] (electronic version). FOR655, 26. http://www.priorisierung-in-der-medizin.de (accessed 17 March 2011).

Hermann, Marie-Louise (2010). *Die Zukunft der seelischen Gesundheit im Alter gestalten. Wirkungen der Münsteringer Zukunftskonferenz* [Shaping the future of psychological well-being in old age: Effects of the Munsterling future search conference]. http://opac.nebis.ch/ediss/20111009_003412412.pdf (accessed 15 April 2011).

Herschinger, Eva (2011). *Constructing global enemies. Hegemony and identity in international discourses on terrorism and drug prohibition*. London: Routledge.

Herzog, Benno, Gómez-Guardeño, Esperanza, Agulló-Calatayud, Victor, Aleixandre-Benavent, Rafael & Valderrama-Zurián, Juan Carlos (2008). Discourses on drugs and immigration: The social construction of a problem. *Forum Qualitative Sozialforschung/ Forum: Qualitative Social Research, 10*(1), Art. 7, http://nbn-resolving.de/urn:nbn:de:0114-fqs090172.

Hogan, Jacqueline (2006*)*: Letters to the Editor in the 'War on Terror': A cross-national study. *Mass Communication & Society, 9*, 63–83.

Holsti, Ole R. (1969). *Content analysis for the social sciences and the humanities*. Reading, MA: Addison-Wesley.

Hsie, Hsiu-Fang & Shannon, Sarah E. (2005). Three approaches to qualitative content analysis. *Qualitative Health Research, 15*, 1277–1288.

Hsu, Clarissa, BlueSpruce, June, Sherman, Karen & Cherkin, Dan (2010). Unanticipated benefits of CAM therapies for back pain: An exploration of patient experiences. *Journal of Alternative and Complementary Medicine, 16*, 157–163.

Hussy, Walter, Schreier, Margrit & Echterhoff, Gerald (2009). *Forschungsmethoden in Psychologie und Sozialwissenschaften. Für Bachelor.* [Research methods in the social and behavioural sciences. For bachelor's students.] Heidelberg: Springer.

Jansen, Harrie (2010). The logic of qualitative survey research and its position in the field of social research methods. *Forum Qualitative Sozialforschung/Forum: Qualitative Social Research, 11*(2), Art. 11, http://nbn-resolving.de/urn:nbn:de:0114-fqs1002110.

Kapustka, Katherine A., Howell, Penny, Clayton, Christine D. & Thomas, Shelley (2009). Social justice in teacher education: A qualitative content analysis of NCATE conceptual frameworks. *Equity and Excellence in Education, 42*(4), 489–505.

Klassen, Michael L., Jasper, Cynthia R. and Schwartz, Anne M. (1993). Men and women: Images of their relationships in magazine advertisements. *Journal of Advertising Research, 33*(2), 30–39.

Klotz, Audie & Prakash, Deepa (2008). *Qualitative methods in international relations*. Basingstoke: Palgrave Macmillan.

Kluge, Susann (2000). Empirically grounded construction of types and typologies in qualitative social research. *Forum Qualitative Sozialforschung/Forum: Qualitative Social Research, 1*(1), Art. 14, http://nbn-resolving.de/urn:nbn:de:0114-fqs0001145.

Kracauer, Siegfried (1952). The challenge of qualitative content analysis. *Public Opinion Quarterly, 16*, 631–642.

Kress, Gunther & van Leeuwen, Theo (1996). *Reading images – the grammar of visual design*. London: Routledge.

Krippendorff, Klaus (2004). *Content analysis. An introduction to its methodology.* Thousand Oaks, CA: Sage.

Kuckartz, Udo (2009). *Einführung in die computergestützte Analyse qualitativer Daten* [Introduction to the computer-aided analysis of qualitative data] (3rd rev. ed.). Wiesbaden: VS Verlag für Sozialwissenschaften.

Lamnek, Siegfried (2010). *Qualitative Sozialforschung* [Qualitative research in the social sciences] (5th rev. ed.) Weinheim: Beltz.

Landis, J. Richard & Koch, Gary G. (1977). The measurement of observer agreement for categorical data. *Biometrics, 33,* 159–174.

Larssen, Steen & Seilman, Uffe (1988). Personal remindings while reading literature. *Text, 8,* 411–429.

Lasswell, Harold D. (1927). *Propaganda technique in the World War.* New York: Knopf.

Lasswell, Harold D. (1941). The world attention survey. *Public Opinion Quarterly, 5,* 456–462.

Lasswell, Harold D. (1948). *Power and personality.* New York: Norton.

Lasswell, Harold D. & Jones, Dorothy B. (1939). *World revolutionary propaganda.* New York: Knopf.

Leites, Nathan, Bernaut, Elsa & Garthoff, Raymond (1951). Politbureau images of Stalin. *World Politics 3,* 317–339.

Lewins, Ann & Silver, Christina (2007). *Using software in qualitative research: A step-by-step guide.* London: Sage.

Lincoln, Yvonne S. & Guba, Egon G. (1985). *Naturalistic inquiry.* Beverly Hills, CA: Sage.

Lisch, Ralf & Kriz, Jürgen (1978). *Grundlagen und Modelle der Inhaltsanalyse* [Basics and models of content analysis]. Reinbek: Rowohlt.

Lissmann, Urban (2008). *Inhaltsanalyse von Texten – ein Lehrbuch zur computerunterstützten und konventionellen Inhaltsanalyse* [The content analysis of verbal data – a textbook on conventional and computer-aided content analysis] (3rd ed.). Landau: Verlag empirische Pädagogik.

MacQueen, Kathleen M., McLellan, Eleanor, Kay, Kelly & Milstein, Bobby (2009). Codebook development for team-based qualitative analysis. *Cultural Anthropology Methods, 10*(2), 31–36.

Maerten, Christian (2008). *What does Al-Qaeda want? The motivation behind terrorism according to high-quality newspapers* (unpublished course paper). Bremen: Jacobs University Bremen.

Marlange, Karen & Vorderer, Peter (1987). Fiktionale Texte: Evasiv-affirmative Textangebote und ihre Gratifikationseffekte [Fictional texts: Evasive-affirmative text formats and their gratifications]. In Peter Vorderer & Norbert Groeben (eds.), *Textanalyse als Kognitionskritik?* (pp. 1–21). Tübingen: Narr.

Marshall, Catherine & Rossman, Gretchen B. (2006). *Designing qualitative research.* Thousand Oaks, CA: Sage

Martin, Helen (1936). Nationalism and children's literature. *Library Quarterly, 6,* 405–418.

Maslow, Abraham (1959). Cognition of being in the peak experience. *Journal of Genetic Psychology, 94,* 43–66.

Mason, Jennifer (2002). *Qualitative researching* (2nd ed.). London: Sage.

Mathes, Werner (1992). Hermeneutisch-klassifikatorische Inhaltsanalyse von Leitfadengesprächen [Hermeneutic-classificatory content analysis of guided interviews]. In Jürgen Hoffmeyer-Zlotnik (ed.), *Analyse verbaler Daten. Über den Umgang mit qualitativen Daten* (pp. 402–424). Opladen: Westdeutscher Verlag.

Mayring, Philipp (2000). Qualitative content analysis. *Forum Qualitative Sozialforschung/ Forum: Qualitative Social Research, 1*(2), Art. 20, http://nbn-resolving.de/urn:nbn:de: 0114-fqs0002204.

Mayring, Philipp (2010). *Qualitative Inhaltsanalyse. Grundlagen und Techniken* [Qualitative content analysis. Basics and techniques] (11th rev. ed.). Weinheim: Beltz.

McClelland, David C., Atkinson, John W., Clark, Russell A. & Lowell, Edgar L. (2008). The scoring manual for the achievement motive. In Charles P. Smith (ed.), *Motivation and personality: Handbook of thematic content analysis* (pp. 153–178). Cambridge: Cambridge University Press.

McDonald, Matthew M., Wearing, Stephen & Ponting, Jess (2009). The nature of peak experience in wilderness. *Humanistic Psychologist, 37*, 370–385.

McMillan, Sally (2000). The microscope and the moving target: The challenge of applying content analysis to the World Wide Web. *Journalism and Mass Communication Quarterly, 77*, 80–98.

Merten, Klaus (1995). *Inhaltsanalyse. Einführung in Theorie, Methode und Praxis* [Content analysis. An introduction to theory, methods and practice] (2nd rev. ed.). Opladen: Westdeutscher Verlag.

Miles, Matthew B. & Huberman, A. Michael (1994). *Qualitative data analysis. An expanded sourcebook*. Thousand Oaks, CA: Sage.

Momani, Kawakib, Bardaneh, Muhammad, Migdadi, Fatih (2009). Gender metaphors in Middle Eastern politics and the Arab receiver. *Social Semiotics, 19*(3), 293–310.

Neuendorf, Kimberly A. (2002). *The content analysis guidebook*. Thousand Oaks, CA: Sage.

Odağ, Özen (2007). *Wenn Männer von der Liebe lesen und Frauen von Abenteuern... Eine empirische Rezeptionsstudie zur emotionalen Beteiligung von Männern und Frauen beim Lesen narrativer Texte* [If men read of love and women of adventures: An empirical reception study of the emotional involvement of men and women when reading narrative texts]. Lengerich: Pabst.

Osgood, Charles E. (1952). The nature and measurement of meaning. *Psychological Bulletin, 49*, 197–237.

Osgood, Charles E. (1959). The representational model and relevant research methods. In Ithiel de Sola Pool (ed.), *Trends in content analysis* (pp. 33–88). Urbana: University of Illinois Press.

Otten, Marina, Schreier, Margrit & Diederich, Adele (2010). *Explorationsstudien zur Priorisierung medizinischer Leistungen: Kriterien und Präferenzen von Vertreter/innen der Krankenkassen* [Exploratory studies about prioritising in health care: Criteria and preferences of representatives of health insurance companies] (electronic version). FOR655, 23 http://www.priorisierung-in-der-medizin.de/documents/FOR655_Nr23_Otten.pdf (accessed 17 March 2011).

Özcan, Ayşe Esra (2009). *Visualization of gender in the Turkish press. A comparative analysis of six Turkish newspapers*. Bremen: Jacobs University Bremen. http://www.jacobs-university.de/phd/files/1276527833.pdf (accessed 16 May 2011).

Pace, Stephen (2004). A grounded theory of the flow experiences of Web users. *International Journal of Human–Computer Studies, 60*, 327–363.

Pallant, Julie (2010). *SPSS survival manual. A step by step guide to data analysis using SPSS* (4th ed.). Maidenhead: Open University Press.

Panofsky, Erwin (1955/1983). *Meaning in the visual arts*. Chicago: University of Chicago Press.

Phillips, Nelson & Hardy, Cynthia (2002). *Discourse analysis. Investigating processes of social construction*. Thousand Oaks, CA: Sage.

Pool, Ithiel de Sola (Ed.) (1959). *Trends in content analysis*. Urbana: Illinois University Press.

Potter, Jonathan & Wetherell, Margaret (1987). *Discourse and social psychology: Beyond attitudes and behaviour*. London: Sage.

Quinn Patton, Michael (2002). *Qualitative evaluation and research methods* (3rd ed.). Newbury Park, CA: Sage.

Rapley, Tim (2007). *Doing conversation, discourse, and document analysis.* London: Sage.

Reisigl, Martin & Wodak, Ruth (2001). *Discourse and discrimination: Rhetorics of racism.* New York: Routledge.

Ritsert, Jürgen (1972). *Inhaltsanalyse und Ideologiekritik. Ein Versuch über kritische Sozialforschung* [Content analysis and ideology. An attempt at critical social research]. Frankfurt: Athenäum.

Rose, Gillian (2007). *Visual methodologies* (2nd ed.). London: Sage.

Rössler, Patrick (2005). *Inhaltsanalyse* [Content analysis]. Konstanz: UVK Verlagsgesellschaft.

Rust, Holger (1980). *Struktur und Bedeutung* [Structure and meaning]. Berlin: Verlag Volker Spiess.

Rustemeyer, Ruth (1992). *Praktisch-methodische Schritte der Inhaltsanalyse* [Content analysis step-by-step]. Münster: Aschendorff.

Ryan, G.W. & Bernard, H.R. (2003). Techniques to identify themes. *Field Methods, 15*(1), 85–109.

Saldana, Johnny (2009). *The coding manual for qualitative researchers.* London: Sage.

Scheufele, Bertram (2001). Notwendigkeit, Nutzen und Aufwand von Mehrfach- und Sondercodierungen [On the necessity for, use of, and effort involved in multiple coding.]. In Werner Wirth & Edmund Lauf (eds.), *Inhaltsanalyse: Perspektiven, Probleme, Potentiale* (pp. 82-97). Köln: Herbert von Halem Verlag.

Schilling, Jan (2006). On the pragmatics of qualitative assessment: Designing the process for content analysis. *European Journal of Psychological Assessment, 22,* 28–37.

Schramm, Wilbur (1997). *The beginnings of communication studies in America. A personal memoir.* Thousand Oaks, CA: Sage.

Seale, Clive (1999). *The quality of qualitative research.* London: Sage.

Shannon, Lyle W. (1954). The opinions of the little orphan Annie and her friends. *Public Opinion Quarterly, 18,* 169–179.

Shapiro, Gilbert & Markoff, John (1997). A matter of definition. In Carl W. Roberts (ed.), *Text analysis for the social sciences* (pp. 9–31). Mahwah, NJ: Erlbaum.

Silverman, David (2000). *Doing qualitative research. A practical handbook.* London: Sage.

Silverman, David (2001). Credible qualitative research. In D. Silverman, *Interpreting qualitative data* (2nd ed., pp. 219–257). London: Sage.

Simpson, George Eaton (1936). *The negro in the Philadelphia press.* Philadelphia: University of Pennsylvania Press.

Skalski, Paul (2002). Computer content analysis software. In Kimberly Neuendorf, *The content analysis guidebook* (pp. 225–240). Thousand Oaks, CA: Sage.

Skorek, Małgorzata (2008). *Gender roles and gender stereotypes in magazine advertisements from Germany, Poland, and the United States* (unpublished MA thesis). Bremen: Jacobs University Bremen.

Skorek, Małgorzata & Schreier, Margrit (2009). *A comparison of gender role portrayals in magazine advertisements from Germany, Poland and the United States.* Paper presented at the 59th Annual Conference of the International Communication Association, Chicago, 21–25 May. http://www.malgorzataskorek.de/academic/Publications.html (accessed 15 April 2011).

Smith, Charles P. (Ed.) (2008). *Motivation and personality. Handbook of thematic content analysis.* Cambridge: Cambridge University Press,

Smith, John K. (1984). The problem of criteria for judging interpretive inquiry. *Educational Evaluation and Policy Analysis, 6,* 379–391.

Sommer, Michael & Vorderer, Peter (1987). Alltags-Rede-Texte: Aspekte von Verdinglichung in (rechtfertigenden) Handlungsbeschreibungen [Everyday speeches: Reification in (justificatory) descriptions of actions]. In Peter Vorderer & Norbert Groeben (eds.),

Textanalyse als Kognitionskritik? Möglichkeiten und Grenzen ideologiekritischer Inhaltsanalyse (pp. 137–193). Tübingen: Narr.

Speed, John Gilmer (1893). Do newspapers now give the news? *Forum, 15,* 705–711.

Stake, Robert (2010). *Qualitative research. Studying how things work.* New York: Guilford Press.

Steinke, Ines (2004). Quality criteria in qualitative research. In Uwe Flick, Ernst von Kardorff & Ines Steinke (eds.), *A companion to qualitative research* (pp. 184–190). London: Sage.

Stewart, Milton D. (1943). Importance in content analysis: A validity problem. *Journalism Quarterly, 20*(4), 286–293.

Stone, Philip J. (1975). Report on the Workshop on Content Analysis in the Social Sciences, Pisa 1974. *Social Science Information, 14,* 107–111.

Stone, Philip J. (1997). Thematic text analysis: New agendas for analyzing text content. In Carl W. Roberts (ed.), *Text analysis for the social sciences* (pp. 35–54). Mahwah, NJ: Erlbaum.

Strauss, Anselm & Corbin, Juliet (1998). *Basics of qualitative research. Techniques and procedures for developing grounded theory* (2nd ed.). Thousand Oaks, CA: Sage.

Swartz, Omar (1997). *Conducting socially responsible research: Critical theory, neo-pragmatism, and rhetorical inquiry.* Thousand Oaks, CA. Sage.

Tambling, Rachel R. & Johnson, Lee N. (2010). Client expectations about couple therapy. *American Journal of Family Therapy, 38,* 322–333.

Tesch, Renata (1990). *Qualitative research: Analysis types and software tools.* New York: Falmer Press.

Todd, Zazie & Harrison, Simon J. (2008). Metaphor analysis. In Sharlene Nagy Hesse-Biber & Patricia Leavy (eds.), *Handbook of emergent methods* (pp. 479–493). New York: Guilford Press.

Van Dijk, Teun (Ed.) (1997a). *Discourse as structure and process.* London: Sage.

Van Dijk, Teun (Ed.) (1997b). *Discourse as social interaction.* London: Sage.

Van Dijk, Teun (2008). *Discourse and power.* Basingstoke: Palgrave.

Van Eemeren, Frans, Grootendorst, Rob & Snoeck Henkemans, Francisca (2002). *Argumentation: Analysis, evaluation, presentation.* Mahwah, NJ: Erlbaum.

Van Leeuwen, Theo (2005). *Introducing social semiotics.* London: Routledge.

Viertel, Katrin (2010). *Most watched. Family life representations in high rating programs on German TV* (unpublished manuscript). Bremen: Jacobs University Bremen.

Vorderer, Peter & Groeben, Norbert (Eds.) (1987). *Textanalyse als Kognitionskritik? Möglichkeiten und Grenzen ideologiekritischer Inhaltsanalyse.* [Textual analysis as cognitive critique?] Tübingen: Narr.

Waples, Douglas (1942) (Ed.). *Print, radio, and film in a democracy.* Chicago: University of Chicago Press.

Weber, Robert P. (1990). *Basic content analysis.* Newbury Park, CA: Sage.

Wengraf, Tom (2001). *Qualitative research interviewing.* London: Sage.

White, Ralph K. (1944). Value analysis. A quantitative method for describing qualitative data. *Journal of Social Psychology, 19,* 351–358.

Winkelhage, Jeannette, Diederich, Adele, Heil, Simone, Lietz, Petra, Schmitz-Justen, Felix & Schreier, Margrit (2007). *Qualitative Stakeholder-Interviews: Entwicklung eines Interviewleitfadens zur Erfassung von Prioritäten in der medizinischen Versorgung* [Qualitative stakeholder interviews: Developing an interview guide for assessing priorities in health care] (electronic version). FOR655, 4. http://www.priorisierung-in-der-medizin.de (accessed 17 March 2011).

Winkelhage, Jeannette, Winkel, Susanne, Schreier, Margrit, Heil, Simone, Lietz, Petra & Diederich, Adele (2008a). *Qualitative Inhaltsanalyse: Entwicklung eines Kategoriensystems zur Analyse von Stakeholder-Interviews zu Prioritäten in der medizinischen Versorgung* [Qualitative content analysis: Developing a coding frame for the analysis of stakeholder interviews about priorities in medical care] (electronic version). FOR655, 15. http://www.priorisierung-in-der-medizin.de (accessed 17 March 2011).

Winkelhage, Jeannette, Winkel, Susanne, Schreier, Margrit, Heil, Simone, Lietz, Petra & Diederich, Adele (2008b). *Anhang zu FOR Working Paper No. 15* [Appendix to FOR Working Paper No. 15] (electronic version). FOR655, 16. http://www.priorisierung-in-der-medizin.de (accessed 17 March 2011).

Winter, David G. (2008a). Power motivation revisited. In Charles P. Smith (Ed.), *Motivation and personality: Handbook of thematic content analysis* (pp. 301–310). Cambridge: Cambridge University Press.

Winter, David G. (2008b). A revised scoring system for the power motive. In Charles P. Smith (Ed.), *Motivation and personality: Handbook of thematic content analysis* (pp. 311–323). Cambridge: Cambridge University Press.

Witzel, Andreas & Reiter, Herwig (in press). *The problem-centred interview*. London: Sage.

Wodak, Ruth & Meyer, Michael (2009). *Methods for critical discourse analysis*. London: Sage.

Yule, George U. (1944). *The statistical study of literary vocabulary*. Cambridge: Cambridge University Press.

INDEX

Figures and Tables are indicated by page numbers printed in bold.